Post-Jungian Psychology and the Short Stories of Ray Bradbury and Kurt Vonnegut

In this book, Steve Gronert Ellerhoff explores short stories by Ray Bradbury and Kurt Vonnegut, written between 1943 and 1968, with a post-Jungian approach. Drawing upon archetypal theories of myth from Joseph Campbell, James Hillman, and their forbearer C. G. Jung, Ellerhoff demonstrates how short fiction follows archetypal patterns that can illuminate our understanding of the authors, their times, and their culture. In practice, a post-Jungian 'mythodology' is shown to yield great insights for the literary criticism of short fiction.

Chapters in this volume carefully contextualize and historicize each story, including Bradbury's and Vonnegut's earliest and most imaginatively fantastic works. The archetypal constellations shaping Vonnegut's early works are shown to be war and fragmentation, while those in Bradbury's are family and the wholeness of the sun. Analysis is complemented by the explored significance of illustrations that featured alongside the stories in their first publications. By uncovering the ways these popular writers redressed old myths in new tropes – and coined new narrative elements for hopes and fears born of their era – the book reveals a fresh method which can be applied to all imaginative short stories, increasing understanding and critical engagement.

Post-Jungian Psychology and the Short Stories of Ray Bradbury and Kurt Vonnegut is an important text for a number of fields, from Jungian and Post-Jungian studies to short story theories and American studies to Bradbury and Vonnegut studies. Scholars and students of literature will come away with a renewed appreciation for an archetypal approach to criticism, while the book will also be of great interest to practising depth psychologists seeking to incorporate short stories into therapy.

Steve Gronert Ellerhoff is a graduate of the Creative Writing MA at Lancaster University, and he also holds an MPhil in Literatures of the Americas and a PhD in English from Trinity College, Dublin. Currently, along with Philip Coleman of Trinity College, Dublin, he is co-editing *George Saunders: Critical Essays*, the first book-length work of criticism on the author. A scholar and writer of fiction, his literary efforts include *Time's Laughingstocks* and *Tales from the Internet*, a story collection. Another novel, *The Hedgehog's Dilemma*, is forthcoming.

Research in Analytical Psychology and Jungian Studies Series
Series Advisor: Andrew Samuels,
Professor of Analytical Psychology, Essex University, UK.

The *Research in Analytical Psychology and Jungian Studies* series features research-focused volumes involving qualitative and quantitative research, historical/archival research, theoretical developments, heuristic research, grounded theory, narrative approaches, collaborative research, practitioner-led research, and self-study. The series also includes focused works by clinical practitioners, and provides new research informed explorations of the work of C. G Jung that will appeal to researchers, academics, and scholars alike.

Books in this series:

Time and Timelessness
Temporality in the theory of Carl Jung
Angeliki Yiassemides

Apophatic Elements in the Theory and Practice of Psychoanalysis
Pseudo-Dionysius and C. G. Jung
David Henderson

C. G. Jung and Hans Urs von Balthasar
God and evil–A critical comparison
Les Oglesby

Bridges to Consciousness
Complexes and complexity
Nancy M. Krieger

The Alchemical Mercurius
Esoteric symbol of Jung's life and works
Mathew Mather

Archetypal Psychotherapy
The clinical legacy of James Hillman
Jason A. Butler

Jung's Theory of Personality
A modern reappraisal
Clare Crellin

Psychological, Archetypal and Phenomenological Perspectives on Soccer
David Huw Burston

Music as Image
Analytical psychology and music in film
Benjamin Nagari

Laws of Inheritance
A post-Jungian study of twins and the relationship between the first and other(s)
Elizabeth Brodersen

Jung and Levinas
An ethics of mediation
Frances Gray

Symptom, Symbol, and the Other of Language
A Jungian interpretation of the linguistic turn
Bret Alderman

Post-Jungian Psychology and the Short Stories of Ray Bradbury and Kurt Vonnegut
Golden apples of the monkey house
Steve Gronert Ellerhoff

Post-Jungian Psychology and the Short Stories of Ray Bradbury and Kurt Vonnegut

Golden apples of the monkey house

Steve Gronert Ellerhoff

Routledge
Taylor & Francis Group
LONDON AND NEW YORK

First published 2016 by Routledge

2 Park Square, Milton Park, Abingdon, Oxfordshire OX14 4RN
711 Third Avenue, New York, NY 10017

Routledge is an imprint of the Taylor & Francis Group, an informa business

First issued in paperback 2017

British Library Cataloguing in Publication Data
A catalogue record for this book is available from the British Library

Library of Congress Cataloging-in-Publication Data
Names: Ellerhoff, Steve Gronert, author.
Title: Post-Jungian psychology and the short stories of Ray Bradbury and Kurt Vonnegut : golden apples of the monkey house / Steve Gronert Ellerhoff.
Description: Milton Park, Abingdon, Oxon ; New York : Routledge, 2016. | Series: Research in analytical psychology and Jungian studies series
Identifiers: LCCN 2015036073 | ISBN 9781138937307 (hardback) | ISBN 9781315676357 (ebook)
Subjects: LCSH: Bradbury, Ray, 1920–2012—Criticism and interpretation. | Vonnegut, Kurt—Criticism and interpretation. | Psychology and literature—United States. | Short stories, American—History and criticism. | Archetypes in literature. | Jungian psychology.
Classification: LCC PS3503.R167 Z675 2016 | DDC 813/.54—dc23
LC record available at http://lccn.loc.gov/2015036073

ISBN: 978-1-138-93730-7 (hbk)
ISBN: 978-0-8153-5994-4 (pbk)

Typeset in Sabon
by Apex CoVantage, LLC

Figure 0.1 Kurt Vonnegut (left) and Ray Bradbury (right) met in person twice. This is the second occasion, captured by photographer Yousuf Karsh in 1988 and unpublished until now.

Photograph by Yousuf Karsh. Reproduced with permission from Camera Press London.

For Peter Nazareth:
a rabbit no hound dog can catch
and a very good friend of mine.

Contents

Figures

Acknowledgments

At Routledge, I first wish to thank Susannah Frearson, who was right in her hunch that this book might be a fit for the Research in Analytical Psychology and Jungian Studies series. Next, my gratitude goes to Clare Ashworth and her editorial assistant, Emily Bedford, for seeing it through the offer to publish and the manuscript preparation. Thanks to Heidi Lee, who took this book into production. My sincerest gratefulness extends finally to Autumn Spalding, whose exuberance and spirit made finishing this book joyful; she is the variety of editor that writers hope exist out there, a true unicorn.

This work was largely conducted in Ireland while I was working on a PhD at Trinity College, Dublin. I am particularly grateful to my supervisor, Philip Coleman, who took me out from behind the wind-up toys counter and made me a scholar. Thanks to Sam Slote, who oversaw my confirmation. I thank the School of English for a two-year studentship and the gift of teaching experiences for two years. Thanks also to the Harborview Medical Center Memorial Scholarship. A deep wellspring of thanks to Melanie Otto and Kasia Boddy for assessing this work and bestowing the PhD with thoughtfulness and true engagement. It is one thing to pass; it is another thing altogether to pass when you have utmost respect for your threshold guardians. Thanks, too, to George Green, Graham Mort, Ailsa Cox, Susan Lohafer, and Michael Trussler for transforming my relationship with short fiction.

I thank the Kurt Vonnegut Society, Sarah Smith, and David K. Frasier at the Lilly Library at Indiana University. Thanks to Chris LaFave, curator of the Kurt Vonnegut Memorial Library, and Vicki Goldsmith, who introduced me to David Goldsmith. Most especially I thank Marc Leeds, who has been helpful and kind. Thanks also to Joe Petro III, literary executor Donald Farber, and Mr. Vonnegut himself, who answered my letter with a signed screenprint in 2005.

Profound thanks go to Jonathan R. Eller and Robin Condon of the Center for Ray Bradbury Studies at Indiana University Indianapolis. I also thank Katie Crawford and John Anthony Miller of the Phantom Bookshop in Ventura, California. They sent rare (and autographed) Bradbury volumes and told Mr. Bradbury of my work not long before he passed away. Thanks to literary executor Cristina Concepcion and Mr. Bradbury, too.

Greatest thanks go, with love, to my dearest teachers and friends – the Storrars chief among them – and to my family – especially Aunt Kay and Unca Tom, my sister Kathryn, brother-in-law Arion and niece Yael, and my parents.

Every effort has been made to contact the copyright holders for their permission to reprint selections of this book. The publishers would be grateful to hear from any copyright holder who is not here acknowledged and we will undertake to rectify any errors or omissions in future editions of this book.

Quotations from the works of Ray Bradbury are published with the permission of Don Congdon Associates, Inc., as agents for Ray Bradbury Literary Works LLC.

"The Shape of Things" (a.k.a. Tomorrow's Child)
© 1947 by Standard Magazines, renewed 1975 by CBS Publications

"The Traveler"
© 1945 by Weird Tales, renewed 1972 by Ray Bradbury

"The Vacation"
© 1963 by HMH Pub. Co., renewed 1991 by Ray Bradbury

"The World the Children Made" (a.k.a. The Veldt)
© 1950 by Curtis Pub. Co., renewed 1977 by Ray Bradbury

"Take Me Home"
© 2012 by Ray Bradbury

"Intro to Ray Bradbury Theater"
© 1991 by Ray Bradbury

"Science Fiction: before Christ and after 2001"
Essay appearing in *Science, Fact/Fiction* Ed. Edmund J. Farrell Glenview, Ill: Scott Foresman, 1974, ix–xv; International Film Exposition. Los Angeles: Filmex
© 1981 by Ray Bradbury

Fahrenheit 451
© 1953 by Ray Bradbury, renewed 1981 by Ray Bradbury

"Zen in the Art of Writing"
© 1990 by Ray Bradbury Enterprises

Quotations from the works of Kurt Vonnegut are published with the following permissions:

Excerpt(s) from *Armageddon in Retrospect: And Other New and Unpublished Writings on War and Peace* by Kurt Vonnegut, copyright © 2008 by the Kurt Vonnegut, Jr. Trust. Used by permission of G. P. Putnam's Sons, an imprint of Penguin Publishing Group, a division of Penguin Random House LLC. Published in the UK by Jonathan Cape and reproduced by permission of The Random House Group Ltd.

Excerpt(s) from *Bagombo Snuff Box: Uncollected Short Fiction* by Kurt Vonnegut, copyright © 1999 by Kurt Vonnegut. Used by permission of G. P. Putnam's Sons, an imprint of Penguin Publishing Group, a division of Penguin Random House LLC. Published in the UK by Jonathan Cape and reproduced by permission of The Random House Group Ltd.

Excerpt(s) and Illustrations from *Breakfast of Champions* by Kurt Vonnegut, copyright © 1973 by Kurt Vonnegut Jr. Used by permission of Dell Publishing, an imprint of Random House, a division of Penguin Random House LLC. All rights reserved.

Excerpt(s) from *Cat's Cradle* by Kurt Vonnegut, copyright © 1963 by Kurt Vonnegut Jr. Used by permission of Dell Publishing, an imprint of Random House, a division of Penguin Random House LLC. All rights reserved.

Excerpt(s) from *Fates Worse Than Death: An Autobiographical Collage of the 1980s* by Kurt Vonnegut, copyright © 1991 by Kurt Vonnegut. Used by permission of G. P. Putnam's Sons, an imprint of Penguin Publishing Group, a division of Penguin Random House LLC. Published in the UK by Jonathan Cape and reproduced by permission of The Random House Group Ltd.

Excerpt from *God Bless You, Dr. Kevorkian* by Kurt Vonnegut, Copyright © 1999 by Kurt Vonnegut. Reprinted with the permission of The Permissions Company, Inc., on behalf of Seven Stories Press, www.sevenstories.com.

Excerpt(s) from *God Bless You, Mr. Rosewater* by Kurt Vonnegut, copyright © 1965 by Kurt Vonnegut, Jr. Used by permission of Dell Publishing, an imprint of Random House, a division of Penguin Random House LLC. All rights reserved.

Excerpt(s) from *Kurt Vonnegut: Letters* edited by Dan Wakfield, copyright © 2012 by The Kurt Vonnegut, Jr. Trust. Used by permission of Delacorte Press, an imprint of Random House, a division of Penguin Random House LLC. All rights reserved.

Excerpt(s) from *Palm Sunday: An Autobiographical Collage* by Kurt Vonnegut, copyright © 1981 by Kurt Vonnegut. Used by permission of Dell Publishing, an imprint of Random House, a division of Penguin Random House LLC. All rights reserved.

Excerpt(s) from *Slaughterhouse-Five: Or the Children's Crusade, a Duty Dance with Death (25th Anniversary)* by Kurt Vonnegut, copyright © 1968, 1969 and copyright renewed © 1996, 1997 by Kurt Vonnegut, Jr. Used by permission of Dell Publishing, an imprint of Random House, a division of Penguin Random House LLC. All rights reserved.

Excerpt(s) from *Wampeters Foma & Granfalloons* by Kurt Vonnegut, copyright © 1965, 1966, 1967, 1968, 1969, 1970, 1971, 1972, 1973, 1974 by Kurt Vonnegut, Jr. Used by permission of Dell Publishing, an imprint of Random House, a division of Penguin Random House LLC. All rights reserved.

Excerpt(s) from *Welcome to the Monkey House* by Kurt Vonnegut, copyright © 1968 by Kurt Vonnegut Jr. Used by permission of Dell Publishing, an imprint of Random House, a division of Penguin Random House LLC. All rights reserved.

Quotations from Joseph Campbell's *Power of Myth* are published with the following permission:

Excerpt(s) from *The Power of Myth* by Joseph Campbell, copyright © 1988 by Apostrophe S Productions, Inc. and Bill Moyers and Alfred Van der Marck Editions, Inc. for itself and the estate of Joseph Campbell. Used by permission of Doubleday, an imprint of the Knopf Doubleday Publishing Group, a division of Penguin Random House LLC. All rights reserved.

A quotation from Inez Martinez is published with the following permission:

Excerpt from "Unconsciousness and Survival: Kafka's *Metamorphosis* and Borowski's 'This Way for the Gas, Ladies and Gentlemen'" by Inez Martinez (*Journal of Jungian Scholarly Studies* 6.2 [2010], 1–25: www.jsss.org), copyright © 2010 by Inez Martinez. Used by permission of Inez Martinez. All rights reserved.

Abbreviations

Quotations from the following books appear often enough to garner parenthetical abbreviations. Full bibliographic entries can be found for each in the list of primary sources. Also, all citations of C. G. Jung follow the format drawing from his twenty-volume *Collected Works (CW)*, which is universally used by scholars of Jungian studies.

BSB	*Bagombo Snuff Box*. Kurt Vonnegut.
BTN	*Behind The Name: The Etymology and History of First Names*. Web.
CDJA	*A Critical Dictionary of Jungian Analysis*. Andrew Samuels, Bani Shorter, and Fred Plaut.
CSRB	*The Collected Stories of Ray Bradbury, A Critical Edition: Vol. I: 1938–1943*. Ray Bradbury.
IROS	*The Inner Reaches of Outer Space*. Joseph Campbell.
MDR	*Memories, Dreams, Reflections*. C. G. Jung.
MGC	*The Masks of God Vol. IV Creative Mythology*. Joseph Campbell.
MGOC	*The Masks of God Vol. III Occidental Mythology*. Joseph Campbell.
MGOM	*The Masks of God Vol. II Oriental Mythology*. Joseph Campbell.
NS	*Novels & Stories 1963–1973*. Kurt Vonnegut.
NSST	*New Short Story Theories*. Ed. Charles E. May.
POM	*The Power of Myth*. Joseph Campbell and Bill Moyers.
SC	*The Soul's Code*. James Hillman.
SFKV	*The Short Fiction of Kurt Vonnegut*. Peter J. Reed.
TGLT1	*Turtle Was Gone a Long Time, Vol. I: Crossing the Kedron*. John Moriarty.
TGLT2	*Turtle Was Gone a Long Time, Vol. II: Horsehead Nebula Neighing*. John Moriarty.
TGLT3	*Turtle Was Gone a Long Time, Vol. III: Anaconda Canoe*. John Moriarty.
TLW	*A Terrible Love of War*. James Hillman.

Chapter 1

A post-Jungian mythology for reading short stories

> "I love you sons of bitches," Eliot said in Milford. "You're all I read any more. You're the only ones who'll talk about the *really* terrific changes going on, the only ones crazy enough to know that life is a space voyage, and not a short one, either, but one that'll last for billions of years. You're the only ones with guts enough to *really* care about the future, who *really* notice what machines do to us, what wars do to us, what cities do to us, what big, simple ideas do to us, what tremendous misunderstandings, mistakes, accidents and catastrophes do to us. You're the only ones zany enough to agonize over time and distances without limit, over mysteries that will never die, over the fact that we are right now determining whether the space voyage for the next billion years or so is going to be Heaven or Hell."
>
> Kurt Vonnegut
> *God Bless You, Mr. Rosewater*
> (*NS* 201–2)

In 1999, Peter Reed published the remainder of Kurt Vonnegut's uncollected short stories in *Bagombo Snuff Box*. Prior to this, in 1977, Jerome Klinkowitz and Donald Lawler encouraged readers to uncover these short works, "a lost art" long out of print and decades from seeing it again (54), at libraries by providing "instructions for an entire book of undiscovered Kurt Vonnegut stories, never collected except in this homemade work you can assemble for yourself" (53). Vonnegut, assessing the "mildness and innocence and clumsiness" of these stories, claimed "there is no greatness in this or my other collection, nor was there meant to be" (*BSB* 2, 3). He tells us that in writing the short stories of his early career, "All I wanted to do was support a family" (*BSB* 1). To date, only one full-length study on his short stories has appeared, Reed's *The Short Fiction of Kurt Vonnegut*. Ray Bradbury's short stories have accrued a similarly meager place in literary criticism, although Jonathan R. Eller is currently editing them in authoritative critical editions. This study is cast with hope of drawing attention to these writers' short fiction, arguing that their practically produced works contain multitudes.

Though Vonnegut abandoned the form, he offers rules for writing short stories – what he, experienced at leading graduate workshops, calls "Creative Writing 101":

1 Use the time of a total stranger in such a way that he or she will not feel the time was wasted.
2 Give the reader at least one character he or she can root for.
3 Every character should want something, even if it is only a glass of water.
4 Every sentence must do one of two things – reveal character or advance the action.
5 Start as close to the end as possible.
6 Be a sadist. No matter how sweet and innocent your leading character, make awful things happen to them – in order that the reader may see what they are made of.
7 Write to please just one person. If you open a window and make love to the world, so to speak, your story will get pneumonia.
8 Give your readers as much information as possible as soon as possible. To heck with suspense. Readers should have such complete understanding of what is going on, where and why, that they could finish the story themselves, should cockroaches eat the last few pages.

(*BSB* 9–10)

Vonnegut also praises Flannery O'Connor, "the greatest American short story writer of my generation" (*BSB* 10), and Ray Bradbury, who he deems "sure as heck prescient" in his future-focused stories (*BSB* 8). Bradbury never taught creative writing but often guest lectured on the craft. In 1990 he published an exuberant manifesto of essays, written between 1961 and 1990, titled *Zen in the Art of Writing*. His advice is evangelical, preaching enjoyment in writing and the creation of short stories in great quantity:

> [T]he first thing a writer should be is – excited. He should be a thing of fevers and enthusiasms. Without such vigor, he might as well be out picking peaches or digging ditches; God knows it'd be better for his health. [. . .]
>
> [Write one]-thousand or two-thousand words every day for the next twenty years. At the start, you might shoot for one short story a week, fifty-two stories a year, for five years. You will have to write and put away or burn a lot of material before you are comfortable in this medium. You might as well start now and get the necessary work done.
>
> For I believe that eventually quantity will make for quality.
>
> (4, 130–131)

Differences individualize these writers' mature positions on advice for those beginning to write. Differences also individualize the stories they wrote.

This study spins a handful of threads through stories by both authors: periodical studies, post-Jungian theories of myth, short story theories, American culture and history. I use initial publications of stories by both authors throughout this volume because they offer glimpses of their own individual historical moments by being printed alongside other stories and advertisements – and in publication formats ranging from pulps to "slicks." As Eller said when I met him at the Center for Ray Bradbury Studies at Indiana University Indianapolis, "You are looking at versions of these stories that hardly anybody has seen since they first appeared." Agreeing with Kasia Boddy that "Where we read the story shapes the expectations we bring to our reading of it, and thus the effect it has on us" (117), I also take artwork published with these stories into account. Vonnegut says, "Illustrators during the golden age of American magazine fiction used to get as much money as the authors whose stories they illustrated. They were often as famous as, or even more famous than, the authors" (*BSB* 4). The art and ads are examined for context and surprising juxtapositions as they arise in striking ways with each story. Another reason for relying on original publications has to do with Bradbury's tendency of tweaking or heavily revising stories when later collected, changing details as first presented in the era in question.

Bradbury published over four hundred short stories in his lifetime; Vonnegut published forty-seven. Selection pools differing in quantity by ten times, with analyses of many stories left on the cutting room floor, I worked to attempt something like balance in selecting Vonnegut's stories while sifting through Bradbury's catalog. Only through this process did I realize the stories I wanted to talk about, save a couple outliers, were published between WWII and the Kennedy assassination. Thus, this study focuses by and large on two decades of American culture, ranging from 1943 to 1963, a time when pulps and "slicks" alike started out thriving and ended up nearly perishing with the spread of television. Reflecting on the health benefits, mental and restful, Vonnegut likened the short story form as akin to a "Buddhist catnap": "[A] short story, because of its physiological and psychological effects on a human being, is more closely related to Buddhist styles of meditation than it is to any other form of narrative entertainment" (5). Sharing an interest in the psychology of stories, research led me to short story theorists and psychoanalysts from Charles E. May to Rollo May. My initial question, prior to applying for this course of study, as I was busy writing my own fiction, was whether or not short stories behave like myths. Sensing a correlation, I sought a way of expressing some ways in which they do.

Vonnegut and Bradbury have received attention for writing myths from the earliest days of scholarship on their work.[1] This continues to this day, for instance, in Gilbert McInnis's exciting contribution to Vonnegut studies: *Evolutionary Mythology in the Writings of Kurt Vonnegut* (2011). What has been missing from these studies is a comprehensive presentation of a theoretical framework for talking about myth. Chapter 1 exists in this study for the sole reason of laying out a "mythodology" for reading short stories with a post-Jungian approach. There are many theories of myth – so many that Robert Segal has built his scholarship on identifying and differentiating them. We proceed with a post-Jungian perspective on myth, particularly that developed by comparative mythologist Joseph Campbell (1904–1987), supporting its application to the interpretation of literature, and specifically short stories. Campbell's work, contemporaneous with what Donald E. Pease calls the Myth and Symbol school of American studies, grew out of the same temporal and cultural context that informed the writing of Bradbury and Vonnegut's short stories. The theoretical pairing with the texts examined is not accidental. It does not, however, pretend to offer anything approaching a final word on how to interpret myths, which I regard as impossible.

The stories analyzed in the following book present opportunities to reflect on and experience aspects of myths – the archetypes – that find expression in a society; are conditioned specifically in time, place, and culture(s); *and* are lived in the broadest universal conditions of life for human beings. Imaginative imagery in these stories may be unrealistic, but all bear relation to reality, for, as Jungian analyst Jean Knox says, "Symbolic meaning depends on the process of evaluation and comparison of experiences with each other – in other words it depends on information from the real world" (201). When it comes to the notion of universality, Jungian literary critic Inez Martinez issues a warning we shall heed:

> Once a story attains the status of myth, it takes on an aura of authorless divine revelation, of numinosity, suggesting a realm beyond human limitation. This aspect of myth can make our lives feel meaningful and purposeful. The shadow of this power, however, is the universalizing of cultural moments of myth as if they apply to all human experience, thus naturalizing or even divinizing a particular cultural moment, thereby creating a brake on what is considered human and natural.
>
> ("Unconsciousness and Survival" 2)

We will all, for instance, live and die, but how and why are nuanced individually by factors beyond conscious organization. Stories, great and crummy, are time capsules for the hopes and anxieties – the complexes – of their own eras. In delving into my selection of Vonnegut and Bradbury's stories, we can see American myths, new and old, packaged and repackaged, in a historical context, in action, and in relation to the complexes of our own day. Before we address those stories, however, we must essay a post-Jungian approach to reading short stories as myths.

What we talk about when we talk about myth

Listen for the word "myth" and you will often hear it taking the fall for others, words like "bunkus," "hooey," and "lies." Today "myth" is popularly synonymous with "falsehood." The widespread understanding of myth syncs with C. S. Lewis's opinion "that myths [are] lies and therefore worthless, even though 'breathed through silver'" (Tolkien 85). Psychiatrist Rollo May (1909–1994), who called the last "our mainly mythless century" (*Cry for Myth* 47), objected to myth's denigration, saying, "This is an error that could be committed only by a society that has become so inebriated with adding up empirical facts that it seals off the deeper wisdom of human history" (*Courage to Create* 28). The twentieth century saw some thinkers, particularly those in the fields of psychology and comparative mythology, arguing against the nineteenth century's intellectual placement of science over myth and the idea that rationality made myth irrelevant. Living amid the collective denial of myth, C. G. Jung (1875–1961), Joseph Campbell (1904–1987), Rollo May, James Hillman (1926–2011), John Moriarty (1938–2007), and others sought to reawaken Westerners' appreciation of myth for its therapeutic, vitalizing properties. They believed rationalism's widespread appeal since the Enlightenment had thrown the Western psyche off balance by showing mystery the back door.

Consider the following extract from the definition of 'myth' in Samuels' *A Critical Dictionary of Jungian Analysis*: "Myths are stories of archetypal encounters. [. . .] Modern psychology [. . .] must treat the products of unconscious fantasy, including mythological motifs, as statements of psyche about itself. We do not invent myths; we experience them" (*CDJA* 95). Not at all meant as a reference guide for the general reader, unlike the *OED* and Merriam-Webster's dictionary, here myth is not equated with lies but respected as a force of human nature. Stories that behave mythically have a dynamism thought to possess a "compulsive hold" that, like feeling and emotion, is not chosen but experienced (*CDJA* 95). In "The Psychology of the Child Archetype" (1951), Jung, in his most concise definition of myth, wrote: "Myths are original revelations of the preconscious psyche, involuntary statements about unconscious psychic happenings, and anything but allegories of physical processes" (1940/1968, *CW 9.I*, 261). That idea of revelation is integral to analytical psychology, which holds myth as abetting mental and spiritual health. Bradbury was no Jungian, but he expressed a similar attitude often: "The ability to fantasize is the ability to survive, and the ability to fantasize is the ability to grow" ("Day at Night").

Hillman, a student of Jung's who broke away to found the field of archetypal psychology in the nineteen-seventies, disagreed on this point with his own polycentric perspective. "For the archetypal school," writes Michael Vannoy Adams, "there are no archetypes as such . . . There are only phenomena, or images, that may be *archetypal*" (Dawson and Young-Eisendrath 109). "This tenet of archetypal psychology," says Hillman, "operates upon every mythic tale and figure, removing them from the realm of story only and pulling them down and in, showing how a myth precisely works in the psyche, in its habits of mind and heart" (*Dream and the Underworld* 24). For Hillman, those figures and presences that rise up from the unconscious in dreams, the imagination, and mythic narrative do not default to beneficence. Their mien can operate under every possible condition of life and beyond if we allow for metaphysics. The millennial Irish mystic John Moriarty is closer to Hillman in this respect: "I don't go all the way with Jung. I don't accept that life in harmony with these images is fullest life. I don't accept that life in harmony with them is wisdom" (*TGLT3* XLIV). But the Jungian approach is not purely positive; Jung believed that a modern manifestation of the Germanic storm god Wotan had possessed the Nazis, destroying not only much of Europe but the Nazis themselves.[2]

Campbell is more optimistic in his appraisal of the potential for our relationship with unconscious contents:

> Fantasy and imagination is a product of the body. The energies that bring forth the fantasies derive from the organs of the body. The organs of the body are the source of our life and of our intentions for life. And they conflict with each other. [. . .] All of these different forces come into conflict within us and the function of mythological imagery is to harmonize them, coordinate the energies of our body, so that we will live a harmonious and fruitful life in accord with our society and with the new mystery that emerges with every human being, namely what are the possibilities of this particular human life?
>
> ("Understanding Mythology with Joseph Campbell")

This perspective gives myth a phenomenological basis, one arising from the body. The biological dimension of these hunches has been supported in recent years in scholarship showing them to be consilient with science today. Knox makes a compelling argument that the concept of the emergent mind "provides the key to our attempts to reconcile biology with psyche" (202), while John Ryan Haule describes today's revisions and validations of Jungian thought as dependent upon a contemporary approach to myth: "A mythic perspective that is out of harmony with the world science describes cannot enchant the world. It can only ignore the world" ("Jung Today"). Literary scholar Loree Rackstraw, whose criticism courts quantum physics, agrees on embracing interdisciplinary consilience: "When we are in accord with these universal processes we, too, may recognize our sense of awareness as a sacred aspect of the universe" ("Quantum" 59).

Key to a post-Jungian approach is the recognition of myth as *dynamic*, as succinctly defined by Lucy Huskinson: "Myth is a story of human behavior, which is continually retold in line with the developing behaviours of the human race, society, or individual personality with which it is concerned" (4). Jung saw the artist as instructing his or her own society by providing narratives in which the myths find expression:

> [Art] is constantly at work educating the spirit of the age, conjuring up forms in which the age is most lacking. The unsatisfied yearning of the

> artist reaches back to the primordial image in the unconscious which is best fitted to compensate the inadequacy and one-sidedness of the present.
>
> (1922/1966, *CW 15*, 130)

As old values fall, new ones are manifesting, emerging. This balancing act plays out unconsciously, spanning eras. Moriarty, not a depth psychologist but a philosopher, also acknowledges this process of change: "Transformed archetypes imply the possibility of an alternative culture" (*TGLT3* xv). From a post-Jungian perspective, as some archetypes dissolve and others crystallize in the psyche of a civilization, myths perpetuate or arise and are expressed, among other places, in narratives. Art provides core samples, as it were, of these unconscious forces demanding conscious attention.

Campbell came to prominence, with *The Hero with a Thousand Faces* (1949), at a time when many scholars in America were reframing the nation's myths. Henry Nash Smith (1906–1986) re-presented the myth of the American West in *Virgin Land* (1950), R. W. B. Lewis (1917–2002) uncovered nineteenth-century American examples of the first man in *The American Adam* (1955), and Perry Miller (1905–1963) humanized the country's Puritan forebears in *Errand into the Wilderness* (1956). Donald E. Pease has called this movement, which includes literary critics Leslie Fiedler (1917–2003) and Leo Marx (1919–), "the Myth and Symbol school of American studies" (162): "The symbolic national tradition that Myth and Symbol scholars invented enabled the symbolic engineers responsible for the forging of the nation's foreign policy to fashion imaginary resolutions for the seemingly intractable political dilemmas that confronted Americans throughout the cold war" (165). Pease, a student of it, once condemned this school with what he describes as "excoriating" rhetoric but has since softened his position: "My real though utterly displaced target was, as I have now come to realize, the myth symbol pedagogy in which Jim Miller had trained me" ("American Studies: An Interview with Donald Pease"). As he conceives it, this school, spanning the forties into the sixties, lost its relevance when the United States faced the crisis of violence in Vietnam (1961–1975).

Campbell – and literary critic Northrop Frye (1912–1991), as a Canadian – stand in relation to the Myth and Symbol school in a curious way. Where Frye sought to unify the human creation of literature under a single theory, Campbell endeavored to look at myths beyond American borders and in the stories of the country's indigenous peoples to deliver to secular Americans a sense of connection with life everywhere on the planet. Frye's project inevitably carries Canadian inflections, just as Campbell's globalizing humanism is born out of an American context. Where other Myth and Symbol scholars concerned themselves with national mythology, Frye and Campbell courted the metanarrative of human myth.

Today Jung and Campbell after him stand branded as romantics. Without regarding recent revisions to Jungian thought, Glen Robert Gill, a devotee of

Frye, has argued that Jung's "orientations and intentions [toward existential empowerment and affirmation] did not prevent him from making certain metaphysical assertions that dilute the phenomenological basis from which he hoped his theories would derive their authority" (48). Hazard Adams, in *Philosophy of the Literary Symbolic* (1983), finds Campbell to be a reductionist reliant on mysticism: "In this theory we find an unconscious return to romantic 'religious' allegory even as the rhetoric of the presentation denigrates allegory in favor of the 'miraculous' symbol" (248). Eric Csapo, in *Theories of Mythology* (2005), dismisses Campbell's monomyth as reductive but falls victim to his own claim by only considering Campbell's first book in a career that spanned forty years. The myth scholar most critical of Campbell is Segal, who sees Campbell as dogmatic, "an evangelist for myth" (*Theorizing About Myth* 137). Segal's worry in "The Romantic Appeal of Joseph Campbell" (1990) is that Campbell's popularity would lead others to see his as the *only* theory of myth: "Campbell's work is an important introduction to myth. It is simply not the last word" (*Theorizing About Myth* 141).

Contrast that to the attitude put forth in "The Dilettante Among Symbols," the introduction to Indologist Heinrich Zimmer's *The King and the Corpse: Tales of the Soul's Conquest of Evil* (1948), edited by Campbell after Zimmer's death:

> What [symbols and stories] demand of us is not the monologue of a coroner's report, but the dialogue of a living conversation. [. . .]They have to be questioned and consulted anew, with every age, each age approaching them with its own variety of ignorance and understanding, its own set of problems, and its own inevitable questions. [. . .] We can never exhaust the depths – of that we may be certain; but then neither can anyone else. And a cupped handful of the fresh waters of life is sweeter than a whole reservoir of dogma, piped and guaranteed. [. . .] No matter what the reading accessible to our present vision, it cannot be final. It can only be a preliminary glimpse. And we should regard it as an inspiration and a stimulation, not as a final definition precluding further insights and differing approaches.
>
> (3–6)

Campbell credited Zimmer (1890–1943) above Jung in his own intellectual development, saying, "If I do have a guru [. . .] it would be Zimmer – the one who really gave me the courage to interpret myths out of what I knew of their common symbol" (Toms 123). The passage above expresses the focus running throughout Campbell's work, so that if he could be accused of being dogmatic, perhaps his is a dogma against dogmatism.

Bernard DeVoto (1897–1955) once noted, "It is a little hard to know what romantic means to those who use the word umbrageously" (Robertson 345). The sense one gets is that the critics are themselves uncomfortable with Jung and Campbell's reliance on metaphysics. Ritske Rensma presents a concise reading of Campbell's metaphysics in *The Innateness of Myth* (2009):

> Campbell felt that when one goes deeply enough into the unconscious one begins to make contact with layers that are truly transpersonal, that connect one to more than just the individual psyche. This is already true for dream consciousness, which contains the collective unconscious: this layer is transpersonal in the sense that it is the same in all of us, and because it is instinctual also connects us to the world of nature. [. . .] Dreams and myths arise from [a 'ground of being'], and by getting in touch with dreams and myths we connect to this source.
>
> (169)

For Jung it manifested in his concept of synchronicity, for Campbell the notion of a transparence to transcendence. In a practical way, Kevin Schilbrack defends metaphysical interpretation, arguing that "to assume that myths cannot involve metaphysics blinds one to the possibility that a myth attempts to describe a culture's understanding of reality as such" (95). Campbell championed the influence of a transcendent source for life. If such belief is concomitant with romanticism, it does not render their approaches to myth invalid, though it does present the opportunity to explore its role.

These modern, secular spiritual stances on myth can be taken as reactionary against the rationalism upheld by earlier scholars like E. B. Tylor (1832–1917) and Sir James Frazer (1854–1941); perhaps rationalism's assumption of superiority over spirituality spurred romantic points of view to arise anew. Kant, Arthur Schopenhauer (1788–1860), Sigmund Freud (1856–1939), Jung, Zimmer, Campbell, Rollo May, Hillman, Moriarty, and others understood pure reason to be incapable of explaining *everything* there is to know about human beings. They did not reject the scientific advances of their day, but felt the acute lacking, the empty spaces, resulting from a complete reliance on rationalism for the difficult and dynamic explanations of one's individual existence. The depths of life's subjective experiences cannot be neatly mapped out like our genome, but their expressions do manifest in works of art, which can then be examined, most formally under the umbrella field we call the humanities.

Campbell's work led him to believe that the benefit of a mythic understanding of life is that it vitalizes, arms against pitfalls, prepares people for and guides them through anxieties, failures, and triumphs. He championed this in the interviews with Bill Moyers that made him a household name when broadcast on American public television as *The Power of Myth* (1988):

> It's important to live life with the experience, and therefore the knowledge, of its mystery and of your own mystery. This gives life a new radiance, a new harmony, a new splendor. Thinking in mythological terms

> helps to put you in accord with the inevitables of this vale of tears. You learn to recognize the positive values in what appear to be the negative moments and aspects of your life.
>
> (163)

He saw myth as the exhaustless repository from which narratives are woven. A myth need not be written, painted, sung, or told – it can be a wholly private story or representation of what lies beyond standard human understanding – but there are people among us, artists, who are compelled to create and share what they discover at the exchange between conscious and unconscious experience.

Archetypes and archetypal images

In 2011, Haule formulated a post-Jungian definition for archetypes that is consilient with current scientific findings:

> 1 An archetype is a species-universal pattern
> 2 of meaningful recognition, imagination and behavior
> 3 that resembles behaviors in closely related species,
> 4 allowing us to trace a hypothetical line of inheritance back to a (possibly extinct) ancestor species,
> 5 and entails identifiable physiological alterations (brain-tracts, hormones, etc.).
> 6 As a result of hormone and autonomic nervous system involvement, archetypes are usually experienced as powerfully emotional, even numinous.
> 7 The archetype itself is an "empty program" that needs life-experience to "fill" it,
> 8 and this filling process "wires" the brain according to local and cultural styles of living,
> 9 with the result that "archetypal," in the sense of "mythic" images and expectations always take culture-specific forms.
>
> (27)

While an archetype can never be captured in our understanding, it will project images by which it can be recognized. Wendy Doniger provides a brilliant simile, drawn from science fiction, to explain the difference between an archetype and an archetypal image: "Like the Invisible Man, who could only be seen when he was wrapped in bandages or dressed in a hat and a coat, the archetype can only be 'seen' when it is enveloped in the bandages that each cultural manifestation swathes it in" (O'Flaherty "The Survival of Myth in Science Fiction" 24). Steven F. Walker adds that where critics of Jungian psychology trip in their assessment of it, and I direct this at Campbell's critics as well, is the distinction between the concepts of myth and archetype: "it is improper to consider a myth as ageless or as universal as an archetype, since it bears the particular stamp of the specific age and culture that produces it" (19). The humanist recognition of universality in the study of mythology points through those specific stamps, while celebrating their unique inflections, to the archetypal situations common to members of the species scientifically named *Homo sapiens sapiens*.

Here it is appropriate to acknowledge Doniger's scholarship because she reads the archetypal approach differently. In "Joseph Campbell, or, rather, the followers of Joseph Campbell" (*Other People's Myths* 175), Doniger sees those who "would reduce all myths to a colorless, minimal, universal form, a common denominator so common that it has no nobility left at all" (35):

> Like their archetypes, myths do not, strictly speaking, have meanings; they provide contexts in which meaning occurs. [. . .] To this degree, a myth is not so much a true story as a story on which truth is based, a story which people may infuse with their truth. [. . .] When the archetype is regarded as the sum total of all the manifestations, when everything is put in, the myth is enriched; when the archetype is regarded as what is left when all the manifestations are removed, when everything is taken out, the myth is impoverished.
>
> (35, 36)

Her respect for Campbell is sincere, noting "he is critically aware of the great gaps in our knowledge, and he usually identifies his hypotheses as no more than that" (O'Flaherty "Origins of Myth-Making Man" 24), but she labels him "a Jungian without shadows" (24), curious given that Campbell deeply influenced George Lucas's ongoing creation of Darth Vader, one of the most infamous shadows in film history. Reviewing his *Atlas of World Mythology* as "good art, not good science" (25), one senses that Doniger's criticism hinges on the romantic aspects of Campbell's perspective.

Campbell was not a scientist; he was a humanist furthering meaningful discussion of the emotional, spiritual, and psychological forces at play in mythic arts and literatures from cultures around the world and throughout time. Moriarty's position on this is fitting: "It has never occurred to me that those of us who aren't scientists should abdicate to scientists the privilege of talking about the universe" (*TGLT3* LXXII). Setting science as the basis for all knowledge creates a one-sided paradigm that renders itself unconscious to matters of the unconscious. As Martinez points out, "symbols can convey numinous experience, not as scientific evidence, but as phenomenological, subjective reality" ("Reading for Psyche: Numinosity" 2). Where Campbell, and Jung before him, reveled was in the sheer diversity of mythic narratives dealing with the same basic archetypal situations. "One of the reasons I lost my temper with Joseph Campbell was because he did it wrong and made it harder for me to persuade people that it was possible to do it right," Doniger writes. "His static monomyth is the very antithesis of the ceaselessly engaged and always subject-filled approach that I argue for" (*Implied Spider* 64). Never mind that the title to his first and most famous work, in which he presents his monomyth, is a perfect metaphor for the difference between archetypes and archetypal images: *The Hero* (archetype) *with a Thousand Faces* (archetypal images).

Doniger, leveling the serious charge of "the archetype as the enemy not only of social change but also of social justice" (*Implied Spider* 137), quotes another eminent critic, Marina Warner:

> When history falls away from a subject, we are left with Otherness, and all its power to compact enmity, recharge it and recirculate it. An archetype is a hollow thing, but a dangerous one, a figure or image which through usage has been uncoupled from the circumstances which brought it into being, and goes on spreading false consciousness. [. . .] The theory of archetypes, which is essentially ahistorical, helps to confirm gender inevitability and to imprison male and female in stock definitions.
>
> (Warner 239, 279)

Warner is right that an archetype is a hollow thing, but it is not fair to assume it is therefore dangerous. The cruel and oppressive manifestations are not the only show in town; some archetypes coo rather than coup. Post-Jungians believe that any archetype is ultimately androgynous and can be expressed across the full valence of human experience. Jung even wrote that mother as archetype, "Like any other archetype [. . .] appears under an almost infinite variety of aspects" (*CW* 9.i ¶156). What we consider is how Mother is inflected and then why. Interpretation must include history *and* histories: personal, societal, ethnic, ancestral, even evolutionary. From a post-Jungian view, Warner has been one of the many voices combating gendered myths supporting patriarchy – what analyst Marion Woodman calls one of "the outworn mythologies" (9) – as its privileged position in the West changes. It is true, too, that Jungians and post-Jungians re-vision the concepts of analytical and archetypal psychology, especially as attitudes toward gender and sexuality change.[3]

The laziest theory of archetypes confuses an archetypal image for the archetype, i.e. an image of a nurturing Mother is read as the Mother archetype.[4] Archetypes are formless, and we haven't chosen them; as conditions of life they simply occur, entirely regardless of the values we perpetually project onto them. We have not invented the patterns of life, but through the diverse effects of living, we experience and elaborate them. We are concerned with inflections of life's energies that run the gamut, from experience to transcendence, not meanings reduced to monoliths. Campbell, maintaining that "one can never exhaust [a work of art's] meaning" or "possibility," jokes about this serious misstep to the archetypal approach: "Ask an artist, 'What does your picture mean?' Well, if he despises you enough, he'll tell you. The point is that if you need him to tell you what it means, then you haven't seen it" (*Pathways to Bliss* 97). If one is going to study the cultural specificity of archetypal images, one must be able to identify the archetypes they constellate and the complexes they feed. An archetypal approach to mythology is incomplete if one only focuses on archetypes *or* archetypal images. Both need to be taken into account, acknowledging the tensions between the human universal and the culturally – and individually – specific.

Campbell's condensed functions of myth

Campbell conceived four functions of myth: the metaphysical, the cosmological, the sociological, and the pedagogical (*MGC* 609–624)[5]:

- The metaphysical function "is to waken and maintain in the individual an experience of awe, humility, and respect, in recognition of that ultimate mystery, transcending names and forms, 'from which,' as we read in the Upanishads, 'words turn back.'"

  (*MGC 609*)

- The cosmological function is "that of rendering an image of the universe through which this sense of the mystery will be experienced, so that the whole world should become as it were a holy picture."

  (*Man and Myth*)

- The sociological function aims "to validate and maintain a certain specific social order."

  (*Man and Myth*)

- The pedagogical function is "the centering and harmonization of the individual, which in traditional systems was supposed to follow upon the giving of oneself, and even giving up of oneself altogether."

  (*MGC* 623)

Key to our understanding of myth's place in the West are Campbell's metaphysical and pedagogical functions, particularly in relation to compensation. Perhaps this is no accident, as he notes:

> Our image of the cosmos is totally different from that of the religious traditions in which we've been brought up. And the social order is totally different from what it was in the days when these laws of Moses and so forth were composed. [. . .] The basic psychological problems of youth, maturity, and age, and death, and the mystical problem of the mystery of the universe, these remain. And so it is largely from the psychological

> standpoint that one can reinterpret, re-experience, and reuse the traditions which science and the new morality seem to have taken away.
>
> (*Man and Myth*)

So whereas we have learned, thanks to the sciences, that Earth is a sphere revolving around the sun, which itself is a star on the outskirts of a galaxy, which itself is one of countless galaxies in the universe, and that we ourselves have come about, like all living things on the planet, through a branching of mutations at the molecular level of DNA, and whereas Westerners have convened to write their own laws instead of relying solely on scriptures for legal and social systems, there are still needs within us right now that can be nourished through an active engagement with myth: a way to metabolize the mystery beyond mystery, and a way, or at least the odd signpost, indicating the stages and ordeals of life commonly experienced, threshold passages such as birth, death, trauma and triumph, war, fear, love. Moriarty says, "Myths are instinct with wonder. Like nothing else perhaps in our culture, they uncompromisingly mediate the difficult strangeness of self and of world. Therefore the philomythos has as good a chance of reaching and living in the Truth as the philosophos does" (*TGLT3* IX).

Campbell believed the cosmological and sociological functions of myth as experienced through religious tradition had failed for many Americans because those institutions have answered reason's smugness toward them by attempting to historicize their scriptures. He stressed that mythic symbols are destroyed as soon as dogma dictates what those symbols should evoke in us: "[All] the historic events that are so important to us in our tradition should not be important to us in any way except as symbols of powers within ourselves" (*Goddesses* 14). Spiritual leaders asking that we accept virgin birth as a human fact does not convince those of us who paid attention in biology class and jeopardizes our chances of experiencing the metaphorical resonances of virgin birth. Campbell's answer to this problem appeals to the myth of individualism and the individual's duty to sift through religion's fractured metaphors to quench our thirsty spirits:

> There are mythologies that are scattered, broken up, all around us. We stand on what I call a terminal moraine of shattered mythic systems that once structured society. They can be detected all around us. You can select any of these fragments that activate your imagination for your own use. Let it help to shape your own relationship to the unconscious system out of which these symbols have come.
>
> (*Thou Art That* 86–7)

The emphasis here falls on the individual to discover for him or herself those stories that affirm and inform the sense of being alive. Here stories are phenomenological expressions of myth, meeting the soul's needs with narratives.

Rensma takes Segal's interpretation of Campbell to task for its denial of Campbell's intellectual development in his relationship with Jung's work over the course of his long career. The same criticism could be leveled at Adams's critique of Campbell in *Philosophy of the Literary Symbolic*, for he only examines *The Hero with a Thousand Faces* (1949) and, like Csapo, fails to consider the rest of Campbell's output. Rensma, showing that what galvanized Campbell's approach was the task of editing *The Portable Jung* for Viking Press (1971), makes a strong argument for reading Campbell's work from 1968 to his death as post-Jungian, because in this final stage of his life he embraced key Jungian concepts with consistency. And while Campbell's work exploring universalities leaves him unpopular with some critics, it is precisely that which won him respect from modern mythmakers and the public. For Americans living with the belief that all men are created equal, universality is one of the most powerful cultural myths. Campbell's humanistic theory of myth embraces the motto of the United States, *E pluribus unum*, making his a uniquely American approach. Where some see in his scholarship a one-sided universalism, others find his kaleidoscopic delight in the diversity of expressions for specific motifs occurring across cultures. In a two-hundred year old country of immigrants from lands, races, and traditions near and far, a system of myth that embraces the diversity of imported and newly-hatched symbols has shown great appeal. Campbell's theory of myth, romantic in its inclusiveness, affirms the ethos set out in United States of America's foundational documents. His theory of myth is one by the people and for the people, whoever they are, wherever they came from, and however they tell their stories.

From Campbell's perspective, the United States is not devoid of myth. Like all societies, the U.S.A. is held together *by* myth, by the collective beliefs, acknowledged and subliminal, shared and fought over by the individuals and groups that make it up. What has changed is the recognition of myth, which Campbell sees as having been repressed by an emphasis on rationalism. In the two decades following WWII, people in the United States faced new situations, which birthed new myths. A major one was the myth of the world superpower. The scientific advances that ended WWII produced only a brief period of weapons superiority, ending 29 August 1949 when the Soviet Union tested their own atom bomb. Though the U.S.A. was (and remains to this day) the only nation to have used nuclear weapons against another country, fear of nuclear annihilation inspired the Cold War with the U.S.S.R., a conflict fought in defense spending and weapons proliferation. The United States, anticipating Soviet discoveries in particle physics, reframed itself from aggressor to defender, renaming the War (and Navy) Department in 1947 to the Defense Department.

This shift, seemingly subtle, changed American consciousness of war. The arena where competition between the U.S.A. and the U.S.S.R. played out most visibly became known as the Space Race. The American myth of the frontier expanded to include low Earth orbit and the moon. Within U.S. borders, the Cold War pitted citizens against each other in the Red Scare, blacklisting, and McCarthyism. This myth of the superpower, which Americans believed in and hold to today, brought with it many anxieties and new dreams for the future.

There were also radical changes in the way Americans viewed race in the fifties and sixties. The old myth of racial hierarchy, with whites above and blacks beneath and others in between, was challenged and legally rejected. Women started entering college and the workplace in greater numbers, and in 1960 took control of contraception with the FDA's approval of the birth control pill, mythically regarded in capital letters as The Pill. Automobile ownership became a mark of normalcy and interstate and highway infrastructure provided a vigorous new circulatory system of freight and travel across the nation. Industry and consumerism invigorated the economy, appliances altered life lived in the American home, and television changed the way America presented itself to itself, repackaging and eventually exporting to other countries, as a globalizing aspiration, the myth of the American Dream. These sweeping changes were not lost on Campbell, whose interest in mythology stretched from prehistory to his present day. An American, shaped by but also aware of the United States' own myths through the nature of his work, Campbell's theory of myth, which is concurrent with their careers as writers of imaginative fiction, provides insight into Vonnegut and Bradbury's America.

Short fiction as myth

Myth's webbing traces through any form of expression, but this study examines myth through the medium of the short story. Compact narratives lend themselves to condensing metaphor, that figure of speech Vico (1668–1744) explained as "a fable in brief" (129). "I speak in tongues. I write metaphors," said Bradbury. "Every one of my stories is a metaphor you can remember. The great religions are all metaphor" (Weller 204). Vonnegut reflected upon this point in a 1999 radio interview: "The short story is a very special art form and almost as artificial as the sonnet, really, because it misrepresents life. Events can't be that meaningful and that compact" (*Bookworm*). A novel, play, or film is oftentimes an anthology of metaphors, whereas short stories, like lyric poems, songs, and some of the visual arts, can single out and distill one with great precision. Campbell insisted metaphors must reveal "that life does not have any one absolutely fixed meaning. These images must point past all meanings given, beyond all definitions and relationships, to that really ineffable mystery that is just the existence, the being of ourselves and of our world. If we give that mystery an exact meaning we diminish the experience of its real depth" (*Thou Art That* 8–9). Short story theorist Charles E. May links the short story back to the impetus for myth: "a feeling – rather than a concept of the systematic pattern of social functioning" (131). May, who rallied around the short story in the nineteen-eighties and nineties as a form deserving of its own criticism, helped found the scholarly movement that has brought forth a suite of short story theories.

May says short fiction's chief reason for existing as a form is "to 'defamiliarize' the everyday. Storytelling does not spring from one's confrontation with the everyday world, but rather from one's encounter with the sacred (in which true reality is revealed in all its plenitude) or with the absurd (in which true reality is revealed in all its vacuity)" (133). May's stance is that the short story disrupts or disturbs those aspects of life most people take for granted, being based upon a receptive, deautomatized perspective, whereas the novel operates in an active, automatized mode. A theoretically promiscuous scholar, he cites psychologist Arthur Deikman's (1929–2013) bimodal automatized/deautomatized world view and Martin Buber's (1878–1965) philosophy of dialogue as fitting the narrative forms: I-It for the novel, I-Thou for short stories. Moment births short fiction, in this view, as opposed to how successive events make a novel.

There is another possibility in short fiction, one reaching past duality, which we might call a reautomatized mode, suprapersonal, or the Thou-I. It fuses awareness of self with awareness of the Other's self and accepts the two as linked, forming an awareness of interconnectedness between and through all. "You can address anything as a 'thou,'" Campbell said, "and if you do it, you can feel the change in your own psychology. The ego that sees a 'thou' is not the same ego that sees an 'it'" (*POM* 78–9). When it comes to this experience with fiction, Martinez urges what she calls reading for psyche, whereby we open ourselves to reading as a rite: "Because imaginative literature engages emotions through narrative and sensuous language, reading it is not merely a sequence of cognitions. Reading for the 'Other' requires an openness to the text as physical, emotional, and conceptual experience of what one does not yet know" ("Ego Readings vs. Reading for Psyche" 6). What we stand to encounter is the interdependence of everything, something we typically all too quickly lose after catching those fleeting glimpses of it over the course of a life. "What literature tells is vital to our survival," says American writer Richard Ford, "[because] the imagination can bring us news about our natures that the other news organs can't and never will" (*New Granta Book of the American Short Story* xxiv).

Campbell often expressed the suprapersonal concept using a Sanskrit phrase from the Chāndogya Upaniṣad: *Tat tvam asi*, translated as "Thou art that." He drew from Schopenhauer's interpretation of the concept in *The World as Will and Representation* (1818):

> "This presupposes," he declares, "that I have to some extent identified myself with the other and therewith removed for the moment the barrier between the 'I' and the 'Not-I'. Only then can the other's situation, his want, his need, become mine. I then no longer see him in the way of an empirical perception, as one strange to me, indifferent to me, completely other than myself; but in him I suffer, in spite of the fact that his skin does not enfold my nerves . . ."
>
> (*IROS* 83–84)

Campbell also cites physicist Erwin Schrödinger's appraisal of the phrase in *My View of the World* (1964):

> Inconceivable as it seems to ordinary reason, you – and all other conscious beings as such – are all in all. Hence this life of yours which you are living is not merely a piece of the entire existence, but is in a certain sense the *whole*; only this whole is not so constituted that it can be surveyed in one single glance. This, as we know, is what the Brahmins express in that sacred, mystic formula which is yet really so simple and so clear: *Tat tvam asi*, this is you.
>
> (22)

This belief in a union of all things pushes beyond rationality into metaphysics to form a suprapersonal perspective. It is evoked by a subjective experience of symbol, which can be rendered within and beyond the confines of fiction. This phenomenon is dynamic and found in many places, arts, even sciences. My decision to focus solely on short fiction is similar to May's, in that the form lends itself to symbolic distillation:

> In their very shortness, short stories have remained close to the original source of narrative in myth, folktale, fable, and fairy tale. They, therefore, are more apt to focus on basic desires, dreams, anxieties, and fears than novels are and thus are more aligned with the original religious nature of narrative. Short stories are therefore more apt to embody a timeless theme and are thus less dependent on a social context than novels. Consequently, short stories are more likely to identify characters in archetypal terms and are more patterned and aesthetically unified than novels are.
>
> (*NSST* xxvi)

May may gambol throughout his scholarship – his essays are grab bags of theorists whose ideas he liberally applies to the short story – but his exuberance succeeded in drawing serious critical attention to the form.

Susan Rowland and Terence Dawson, especially, have emulsified post-Jungian psychology and literary criticism in the theory-driven (and oftentimes theory-obsessed) field of literary studies. Rowland identifies the cross-pollinating potentials of post-Jungian criticism and feminist, postcolonial, historicist, deconstructionist, and postmodern theories. As she argues in *C. G. Jung and Literary Theory* (1999), Jungian theory needs to be critiqued by contemporary paradigms but also stands to enrich them in the process. Luckily, the aim in literary studies, more and more, is not textual mastery but what Dawson calls "polyphonic" discourse (286). He claims that "The defining characteristic of Jungian interpretation is *not* an interest in archetypal images, but the concept of *compensation*" (*The Effective Protagonist in the Nineteenth-Century British Novel*, 13). Studying archetypal images is the key to unlocking the nature of compensation present in a literary work. Even if one is reading stories written in his or her own culture, the critical reader must not assume definitive knowledge of the societal dynamics in which they were written, particularly if those stories were written before one's lifetime. Martinez urges us to learn whatever we can about what mattered to people in the time and place a narrative appeared: "Obviously, one should know as much about those times as one can, not only imaginatively to approach what experiencing the work could have been like, but precisely because what was consciously valued provides clues as to what was missing from a culture's attitude" ("Re-reading Sophocles's Oedipus Plays" 4).

Dawson calls post-Jungian criticism an "approach" (275), not a dogma. At its best, he finds it operating not so much as a theory but as a "working hypothesis" (289). His challenge to those who would pursue this approach is to emulate Jung's habit of being unpredictable. Instead of expected arguments built too heavily upon Jungian terms, what Dawson calls "instant Jung," the post-Jungian literary critic should strive to make new discoveries and bring forth the unexpected. This complements the endeavor of short fiction, for, as Ford notes:

> Imaginative literature, at least initially, means to tell us something different, something made-up and for which we may have to suspend our disbelief, something whose existence is specific to a piece of writing and can't be accurately paraphrased, and which often deals with those consequences of our acts which we are likely to overlook because they're small, or buried in our interior selves, or both; or because language turns out to be an ambiguous thing which doesn't always announce what it seems to be announcing so that we are forced to act out of confusion. [. . . It's] frequently about things that *aren't* clear but that need clearing up so that we can lead more morally responsible or even pleasurable lives – things we may not want to do because they're difficult.
>
> (*Granta Book of the American Short Story* xii–xiii)

If mystery is inherent and crucial to the art form – and it certainly is – a predictable approach will never do. Let us not fall into the trap cynically identified by critic Frank Lentricchia when he says, "Tell me your theory and I'll tell you in advance what you'll say about any work of literature, especially those you haven't read" (Boyd 388). Let us dare to honor the uniqueness of each work of art in our own unique ways, for as post-Jungians we respect our subjectivities as peculiar to each of us, allowing us greater freedom to synthesize and essay one-of-a-kind readings than those working (or suffering) under other paradigms.

A post-Jungian approach favors criticism of the short story in that, as Dawson notes, Jungian interpretations require a lot of space on the page. More can be unpacked in an article about a short story's details than those found in a novel for, when it comes to details, novels dwarf short stories. Post-Jungian close readings and the psychoanalytic case studies of dreams share much in common: they are extrapolations, detail-conscious, and they build upon the content available in order to get at archetypal underpinnings. At the same time, short stories share with dreams the quality of brevity. For the post-Jungian literary scholar, it is all the more possible to build an insightful reading of a short story in six to seven thousand words than it would be to do so for an entire novel. Jung and his descendants, working from a therapeutic basis, have produced book-length studies analyzing dream cycles experienced by individual analysands much the way literary critics produce research monographs on single novels and story cycles by single authors. Covering more with less space can and has been done well, particularly by Dawson and Rowland, but the potential for the uses of a post-Jungian approach with the study of short fiction is fertile ground. Criticism and art form meld in compelling ways heretofore unrecognized as an approach complementary to both. All short stories can be read archetypally, but the approach may also be most convincing in the instance of those stories that feature the sort of fantasy met in dreams and mythology.

Perhaps the greatest contribution May has made to the field of short fiction studies was the decision to recognize short story *theories* over short story *theory*. Scholars working on the criticism of short stories after decades of critical neglect already honor a polyphony of theoretical approaches. The field is progressive in this sense, moving away from the outworn notion of mastering a text and into a vast realm of readings. Here is another place in which short fiction studies and post-Jungian perspectives coexist. Critics are able to put forth their own readings of a story without the insistence upon invoking the same few theorists and movements over and over again. This works so long as they produce relevant readings and bring forth ideas heretofore unexpressed. And while a project such as Northrop Frye's, seeking the "coordinated principle" of myth and literature (*Anatomy of Criticism* 16), need not be dismissed, it is exciting to see critics incorporating perspectives ancient and new to collectively achieve a body of criticism that defies reductive techniques by undertaking synthesizing explorations.

Regarding myth, Dawson notes that "One of the most pressing challenges facing Jungian criticism is to formulate a theory of myth that can be respected by a sufficient number of scholars of myth to allow it to enter wider debate" (289). Here he sidesteps his own claim for polyphony. Citing Csapo's lack of engagement with Jung and Campbell is appropriate, but let us not surrender to the hollow Jungian ring in others' scholarship as a call to a unified theory of myth. Segal has devoted much of his work to favorably critiquing the mechanics of Jung's ideas of myth in comparison with others. But here I make a humble suggestion: let us consult Segal's and Csapo's works as references, for that is the nature of their projects. They have collated and critiqued critical theories of myth but are not themselves theorists of myth, having yet to put forth models or approaches we can recognize as their own. If anything, they have shown us that there is not a single paradigm to explain myth. Should there be? A living theory of myth is the embrace of diverse theories of myth. Again, ours in post-Jungian scholarship is an approach, one of many, and it need not exist merely to bat others down and claim dominance. Let us, in the spirit of those attending Olga Fröbe's Eranos conferences, invite all to sit at the round table and there appreciate our consilience and differences alike.

A useful method in a post-Jungian reading of myth in short stories is amplification. Jung said that "we resort to amplification in the interpretation of dreams, for a dream is too slender a hint to be understood until it is enriched by the stuff of association and analogy and thus amplified to the point of intelligibility" (1968, *CW 12*, ¶403). We can do as much with short stories so as to draw out and better discuss what cultural imbalance is being compensated for. Hillman championed the way amplification honors multiplicities inherent in dream and fantasy images to create a dynamic sense of what is present, opposing reductive reading – what he calls "singleness of meaning" and "the scientific fallacy" (*Animal Presences* 21). Literary critics are already amplifying when we "unpack" those images, names, characters, and situations as they are encountered in fiction. In applying a range of cultural, historical, political, periodical, scientific, and subjective reader response perspectives to those story images, we can contextualize them in any number of ways. Rowland writes that "words on the page are one step removed from visual images. Reading a fiction will provoke mental images and these will be affected by the Jungian unconscious" (196). Amplification is our key to drawing the myth out of the narrative spurring those images in readers' imaginations.

Building from Campbell's four functions of myth can guide us, initially, in asking questions that will amplify a short story:

- Is there a metaphysical aspect to this story, pointing through its metaphors to the mystery of being?

- Is there a cosmological aspect to this story, iterating (super)natural rules and laws by which the universe is believed to operate?
- What are the sociological dimensions of the story? How do we place it in terms of history, socioeconomics, race and ethnicity, gender, nationality, and other social identities?
- Pedagogically, what is this story depicting in its characters at the individual level? Where are they in life, and what have we to learn from it? Where have they grown from and what do they grow toward?

The metaphysical question ponders the ineffable, of which there will only be so much a critic can express, its ultimate nature being inexpressible. For the second, particularly in addressing stories taking place in fantastic realms, we elbow up to scholars whose concern is the construction of an imaginary setting: worldbuilding. If a story opens on a Martian landscape, what is the nature of this specific version of Mars? How does it relate to contemporary findings about our cosmos? In short stories these details are presented quickly, for there is no room to elaborately describe an otherworldly environment the way, say, Frank Herbert could in his epic novel *Dune* (1965). But again, it is the sociological and pedagogical questions which may very well receive the most attention for they expand upon the more immediate conditions of human life. Dawson tells us to ask "how a work reflects *the society of the time in which it was created*" with an emphasis on considering the "possible *psychological implications of the text as a whole*" (277). Elaborating upon these questions allows us to parse a story for its myth. The answers amplify its contents, revealing the nature of its compensatory aspect. Interpretation, as with dreams, unfurls and validates the myth at work in the narrative.

If archetypal theory is lifted from religious interpretation and applied to secular literature, we may see in the characters and situations depicted the culture's archetypes in action. May argues that "the tradition of the short story as descended from myth, folktale, fable, and romance forms, drives it toward focusing on eternal values rather than temporal ones and sacred/unconscious reality rather than profane/everyday reality" (*NSST* xviii). I do not disagree, but add that in the short fiction we examine, the eternal and sacred/unconscious will be dressed in temporal and profane/everyday outfits and idioms. Applied to Vonnegut's and Bradbury's popular short fiction, we shall discover the undeniably postwar American-ness of the extraterrestrials, time machines, and monsters as they expound problems and situations both ancient and new to those people who identified themselves as twentieth-century Americans. The editors of *It Came From the 1950s!*, Darryl Jones, Elizabeth McCarthy, and Bernice Murphy, set a complementary aim in exploring postwar pop culture:

> Popular culture was the perfect medium for securing and enforcing cultural-imperial hegemony. And yet, as we have seen, popular culture

> also became a means of expressing themes and concerns which openly contradicted the cozily consensual message being disseminated by the military-industrial complex of which it might be viewed as the cultural arm. This duality, we would argue, is at the very heart of popular culture and its appeal.
>
> (14–15)

There are those who fight to uphold fading cultural norms and those who undermine their task to do so; there are those who attack new cultural conditions and those who seek to establish them against great odds. The anxiety arising from this struggle, which is itself a culture's attempt to find balance under shifting archetypes, provided Vonnegut and Bradbury with the wellspring from which they crafted their fiction. Again we should consider Jung's statement that, "[Art] is constantly at work educating the spirit of the age, conjuring up forms in which the age is most lacking." These two writers were anything but poster boys for American hegemony, but they were not pure rebels either. While Vonnegut and Bradbury's stories often confront and criticize postwar American life, they also embrace many of the foundational and adaptive ideals thought to be idiosyncratically – or, if you prefer, exceptionally – American.

The time and place for metaphors

If we pan out hemispherically and consider differing perspectives on literature from other parts of the Americas, we see the writer's individual mythic impulse while heeding the mythic pulse of his or her own society – and how these are inflected in a Pan-American way. Given the European colonial history of North and South America, there can be traced a common effort in the many cultures there to represent themselves as independent from Europe, to inflect archetypes by their own distinct warp and woof. "In this new world, the old stories break down," says Canadian writer Robert Kroetsch (1927–2011) (29). New stories based on American archetypes – newly hatched and ethnographically uprising – offer recognitions where those imposed from Europe fall short. Another Canadian, Frye, who carried the torch of archetypal literary criticism from the nineteen-fifties to his death in 1991, articulated a possible marriage through literature of those individuating myths we live by and the myths that uphold a society:

> Literature [. . .] is conscious mythology: it creates an autonomous world that gives us an imaginative perspective on the actual one. But there is another kind of mythology, one produced by society itself, the object of which is to persuade us to accept existing social values. "Popular" literature, the kind that is read for relaxation and the quieting of the mind, expresses this social mythology. [. . .] I know of no critical rule for

> distinguishing them. [. . .] The same work may belong to both mythologies at once, and in fact the separation between them is largely a perspective of our own revolutionary age.
>
> (*Bush Garden* 237)

Bradbury and Vonnegut worked in this final mode, aiming at psychological relevancy with mainstream appeal in the U.S.A. Each of their stories becomes a new creation of narrative expressing and expanding American mythology. "[The] imaginative writer is finding his identity within the world of literature itself," Frye argued. "He is withdrawing from what Douglas LePan calls a country without a mythology into the country of mythology" (*Bush Garden* 240). LePan's (1914–1998) poem, "A Country Without a Mythology," imagines a "stranger" wandering through the Canadian wilderness, overwhelmed by the natural world and the "savage people" living there (75–76). The descendant of Europeans in North America, as Frye reads it, must write his or her new culture's mythology in order to survive.

Vonnegut and Bradbury's work is free, by virtue of our collective attitude toward fiction, from religion's tendency to historicize. Most will never read a science fiction, fantasy, or even a so-called realistic short story or novel and say, "Yes, this actually happened, is happening, or will happen, just like this, to the *t*." Readers do not demand that fiction maintain nonfiction's implied authenticity or factuality. Doniger expresses this as reading without commitment: "[W]e have no *commitment* to the myths of 'Star Trek' or Tolkien; there is no group that will hold us responsible to live in a certain way because of these myths. Our suspension of disbelief when we read such stories is only momentary; it has no lasting effect upon us" ("The Survival of Myth in Science Fiction" 23). I disagree with the lengths to which she takes the point; joking or not, in the first decade of the twenty-first century tens of thousands identified their faith as Jedi in censuses taken in Ireland, the U.K., Canada, Australia, New Zealand, and the Czech Republic. While there is not (yet?) a Church of Star Wars with a substantial following, it is too much to say myths of this type have no lasting effect. But Doniger is correct that we are not expected to believe these stories to the degree religious institutions expect their faithful to believe holy writ. The often unrecognized acceptance that a science fiction story is not a factual or religious account grants the reader more immediate and less scrutinizing access to the imaginative realm as invoked by its author. In *The Short Story: The Reality of Artifice*, May tunes his approach upon this tension:

> Short fiction [. . .] often features characters caught between their "as-if-real" nature and their status as functions of the fable in which they exist. As a result of this dual nature of character in the short story, the form takes on some of the metaphoric qualities that we usually associate

> with poetry: conflicts are not resolved solely by preestablished plot or by realistic characterization. Instead [. . .] characters ultimately confront a metaphoric embodiment of their dilemma.
>
> (72–3)

This is a major reason why Vonnegut and Bradbury's short stories succeed in their blend of fantasy, science-fiction, or gothic motifs with characters who exhibit a twentieth-century American psychology. Much has been written on metaphor in their most famous novels, on the book-burning firefighters of *Fahrenheit 451* as metaphor for censorship and McCarthyism, on Billy Pilgrim's coming unstuck in time in *Slaughterhouse-Five* as a metaphor for Post-Traumatic Stress.

Even more waits to be unpacked in these writers' short stories, which, with little space and time to establish atmosphere, character, and plot, are marked by a necessary confidence of expression. The boldness of a Venusian landscape or the unreality of a gadget that will ruin a housewife's life by whispering her worst insecurities to her are tempered by characters whose behavior was believable to a mainstream audience. Encountered in "slick" magazines that boasted interviews, articles, and advertisements appealing to the American white middle class, these tales had an uphill fight in suspending the disbelief of their readers, who likely would not have come to the periodical with science fiction or fantastic expectations. While many of their stories were indeed published in genre pulps catering to an audience seeking precisely that, others found publication in the pages of *Collier's, The Saturday Evening Post, Cosmopolitan, McCall's* – everything from *Ladies' Home Journal* to *Playboy*. In the case of Vonnegut, Myth and Symbol critic Fiedler hammers home the legitimacy of myth in his work as it was published in the forum of popular culture:

> [H]e began as a Pop writer, the author of "slick" fiction, written to earn money, which is to say, to fit formulas which are often genuine myths, frozen and waiting to be released. Fortunately, though he has sometimes written to suit the tastes of middle-aged ladies who constitute the readership of *Ladies' Home Journal*, he has tended more to exploit the mythology of the future. But he has, in any case – as writers of, rather than *about*, mythology must – written books that are thin and wide, rather than deep and narrow, books which open out into fantasy and magic by means of linear narration rather than deep analysis; and so happen on wisdom, fall into it through grace, rather than pursue it doggedly or seek to earn it by hard work. Moreover, like all literature which tries to close the gap between the elite and the popular audiences rather than to confirm it, Vonnegut's books tend to temper irony with sentimentality and to dissolve both in wonder.
>
> (7)

What the stories share is a consistency of clarity in their fantastic elements, which come through as culturally specific metaphors for the energies of life. Through power of suggestion we are challenged beyond a mundane, concrete, positivistic understanding to a poetic, symbolic, mythic understanding reachable only through the imagination, allowing uncomfortable truths, notions, or feelings to be addressed – ones that may have gone unexpressed, unexplored, or unrecognized elsewhere.

Jung, fascinated by the UFO phenomena that arose in the late forties, devoted one of his final studies to it. His focus was not the physical existence of UFOs but how people dealt with such sightings. He found a historical precedent of shapes seen in the sky and determined that what had changed in the middle of the twentieth century was the way people defined what they saw: "Anything that looks technological goes down without difficulty with modern man" (1958/1970, *CW 10*, ¶624). Walker's analysis of this work applies to our own: "Our modern age no longer believes in personifications of psychic forces in the form of gods or spirits of other kinds. For that reason, when the UFO as a modern projected image of wholeness is visualized in terms of the modern mythological imagery of contemporary science fiction, it can easily become part of a modern mythic narrative" (99). The nineteen-fifties saw the body of literature in film, television, and fiction featuring contact with aliens from outer space expand at the same time Westerners started reporting flying saucers in their skies. Symptomatic of a need for new symbols, science fiction itself blossomed as a genre.

"In the forties," Bradbury later reflected, "only a handful of paperback s-f collections had begun to pop up. Science was exploding all over the place but s-f was still [. . .] Sleeping Beauty waiting to be kissed awake by atomic bombs, hydrogen explosions but, above all, Sputnik, and Neil Armstrong bootprinting the lunar soil for all mankind" ("Science Fiction: Before Christ and After 2001" IX, XI). Once kissed, science fiction and fantasy experienced a profound expansion in quantity, visibility, and variety. Doniger allows that the best (and worst) of it carries forth mythic dimensions:

> Science fiction provides a body of literature in which great mythological classics take refuge in a demythologized age. [. . . Nowadays] in writers like Ray Bradbury and Ursula LeGuin, mythology takes on a new form, devoid of a formal, communal, ritual religious element, but not necessarily devoid of an individual, personal, mythical religious element. Such works of literature, like the great science-fiction films, present a genuine instance of that ephemeral swinging door through which myth and reality eternally pass one another, like star-ships in the night.
>
> ("The Survival of Myth in Science Fiction" 32)

A point David Goldsmith makes about Vonnegut carries over to Bradbury as well: "Certainly he is fond of space ships, time travel, and other gimmickry, but these phenomena, after all, represent the latter half of the twentieth century far better than would the riverboat journeys of Twain, the small town life of Sherwood Anderson, or the physical encounters with death of Ernest Hemingway" (6).

The magazine industry of the time in question, those twenty years between WWII and the first Kennedy assassination, started out verdant and, with the proliferation of TV in the American household, came out withered. There were the highbrow magazines, chief among them the *New Yorker*, which survives, but there were also large format magazines – *The Saturday Evening Post, Collier's, McCall's, Esquire, Cosmopolitan*, and others – that published multiple short stories weekly or monthly. These were aimed at the mainstream, containing articles on an array of topics considered to be of general interest to white middle class readers. One magazine editor Bradbury and Vonnegut shared is Knox Burger. He "cultivated a fruitful relationship with Bradbury by publishing six of his stories" in *Collier's* between 1950 and 1952 (Eller *Becoming Ray Bradbury* 206). More fortuitous was Vonnegut's relationship with Burger, who gave his work a chance because they were acquaintances from Vonnegut's time writing for the *Cornell Daily Sun* before the war. Burger gave Vonnegut his big break and published twelve of his stories in *Collier's* between 1950 and 1953. Charles Shields provides some context for these magazines:

> The pages of *Collier's* or the *Saturday Evening Post* indicated that most popular magazine fiction was an extension of consumers' wish fulfillment. Attractive, smartly dressed young couples were perpetually entertaining or, in the case of male professionals, working at executive level jobs. Big blocks of advertising, quarried from the same happy landscape, featured young men and women enjoying the good life – house, car, television, and home appliances. "The Golden Age of White People" was how Vonnegut later referred to the era.
>
> (104–5)

There were also inexpensive pulp magazines, printed on cheap paper, that catered specifically to science fiction and fantasy enthusiasts. The pulps, as they were known, championed imaginative work and Bradbury and Vonnegut both found success there, particularly as the middlebrow market dried up. But we truly have to thank plucky young editors like Burger, who was only twenty-six when he took over fiction at *Collier's* in 1948, for bringing these writers and their mythic stories to a wider national audience. Room was made, amid these magazines' stories about middle class romance and careers in business, for the palatable sort of fantasies Bradbury and Vonnegut were writing, stories that coyly brought a sense of mystery into their readers' consciousness.

Vonnegut and Bradbury as mythmakers

Pairing Bradbury and Vonnegut works for several reasons: both are white and of the same generation, Bradbury born in 1920 and Vonnegut in 1922; both spent their childhoods in the American Midwest, Bradbury in Waukegan, Illinois, and Vonnegut in Indianapolis, Indiana; both left the Midwest to live on an American coast, Bradbury the Pacific and Vonnegut the Atlantic; both enjoyed publication in the pulps and "slicks" in the nineteen-fifties and sixties, a time when short story writers received widespread attention and handsome payment; both achieved widespread success through their work, becoming household names in North America and translated into many languages around the world; both are regularly taught to this day in American public schools, have had their work adapted for stage, screen, TV, and radio, and show no sign of going out of print; both lived secular lives, neither committing to a religious tradition, although Vonnegut became honorary president of the American Humanists after its previous president, Isaac Asimov (1920–1992), died; and, perhaps most integral to our study, both wrote using a variety of fantastic motifs, refusing to limit themselves to any single style or genre, so that while we can identify the voice of Vonnegut or Bradbury when blindly picking up and reading a story, we know to be on the lookout for elements of science fiction, fantasy, magic realism, prairie realism, and so on.

In his 1972 study on Vonnegut, David Goldsmith uses the term fantasist and also pairs these men with a third wheel writer who remains quite neglected: "A list of contemporary American fantasists who have achieved some measure of respectability would include, besides Vonnegut, only Ray Bradbury, and perhaps John Collier" (31). As Bradbury put it, "I grew up in the one field that reached out and embraced every sector of the human imagination, every endeavor, every idea, every technological development, and every dream" ("Science Fiction: Before Christ and After 2001" xi). Vonnegut, self-conscious of his work's reception, worried that his use of such motifs kept people from taking his work seriously: "I have been a soreheaded occupant of a file drawer labeled 'science fiction' [. . .] and I would like out, particularly since so many serious critics regularly mistake the drawer for a urinal" (*Wampeters* 1). And here we have a sense also of how different these writers were.

Pairing them works quite as well for their dissimilarities: Vonnegut was shaped by personal and collective tragedies in his life, from his mother's suicide to surviving the firebombing of Dresden in World War II to losing his sister to cancer and brother in-law to a train wreck, which saw him and his first wife adopting three of their sons and doubling the size of their own family, as well as surviving a suicide attempt in the nineteen-eighties, while Bradbury, who did lose a sister in childhood, did not serve in the war and lived, by his accounts, poor and then comfortably in southern California; Vonnegut eventually rubbed elbows with New York's literary crowd while Bradbury preferred lifelong friendships with science fiction writers on the west coast; when the market for profitably writing short stories dried up, Vonnegut switched almost solely to writing novels, whereas Bradbury held to the form all his life, many of his novels being groups of his stories sewn together in new ways; Vonnegut eventually placed himself in his fiction, collaging his public persona, whereas Bradbury hid once-removed in characters who shared his middle name, Douglas, and his father's middle name, Spaulding; Vonnegut's black humor became a trademark while Bradbury preached a robust enthusiasm for life.

Just consider the bios written for each author when their short stories were published in the same issue of *Wonder Stories: An Anthology of the Best in Science Fiction* (1957 Vol XLV, No 1). The first appears inside the front cover:

> RAY BRADBURY
> Speaking of places in the sun, few if any writers in the field of fantasy and science fiction occupy the high, bright seat that Ray Bradbury does. The dean of his genre at the ripe old age of 36, Ray began writing at the age of 12, selling when he was 20. His short stories have been published in most of the top literary and slickpaper magazines, and have been repeatedly anthologized. Collections of his own work in book form include THE ILLUSTRATED MAN, THE MARTIAN CHRONICLES, GOLDEN APPLES OF THE SUN, FAHRENHEIT 451 and OCTOBER COUNTRY, at least two of which are being transformed at this moment to Broadway plays. He is the author of the new novel, DANDELION WINE, wrote the screen-play for MOBY DICK and is at work on 28 new short stories, simultaneously. Married and the father of three girls, Ray basks in California sun.

The other appears inside the back cover:

> KURT VONNEGUT, JR.
> Author of short stories published principally in *The Saturday Evening Post, Collier's, Cosmopolitan* and *The Ladies' Home Journal*, Kurt Vonnegut, Jr., also wrote the novel, PLAYER PIANO. He became a science-fiction writer by way of the study of biochemistry at Cornell, mechanical engineering at Carnegie Tech and anthropology at the U. of Chicago, some of which was segmented by a tour of duty in World War II which resulted in his being captured by the Germans, liberated by the Russians and rehabilitated at Miami. He lives with wife and children in Osterville, U.S.A.

Here we find adumbrations of the archetypes that most inform their early short fiction. In Vonnegut, we see the emphasis on his wartime experience, which informs his earliest stories, each providing new narratives for the War archetype (see Chapter 2). The mentions of capture, liberation, and rehabilitation, as well as our knowledge that he never completed any of those degrees listed as his studies, points to fragmentation which shapes so much of his work throughout his career. Here we find a person who was picked apart by events international and personal, which made him uniquely capable of critiquing his own culture in his stories (see Chapter 3). Bradbury's exuberance is nearly boastful in the brief biography, touting his success and ending with a sentence that points to the archetypes greatly informing his short stories. First is his investment in exploring the family, which he does in many configurations and crises that show what white middle class Americans feared and hoped for at home (see Chapter 4). Then there is the sun, a symbol many have pointed to as embodying wholeness. Bradbury wrote many stories in the fifties that bring the sun in as a force operative in the lives of his characters (see Chapter 5). And here it is important to point out that Vonnegut's fragmentation and Bradbury's wholeness are two sides of the same archetype. Fragmentation is the breaking of a whole; and something whole can be fragmented – even, if it is to be absolutely whole, *must* be fragmented if it is to encompass all things. In both, in this regard, we find a tension between what is American and what is human, with the emphasis on linking back to a common humanity, which has always been a problem for the collective project of the United States of America.

Bradbury later said, "[I]f I heard that Kurt Vonnegut suddenly liked me a whole lot, I would worry; I'd begin to think I was going around the bend. He has problems, he has terrible problems. He cannot see the world the way I see it. I suppose I'm too much Pollyanna, he's too much Cassandra" (Weller 291). Vonnegut did like Bradbury a whole lot, and wrote him a letter in 1959 to which he replied. In a letter to Knox Burger, Vonnegut summarized the exchange:

> I got an extremely friendly letter back from Ray Bradbury. I called him Mr. Bradbury and he called me Kurt. I told him I was thinking of moving to California, and he said sure, come ahead. He said he would introduce me to some people, and he said it was warm all the time out there. Can you imagine someplace where it's warm all the time?
>
> (*Letters* 68)

Vonnegut praises Bradbury in *Fates Worse Than Death* (1991) as a "great fiction writer" and riffs on "The Kilimanjaro Device," his short story reimagining Hemingway's suicide, when bringing up his own suicide attempt (182). In *Palm Sunday* (1981), he also lists Bradbury as one of the "friends" he has met at least once (111).

Each of Bradbury's and Vonnegut's stories are Invisible Men à la Doniger's analogy for archetypes, carefully donning contents pulled from Benjamin

Franklin's junk drawer of American life, and in them we can read the myths that possessed and enriched people's lives in the United States in the middle of the twentieth century. In "Open Letter to Ray Bradbury" (2001), Russian physicist and artist Bulat Galeyev (1940–2009) criticizes Bradbury for U.S.-centricism. While expressing profound appreciation and sharing that he memorized Bradbury's stories like poems when he worked in the Aircraft Engineering Institute for the Soviet Union, he asks why Bradbury's future-focused fiction never depicts Russia's presence across the solar system:

> How is it that you, being so much "our" writer, never let representatives of other planets know that "our" country is also on Earth? How was it possible not to note the huge red spot on the geographical map of our planet?
>
> (25)

Bradbury, to my knowledge, did not respond to Galeyev. But here I defend Bradbury as an artist offering archetypal images, which always bear ethnic, localized inflections. Is it wrong that Bradbury did not shoehorn Russia into his stories? He wrote about Americans colonizing other planets because his is an American heritage. While Arthur C. Clarke and others put Russians out there, Bradbury's scope was much more regional, growing out of his ethnicity as a child of the American Midwest. Though not depicting Russians in space, there is still something present in Bradbury's work that spoke to Galeyev. Though frustrated by not being nationally represented in them, he still credits their cross-cultural, archetypal significance.

It is true that while Bradbury may have overlooked Russians in space, Vonnegut did not. "The Manned Missiles," first published in the July 1958 issue of *Cosmopolitan*, is an epistolary story, pairing two letters written between fathers. Mikhail Ivankov's letter to Charles M. Ashland expresses sorrow that their respective sons, Stepan and Bud, the first two men in space, died as a result of their rockets colliding. Ashland's response to Mr. Ivankov is one of respect and commiseration. Historian Hugh Brogan notes that "When the Soviet Union put the first satellite into space in 1957 the shock to American vanity was almost unbearable; the cry went up that something was badly wrong with American society, American science, American education" (612). In his own moralistic way, Vonnegut gives voice to anxieties running hot at that time and appeals for a humane response to the burgeoning space race between the U.S.S.R. and the U.S.A., humanizing it for a mainstream American audience. He breaks the conflict down to the level of two men, separated by geography and culture, who can relate as fathers who lost their sons in war games playing out above the global stage. The story's title, "The Manned Missiles," underlines the urgency felt in America at the time and provides, as it were, a preemptive myth of mutual assured conciliation. "[Our sons] will be forgotten only when men no longer look up at the

Figure 1.1 Three pages of art by Paul Nonnast for "The Manned Missiles." (© *Cosmopolitan* magazine, 1958)

sky. They are like the moon and the planets and the sun and the stars," Alexei writes in English on his father's behalf (83); "I never got it straight in my mind about religion in Russia. You don't mention it," Ashland writes back, "Anyway, we are religious, and we think God singled out Bud and your boy, too, to die in a special way for a special reason. [. . .] I like to think they lived a little while after the crash, and tried to save each other" (88). However universal Vonnegut and Bradbury's mythologizing, they nonetheless need to be read as American writers. So concerned with the issues of their time and place, their work was twofold, that of presenting appropriate images for new archetypes and re-presenting old archetypes with fresh images.

Lifting the lid on the unconscious

Before delving into each writer and his stories' constellating archetypes, let us remind ourselves that there is always the possibility of a diversity of readings present in a sole symbol by analyzing Bradbury's short story "The Jar" (1944). Charlie lives in Louisiana, in a place called the Hollow, and gains agency by mystifying his community with a thing in a jar he buys for twelve dollars from a carnival man. The story begins with this paragraph, presenting a murky image evading specifics:

> It was one of those things they keep in a jar in the tent of a sideshow on the outskirts of a little, drowsy town. One of those pale things drifting in alcohol plasma, forever dreaming and circling, with its peeled dead eyes staring out at you and never seeing you. It went with the noiselessness of late night, and only the crickets chirping, the frogs sobbing off in the moist swampland. One of those things in a big jar that makes your stomach jump like it does when you see an amputated arm in a laboratory vat.
>
> (49)

The gothic elements stack into a recognition of the ineffability of death, which is granted both the inanimate qualities of dead eyes and a preserved arm and the unconscious force of "forever dreaming." The hypothetical "outskirts of a little, drowsy town" and the noiselessness paired with crickets and "frogs sobbing off in the moist swampland" provide melancholic harmonies to "one of those things they keep in a jar." It is the undefined nature of the thing in the jar – its being at its most specific a *thing*, and therefore ultimately unknowable – that imbues it with power.

The jar is a container not unlike that of Wallace Stevens's 1919 poem "Anecdote of the Jar," in which practitioners of practically every branch of literary theory, from new critics to feminists and beyond, have seen the contents of their own intellectual focus.[6] Each of Bradbury's neighbors in the Hollow makes sense of the thing in the jar in his or her own subjective way. Thedy, Charlie's unloving wife, initially sees him in the jar; Gramps Medknowe sees something genderless, a brain, an octopus; Juke Marmer sees a kitten his mother made him drown as a boy; Jahdoo sees "the center of Life": Middibamboo Mama, primordial progenitor of all humankind, "from which we all come ten thousand year ago" (53); Mrs. Tridden sees her young son Foley, who vanished in the swamp; pipe-smoking Granny Carnation relishes the thing's ambiguity, asking, "why couldn't it be sort of – all things? [. . .] That's it. Symbol. Symbol of all the nights and days in the dead canebrake. Why's it have to be one thing? Maybe it's lots" (54); and Tom Carmody, who is likely having an affair with Charlie's wife, refuses to look into the jar, declaring, "I don't think it's nothin'!" (54). They all see different colors in its eyes, its hair.

The thing in the jar is numinous, the evenings spent discussing it described as "kind of a rude church gathering" (52). Threatened by Charlie's newfound respect in the community and the awe he has awakened, Thedy and Tom Carmody take it upon themselves to spoil the mystery by tracing the thing in the jar to its source. She takes a cruel pleasure in telling Charlie what they discover:

> "We talked to that carny-boss, and he – he almost died laughin', he said he sold it to some – hick – for twelve bucks. And it ain't worth more than two dollars at most!"
>
> Laughter bloomed in the dark, right out of her mouth, an awful kind of flower with her breath as its perfume.
>
> She finished it, snapping, quick:
>
> "It's just junk, Charlie! Liquid rubber, paper-mache, silk, cotton, chemicals! That's all! Got a metal-framework inside it! That's all! That's all it is, Charlie! That's all!" she shrilled in triumph.
>
> (55)

Here Thedy reveals herself as a rationalist and, with her threat to reveal the truth to the community, we see played out the schism between concretized and transcendent consciousnesses. Her perspective denies metaphor its opportunity to speak past the categories of definition because she thinks the world can be explained. That concretism is an utterly unlivable mindset for Charlie, who has won respect by introducing something mysterious into his neighbors' lives. "Thedy, this jar HAS to have somethin' in it. Somethin' besides the junk you say," Charlie pleads with her, "Too many people believe there's somethin' in it, Thedy. You can't change that" (56). When unconscious contents are consciously denied, they oftentimes rise with force, and that is precisely what happens. Thedy thinks her rational explanation trumps, defeats, contains Charlie's object of mystery. But before she has a chance to tell the others, he replaces the thing in the jar with her head. Though switched out, the individual members of the community *still* see what they project into it.

"The Jar" not only provides a glimpse of the potential diversity found in a symbol, it also exposes the danger of literalism to an image or motif. Campbell often warned against the literal interpretation of a symbol, the stock example being a creationist reading of *Genesis*, which does not hold up factually against scientific understanding. Bradbury's story shows how a literal interpretation from a rationalist stance is just as destructive to a metaphor's mythic potential. Thedy's understanding of the thing as crafted and manmade does not change the subjective, psychic realities it has already inspired in the neighbors' minds, but her use of reason to debunk its mysteriousness is as much an attack to its poetic vitality as would be identifying it as any single one of the neighbors' imagined interpretations and demanding everybody accept it as such. Rationalism itself is exposed as a dogma, a narrative that both threatens and fails to grasp the value of the unconscious.

Bradbury's title, "The Jar," is an intriguing choice for the story. He could have very well called it "The Thing in the Jar," for it is the thing that manifests so differently for all of the characters, but "The Jar" points instead to

Figure 1.2 Boris Dolgov's illustration for "The Jar" from *Weird Tales*. (© *Weird Tales*, 1944)

the seemingly benign container that holds the thing. Boris Dolgov's illustration that accompanies its first publication, in pulp digest *Weird Tales* (Nov. 1944), highlights the subjective nature of its contents: a human skull is crosshatched dark behind the heads of those looking into the jar, which holds only the story's title in a field of white. We recall Warner's observation that an archetype is a hollow thing, rendered here artistically. The jar within the story can be read as a representation of archetype itself, making the thing within it the subjective archetypal image that manifests to express the archetype. "Myth is a conscious interpretation of unconscious communication," writes Huskinson, "and as such its nature is both rational and non-rational, archetypal image and ineffable, numinous 'content'" (9). And so while Thedy and Tom Carmody see an ineffective sign in a mere jar, Charlie and his neighbors, according to their own orientations, don't see the jar at all but find themselves looking through it at untold mysteries of death, origins, regret, loss, multitude.

Most symbols are not as ambiguous as Bradbury's thing in the jar. Most are experienced with some similarity of meaning by members of a society because of overlaps in their biological and cultural connotations with any specific image. Campbell also stressed that symbols have shelf-lives: "[T]he metaphors of one historically conditioned period, and the symbols they innervate, may not speak to the persons who are living long after that historical moment and whose consciousness has been formed through altogether different experiences" (*Thou Art That* 6). In the United States after WWII, two-thousand-year-old pastoral religious traditions simply fell flat – not for all but for many. The world looked different, life was changing in how it was lived, and new symbols appeared to replace old ones.

Rollo May declared that "we in America want to find a new self, a new set of expectations" (*Cry for Myth* 102). Vonnegut, reflecting on Joseph Heller's *Catch-22* being hailed as the American myth of WWII, understood the field in which he wrote, that of popular fiction, to be the vehicle for those new expectations:

> To accept a new myth about ourselves is to simplify our memories – and to place our stamp of approval on what might become an epitaph for our era in the shorthand of history. This, in my opinion, is why critics often condemn our most significant books and poems and plays when they first appear, while praising feebler creations. The birth of a new myth fills them with primitive dread, for myths are so effective.
>
> (*Palm Sunday* 121–2)

An artist thrusts contents from the unconscious into the field of a reader's awareness and forces him or her to confront what has been denied, avoided, or not yet seen. By following specific mythic motifs that appear across stories written by Bradbury and Vonnegut, we can map constellations of certain archetypes as filtered through the white American psyche of the mid-twentieth century. The path is not easy, as Walker warns: "Reductive interpretation may be useful in discussions of psychological matters, but it does not make for good literary criticism. A literary critic's first duty is to the text" (148). The temptation to essentialize a symbol, to cherry pick and ascribe how it should make us feel, what it should make us think, is perilous. Our work, rather, is to engage the valence of connotations present in archetypal images that recur in Bradbury and Vonnegut's short fiction, read as narrative projections of both crumbling and load-bearing cultural archetypes, to bear witness to myths informing American society in the decades following WWII. By following specific archetypes and analyzing how they manifest, we shall examine how Bradbury and Vonnegut expressed these collective animating psychological forces in and from their own time, place, and culture. Their stories may not have overt rites and rituals attached to them but, as we shall see, they do behave in mythic ways.

Notes

1 See Willis McNelly, "Science Fiction: The Modern Mythology." *America* 123.5 (1970): 125; Gail Landsman, "Science Fiction: The Rebirth of Mythology." *Journal of Popular Culture* 5.4 (1972): 989–992; Robert Nadeau, "Physics and Metaphysics in the Novels of Kurt Vonnegut." *Mosaic* 13 (1980): 37–47; Gary K. Wolfe, "The Frontier Myth in Ray Bradbury." *Ray Bradbury*. Eds. M. H. Greenberg and J. D.Olander. New York, NY: Taplinger, 1980. 33–54; Sallye Sheppeard, "Kurt Vonnegut and the Myth of Scientific Progress." *Journal of the American Studies Association of Texas* 16.1 (1985): 14–19; "The Survival of Myth in Science Fiction." *Mindscapes*. Ed. Slusser and Rabkin. Carbondale, IL: Southern Illinois University, 1989. 16–33.

2 See "Wotan" (1936/1970, *CW 10*, ¶371–99).

3 See, among others, Susan Rowland's *C.G. Jung and Literary Theory* (London: Palgrave, 1999) and *Jung: A Feminist Revision* (Cambridge: Polity Press, 2002); Marion Woodman's *Ravaged Bridegroom: Masculinity in Women* (Toronto: Inner City Books, 1990) and *Dancing in the Flames* with Elinor Dickson (Boulder, CO: Shambhala, 1996); Baumlin, Baumlin, and Jensen's *Post-Jungian Criticism* (Albany, NY: State University of New York Press, 2004); Lucy Huskinson's *Dreaming the Myth Onwards: New Directions in Jungian Therapy and Thought* (London: Routledge, 2008); Mitch Walker's *Gay Liberation at a Psychological Crossroads* (North Charleston, SC: BookSurge, 2009); and Lin Fraser's "Depth Psychotherapy with Transgender People" in *Sexual and Relationship Therapy* 24.2 (Routledge 2009: 126–142).

4 This is the problem behind most symbol dictionaries, which present finite definitions for archetypes, which are always multivalent. There are two exceptions: Chevalier and Gheerbrant's *Dictionary of Symbols* and the Archive for Research in Archetypal Symbolism's *Book of Symbols*. Both are consulted often by Jungians (ARAS is a Jungian Institute) and post-Jungians because they compile examples of images and how they are inflected in cultures around the world, living and dead. Each entry is an anthology of meanings, not a monolithic definition.

5 Readers consulting *The Masks of God: Creative Mythology* will find that Campbell initially called this the "psychological function" of myth. In his final years, Campbell renamed it the "pedagogical function." This change is foundational, especially since he stressed this was the most important of the major functions. "Psychological" is too vague to truly address what he was getting at, which is that myths can teach us "how to live a human lifetime under any circumstances" (*POM* 31), "guiding individuals in a harmonious way through the inevitable crises of a lifetime" (*The Hero's Journey* 164). That emphasis on education, coming from a professional educator toward the end of his own life, makes the change to "pedagogical" a refinement in Campbell's striving for clarity. It also shows that his own process of thinking, as with any active theorist, was open and subject to revision as he learned more, on into his eighties.

6 See Jacqueline Vaught Brogan's essay "Introducing Stevens: Or, the Sheerly Playful and the Display of Theory." *Teaching Wallace Stevens*. Eds. John N. Serio and Bobby J. Leggett. Knoxville, TN: University of Tennessee, 1994. 51–62. Print.

Part I

Kurt Vonnegut

A comedic Cassandra

Figure 2.1 "Kurt," reproduced with permission from the artist. (© 2014 Kevin Storrar)

Chapter 2

War's shadow

Vonnegut's conflicts with arms

"Dear people," Pfc. K. Vonnegut, Jr., wrote home from the Le Havre P.O.W. Repatriation Camp on 29 May 1945, "I'm told that you were probably never informed that I was anything other than 'missing in action.' Chances are that you also failed to receive any of the letters I wrote from Germany. That leaves me a lot of explaining to do" (*Armageddon In Retrospect* 11). This explaining continued for the rest of Vonnegut's life, culminating most overtly in two novels: *Slaughterhouse-Five* (1969) and *Bluebeard* (1987). Before those he also portrayed the bewilderment of military service in *The Sirens of Titan* (1958), ethics of war in *Mother Night* (1961), and produced a series of posthumously published short stories inspired by his service, which remained the pivot of his psyche for the rest of his life. Saying in 1977 that he wanted a military funeral, he explained that, "It will be a way of achieving what I've always wanted more than anything – something I could have had, if only I'd managed to get myself killed in the war. [. . .] The unqualified approval of my community" (Allen 169).

Early adulthood was a traumatic time in Vonnegut's life. Historian Paul Fussell, a veteran of the same war, provides perspective on Vonnegut's Division and what they experienced in the Battle of the Bulge, where he was taken prisoner:

> It would not be fair to depict what happened to the 106th Division as typical. The boys were young and they had been drafted and were not terribly well trained. Charles Whiting puts it bluntly: "There was no 'Crusade in Europe' for the young soldiers of the 106th Infantry Division." Those not immediately captured fled to the rear, many throwing away their weapons and howling, "The Krauts are coming." Those remaining on the line or close to it were hustled back east for long marches into prisoner-of-war cages. They were the eight thousand boys of two whole regiments of the 106th. Later narrative tried to brighten things up by noting that they said they were out of ammunition. This mass surrender was one of the most embarrassing moments in the history of the American military. Because an event

> like this was unthinkable, neither officers nor men were prepared for its ever happening.
>
> (129)

The surrender was merely one of a series of wounds Vonnegut suffered in a short span of time: "In 1944 he had to confront the suicide of his mother, capture by the Germans, the loss of over forty pounds while in captivity, and a second narrow escape from death in the firebombing of Dresden – traumas that would later fuel his fiction and impact the nature of his humor" (*SFKV* 3). The result of his survival was induction into the rest of his life as a veteran, here contextualized by Hillman: "The veteran has survived an initiation; the fact of that survival, that chance or miracle, forces upon one the deepest questioning and the veteran's burden of carrying the dead into life" (*TLW* 34).

Such survival is rarely, if ever, cleanly achieved. The ancient Greeks interpreted war trauma as a polluting of the person that must be cleansed. "The answer to *miasma* [translated as defilement or pollution]," writes classicist Robert Emmet Meagher, "its cure or antidote, as it were, was called *katharsis*, an elusive word meaning something like purgation, cleansing, and the restoration of normalcy" (19). Unfortunately, shell-shock/combat fatigue/PTSD – each designation being a euphemism for this same *miasma*, this lasting agony earned in combat – has repeatedly gone untreated collectively in modern times. The burden of achieving *katharsis* in all modern American wars has been placed squarely on the shoulders of the individual soldiers suffering long-term effects. This continues to be a major problem today, despite studies and worries for the health of veterans.[1] For those who suffered during World War II, part of the problem of adjusting to life after it was due to the collective notion of normalcy. Historian James Oliver Robertson writes that, given the Great Depression that had preceded it, after WWII "there was no acceptable vision of normalcy to go back to" (334):

> The myth of war, with all its analogies, its aggressive and heroic metaphors, its visions of loyalty and victory, its promises of defense and security, its focus on an enemy, its image of supreme effort and efficiency, its appeal of "the game well played" and of sacrifice, and its implications of national unity, national prosperity, and national success, has become the most important model for American behavior since World War II.
>
> (335)

This state of affairs, this mythological alignment, is hardly conducive to healing those so-called unseen wounds of war.

Evolutionary psychologist David Livingstone Smith reminds us that the ways we imagine war often exacerbate our inability to understand it at all:

> In the popular imagination, soldiers unflinchingly perform their duties and are emotionally unscathed by their experiences. But this image is

> tragically flawed. It is a convenient fiction that occludes a more disturbing reality. [. . .] War is not only an assault upon a soldier's body, it is an assault upon his sense of his own humanity. It requires him to perform acts that no human being should have to perform, exposes him to perpetual fear, and threatens him with crushing guilt. One way to minimize these pressures is to become distant, to close down, to enter into spiritual hibernation. When this happens, the world seems to become unreal. (152, 160)

Vonnegut, left like others to conjure his own *katharsis*, sought a cure in the arts. The task of working to correct the popular narrative of war was so great, so much bigger than himself, that its achievement proved evasive. He later admitted that his "war book" was beyond reach in his first twenty years of writing, and yet he tried to produce something of the sort through much of his earliest work. Realism had its day in his WWII short stories never published in his lifetime but fantasy asserted itself early and became a useful tool in Vonnegut's exploration of war. From a post-Jungian standpoint, the fantastic events, settings, and devices in Vonnegut's war stories are born of conscious engagement with the unreal *miasma* Smith acknowledges.

In the short stories we examine here, we sense Vonnegut, in his later twenties and thirties, already understood that war dominated his personal myths. He knew the myth he lived by but articulating it, his life's work, was his primary artistic struggle. These stories are more than attempts, however. Most were published. Some were not. Hillman states that, "Writers, especially writers of war, do not create; they re-create" (*TLW* 29). What was required was a submersion into that forgotten past and, through active imagination, Vonnegut finally surfaced with Billy Pilgrim and his condition of schizoid temporality. "Report on the Barnhouse Effect," "All the King's Horses," "Great Day," and "Armageddon in Retrospect" deliver instances of experiential and creative engagement with the war archetype. "If we want war's horror to be abated so that life may go on, it is necessary to understand and imagine," Hillman urges. "Perhaps that is what we are here for: to bring appreciative understanding to the phenomena that have no need to understand themselves [. . . A] rational science of war can only go so far, only to the edge of understanding. At that point a leap of imagination is called for, a leap into myth" (*TLW* 5, 9). Vonnegut, an accidental survivor, practiced this leap in crafting stories.

The ancient Athenian dramatists were veterans producing art for audiences of veterans. With military service reaching to the age of sixty for all men, the Greeks were no strangers to war and embraced tragedy as a means of collectively addressing its wounds. Vonnegut's early stories sought to provide the same collective benefit in the advertisement-laden pages of magazines. His own literary hero, Mark Twain, left his most damning condemnations of war to be published after his death, *The Mysterious Stranger* going unfinished and "The War Prayer" appearing during World War I in

Harper's Monthly (November 1916). But Vonnegut, like Euripides, was a veteran who openly crafted his work as a veteran, airing conflicts with and of war from the very beginning of his career.

Thomas F. Marvin points out Vonnegut's "basic belief that, except in extraordinary circumstances, wars should be avoided" (131). While his work expresses anti-war sentiments, he allows for the occurrence of a just war. He even expressed gratitude for World War II altering the course of his life:

> World War II made war reputable because it was a just war. I wouldn't have missed it for anything. You know how many other just wars there have been? Not many. And the guys I served with became my brothers. If it weren't for World War II, I'd now be the garden editor of *The Indianapolis Star*.
>
> (*Rolling Stone*, 24 Aug. 2006)

We do not find prescriptions for absolute pacifism in his writings. His fiction depicts war as horrible, terrible, awful – which it surely is – and, once every now and again, necessary. This paradox is a complexity misunderstood by anyone enlisting him simply as an anti-war author with a ho-hum Midwestern voice. Exploring the attitudes of war in the following selection of stories reveals a far more dynamic engagement with the problem; we bear witness to the valence of the archetype of war. Though Vonnegut's work is at times funny, it never shies from the seriousness or the magnitude of war, elbowing right up to it. Here we find the short story as testimonial, as lament, as warning. Sublimity, in these fictions, as in life itself, is war's overpowering energy:

> MOYERS: I once interviewed a veteran of the Second World War. I talked to him about his experience at the Battle of the Bulge, in that bitter winter when the surprise German assault was about to succeed. I said, "As you look back on it, what was it?" And he said, "It was sublime."
>
> CAMPBELL: And so the monster comes through as a kind of god.
>
> (*POM* 117)

Before signing off at the end of the letter home to his father and siblings, who had known him as Missing In Action, he wrote, "I've too damned much to say, the rest will have to wait" (13). The rest, we might say, was Vonnegut's career in the literary arts.

Barnstorming debut

Vonnegut's first published story was "Report on the Barnhouse Effect," a fantasy of worldwide disarmament. On 29 August 1949 the Soviet Union successfully tested a nuclear bomb, becoming the first nation after the U.S.A.

to do so and starting the Cold War arms race. Appearing four and a half months later in the 11 February 1950 issue of *Collier's*, Vonnegut's story plays upon the timely fear while criticizing the exploitation of individuals for purposes of national security. Written as a dossier regarding the discovery and use of "dynamopsychism," the ability to move objects with the mind, Vonnegut's narrator provides a sympathetic evaluation of what has happened to Professor Arthur Barnhouse. Desired by the state as a weapon, Barnhouse has disappeared and gone on a rampage in exile – disarming the world's weaponry. In a final twist, the author of the report admits that he, too, has developed the skill and, with a threat to the sabre-rattlers of the world, has decided to vanish too.

Names always carry associative significance, and here Arthur evokes the monarch of greater Britain's medieval romances: King Arthur. The legend is well known in North America (for instance, Twain's *A Connecticut Yankee in King Arthur's Court*) of how Arthur lies dormant in Avalon until needed once again to vanquish Britain's enemies. When Vonnegut's Arthur unleashes his might in a military demonstration, the professor spirits himself away to his own undisclosed Avalon to precipitate "a bloodless and entertaining sort of war that might be called the 'War of the Tattletales'" (185), in which fear of his return has all but quashed the world's militaries and reduced them to revealing each other's hidden arms. Arthur Barnhouse is presented as a humane phantom sentry, ever-vigilant against the use of weapons around the globe.

His surname, Barnhouse, could point toward Donald Barnhouse, an evangelical pastor from Pennsylvania and a pioneer of radio preaching. His sermons played on stations across the country from the twenties until his death in 1960. *Collier's* readers in 1950 would have known of Dr. Barnhouse, whose reputation may have triggered a sense of Professor Barnhouse as a holy man. Most readers today will lack this association, as Donald Barnhouse is not widely remembered; the reference is something of a cultural timestamp. The name also bluntly summons a barn that has been converted into a home, an image of architectural metamorphosis in line with America's postwar transition from the Depression's ailing pastoral identity to suburban possibility – not to mention that the majority of Americans in 1950 (and to this day) are no stranger to the concept of a savior born in a barn.

Beyond the professor, Vonnegut names characters with Dickensian glee. The Soviets, Premier Slezak and Commisar Kropotnik, carry associations sophomoric and sophisticated. Slezak, apart from the punning of "sleaze," was also the surname of an Austrian character actor, Walter Slezak, who often portrayed villains in Hollywood films. Kropotnik plays on Pyotr Kropotkin, a Russian communist revolutionary and astute critic of capitalism. Kropotnik's American counterpart is Senator Warren Foust, who declares, "He who rules the Barnhouse Effect rules the world!" (175). His name is a nod to soul-selling Dr. Faust of German folklore. There is also the State

Department's William K. Cuthrell and General Honus Barker, a thrall-cutter and a barker who engineer "Operation Brainstorm" and wish to use Barnhouse for military purposes. He confronts their desire to exploit him in his parting letter: "*as the first superweapon with a conscience, I am removing myself from your national defense stockpile. Setting a new precedent in the behavior of ordnance, I have humane reasons for going off*" (185; italics in original).

And yet, with all of these playful names, the author of the report remains nameless. He provides plenty of personal details, but refrains from signing his name at the end. Context tells us the report's recipient is likely the U.S. government, as the author's refusal to share the method of the Barnhouse Effect and final note of "Good-by" (188) imply that he does not trust those who will be reading it. One effect of reading the story is titillation, of having something in our hands that is only meant for other eyes and probably classified information. As a method of hooking a reader, it will come off as a gimmick to some while others will find it irresistible.

Jeff Karon, in an article applying science to Vonnegut's early short fiction, says, "We can easily condemn dynamopsychism – because it [disobeys the] fundamental forces of nature [. . .] – and thus kick away the story's central prop" (*At Millennium's End* 113). This move limits the story to rationalistic interpretation, under which it befalls a fate suffered by all mythopoetic texts that are read literally: reduction, ridicule, and dismissal. Reed, on the other hand, is more accepting: "The central premise may seem farfetched, especially when taken to such extremes, but it retains just enough plausibility to sustain the plot" (*SFKV* 29). We should remember that plenty accept paranormal phenomena as real. This is not to say that we should accept Vonnegut's invention as a reality; that is the other pole of literalism, and reading fiction as fact is out of the question. Rather, we might attempt a more dynamic deconstruction of dynamopsychism.

The report's author defines the phenomenon as "*force of the mind*" (173), but consider the word's parts in finer detail. The *OED* lists "dynamo-" as a combining form "pertaining to current (formerly called dynamic) electricity." A "dynamo" is also a machine that converts mechanical power into electrical energy by rotating conductors in a magnetic field. "Psychism" pertains to "[t]he theory or doctrine that there is a single vital force diffused throughout all animate nature," "[a]nimism," and "[t]he doctrine proposing the existence of psychic phenomena." We should also note the Greek root, "psyche," for "soul" or even "butterfly." Read etymologically, dynamopsychism is the effect of an electrified, conducting, rotating, magnetic soul. It is the product of a metamorphic life set apart, of metabolized internal trauma coiled in copper and emitting a powerful field "undiminished by distance" (174). It manifests only in Professor Barnhouse and the story's narrator, who, along with scholarship, share the distinction of being war veterans. The superhuman quality remains out of reach for all other characters.

Dynamopsychism also provides the story with a MacGuffin: Barnhouse has it and everybody else wants it. What complicates matters is not only the fact that the Effect is stupendously powerful but that it is also an ability arising within a person who bears a conscience against killing. It is bodily inseparable from the character at the heart of the story. In this way, Professor Barnhouse bears much in common with comic book superheroes of his day, particularly Captain America, who was infused with Super Soldier Serum and employed against the Nazis in WWII. Vonnegut's combat vet, however, has no interest in cooperating. We are told he discovered his skill in May 1942, while serving in the U.S. military. He kept the ability to land sevens in games of craps to himself, and "[b]y the time of his discharge in 1945, he could knock bricks loose from chimneys" (177).

We know nothing of the action he saw as a soldier; his war stories remain untold. A detail that reveals Barnhouse's humility emerges in his enlistment, whereby he shrugged off the chance to enter the military as an officer and willingly stepped into a role as an artillery private at the bottom of the ranks. It is a sacrificial move, as an artillery private was far more likely to experience combat than an officer. Being older than his comrades, he was given the nickname Pop, a colloquially disarming and fatherly designation. The narrator, himself an overseas WWII veteran, scoffs at the notion that Barnhouse's ability could have ended that war singlehandedly. They share a bond as veterans, protecting one another from others who do not understand them or would seek to exploit them. The dean of students at Wyandotte College, where Barnhouse teaches, describes him as "Difficult to know since his return, perhaps, but his work before the war brought a great deal of credit to our little school" (177). He sees him as a hapless casualty of the war, only to be pitied and tolerated. But Barnhouse warms to the narrator, his advisee, assigning him done-and-dusted experiments while he "annoyed me further with irrelevant questions. His favorites were: 'Think we should have dropped the atomic bomb on Hiroshima?' and 'Think every new piece of scientific information is a good thing for humanity?'" (178–179). Later, after he vanishes, Barnhouse entrusts a list of nine riddled instructions to the narrator, which pass along the Effect and unlock the ability.

Their camaraderie bonds almost instantaneously upon meeting. The narrator's account of this event depicts someone suffering what was then called "war fatigue": Barnhouse is napping at the desk in his dusty lab alongside three full ashtrays. The professor is portrayed as stagnating, presumably from the psychological effects of his service. He is the veteran who returns home "changed" and "unfit for work," misunderstood or *not* understood by those around him, those who did not serve. But another legend is hiding within this passage, that of Albert Einstein, whose naps on the job as a young man are legendary for furthering his development of the theory of relativity. As Peter Venkman quips in *Ghostbusters* (1984), "Einstein did his best stuff when he was working as a patent clerk!" The trope of eccentric genius applies to Barnhouse as much as that of the vet suffering long-term effects of war.

Selective in whom he trusts, Barnhouse screens and approves of the narrator with a brief exchange in which he asks if he enjoyed WWII, whereby the narrator answers in the negative. He also asks if it looks like a new war is on the horizon, which the narrator modestly intones as possibly unavoidable. This establishment of common ground as veterans opens the professor to human connection. Details of their experiences are not necessary yet; what counts is their attitude toward those guarded experiences. Discovering mutuality in their understated lack of enjoyment of the war makes possible a relationship exclusive to individuals who have lived and suffered as soldiers. A month later Barnhouse implores his advisee for help: "I wish you'd help me look into a more interesting problem – namely, my sanity," he says, and, "It's fear of myself that's made me odd" (179). The narrator does not spell out where he thinks this was going but we assume he, like others, feels that Barnhouse has lost touch with reality. However, where others would fall impatient, the narrator shows respect when the professor admits that he may be delusional:

> "To give you an idea of how crazy, I'll tell you what's been running through my mind when I should have been sleeping. I think maybe I can save the world. I think maybe I can make every nation a have nation, and do away with war for good. I think maybe I can clear roads through jungles, irrigate deserts, build dams overnight."
>
> (179)

On the precipice of witnessing dynamopsychism, a phenomenon he was unaware of, the narrator is confronted with what appear to be delusions of grandeur. His response is not to confront Barnhouse as a madman but rather to treat him with dignity, saying, "Yes, sir" (179).

"War is venomous to the human spirit," writes Meagher, "and friendship is the anti-venom. Like air, it allows us to breathe rather than suffocate" (32). Vonnegut wrote many times of his war-forged friendship with Bernard V. O'Hare, Jr., how this relationship was important to his own wellbeing: "We were paired off to look out for each other before being sent into battle [. . .] the buddy system. After we were captured, that continued. It's a very close bond, so he's a very close friend" (Rhodin). Though they are not war buddies, Professor Barnhouse and the narrator develop a bond that allows the former to share his most guarded secret, and the latter to rise to the occasion of guarding it. When circumstance calls for *peace-minded* Barnhouse to vanish into a self-imposed exile, the narrator is the person who receives his recipe for dynamopsychism in the mail.

If we read dynamopsychism as the precipitation of Barnhouse's wartime *miasma*, his friendship with the narrator brings about *katharsis*. Consider how the war machines Barnhouse destroys in "Operation Brainstorm" are deployed by the American military; despite being a demonstration, he strikes down 120 ships, ten V-2 rockets, and fifty radio-controlled jets. Barnhouse is put in a position of demolishing weapons launched by his *own* nation. Vonnegut was nearly killed by Allied firepower while he was a P.O.W. The fantasy of bringing down the war machinery one once used in the name of his nation is raised like a banner in this story, which was sold to a mainstream middle class American reading audience alongside ads for Cohama ties, Old Spice, Ex-Lax, and Dr. Edwards' Complete Relief from Constipation. It is a *katharsis* not only for the character of Professor Arthur "Pop" Barnhouse but for real-life Americans in 1950 feeling helpless against the escalation of nuclear armament.

The aspect of psychological cleansing that simmers between the lines of the report comes across as minimized, held privately, because the narrator is invested in protecting Barnhouse. Through an act of compassion, he shoulders the professor's burden. Like Simon of Cyrene, commanded by the Romans in the Synoptic Gospels to carry Christ's cross when he drops it, Vonnegut's nameless narrator is compelled by the ruthlessness of the world's militaries to take up Barnhouse's dynamopsychic cross. His given reason is that Barnhouse's parents died young and he may, too – a passing which will send the world's militaries back into war – but he himself is of long-lived stock, which should keep war at bay. With the narrator being a disciple of Barnhouse, we may read his report as an epistle in the vein of those found in the New Testament. The author even expects this of the reader, mentioning the First Church of Barnhouse, which has a sizable congregation in Los Angeles, though he insists nothing supernatural is at work: "He is godlike in neither appearance nor intellect. [. . .] Neither he nor his powers fall outside the sphere of Nature" (174).

This is a lukewarm attempt at rationalizing a paranormal phenomenon to an American audience whose majority identified as Christians accepting, literally or metaphorically, the son of God as having assumed human form. Furthermore, Vonnegut's capitalization of Nature implies divinity of a feminine order – all that is lacking is "Mother" before it. Barnhouse's personal intentions incline him toward improving the world's infrastructure, both transportational and agricultural, and moving rainclouds to relieve countries suffering drought. Left to his own devices, he would be a real Child of Nature, but the weight of responsibility that accompanies his power leads him to seek help in regulating it: "Now I realize that I haven't any more right to it than a man has a right to own an atomic bomb" (180). There is also the detail in the story's second sentence, of receiving "one short, enigmatic message left in my mailbox on Christmas Eve" (173), activating our awareness of Santa Claus and the birth of Christ.

The professor's ethical obligation "to single out critical individuals and objects instead of slaughtering whole populations in the process of maintaining international equilibrium" (175) casts him as nothing short of Christlike, a savior for the dead center of the twentieth century. Also worth considering is the apocalyptic full-page painting that accompanied the story in *Collier's*. Tran Mawicke's infernal illustration portrays a serious, concentrating Barnhouse in eyeless, orange-fire silhouette as jets, engulfed in

Figure 2.2 Tran Mawicke's title illustration for "Report on the Barnhouse Effect." (© *Collier's* magazine, 1950)

flames and smoke, crash toward Earth and battleships burn on the water. The image is a descendant of romantic apocalyptic paintings, such as John Martin's *The Destruction of Sodom and Gomorrah* (1852).

Fiedler writes that when first encountering Vonnegut's novels, "his books seemed more scriptures than commodities" (5). In this light, "Report on the Barnhouse Effect," delivered to American mailboxes and porches on 11 February 1950 in the pages of *Collier's*, may very well be received as the inaugural epistle in a humanistic literary career that, taken all together, might be thought of as the Gospel According to Kurt. It is a tale of war vets who lead a two-man insurgency against the system that made them who they are. It is also a serious meditation upon the potential agency lurking within the individual, dynamic in the breadth of its possible uses, as well as a withering critique of the exploitative motivations of the military-industrial complex. "The potential for the disastrous rise of misplaced power exists and will persist," Dwight D. Eisenhower would warn in his final speech as President of the United States. A full eleven years earlier, Vonnegut made the same warning in this story.

Only a pawn in their game

With a title evoking the nursery-rhyme futility of trying to repair a broken eggshell, "All the King's Horses" presents a fanciful micro-drama of international relations edging on war, what Jerome Klinkowitz and John Somer call one of Vonnegut's "early fables" (38). His fourth published story (*Collier's* 10 Feb. 1951), it stands out in Vonnegut's oeuvre for its unambiguous designation of heroes and villains. Where much of his fiction refuses to establish or subverts binary oppositions, there is no question here when it comes to who to root for and who to despise. The story follows sixteen American P.O.W.s who have suffered a plane crash and been captured on the vaguely designated Asiatic mainland by Pi Ying, "a Communist guerilla chief" (91). In pulp-fiction style, the warlord offers safe travel through his territory if American Colonel Bryan Kelly can beat him in a life-size game of chess. Kelly plays with his fellow P.O.W.s, his wife Margaret, and twin sons Jerry and Paul as the game pieces, while Pi uses massive wooden pieces. Every time Kelly loses a player to Pi, that person is taken to an adjoining room and shot dead.

Chess was used to similar ends in earlier fiction. *The Chessmen of Mars* (1922) by Edgar Rice Burroughs, fifth volume in his Barsoom series, features a similar game, called jetan. Warlords play the game in an arena with a life-size playing field and death to players lost. There is also the chessboard layout of the Victorian classic *Through the Looking-Glass, and What Alice Found There* (1871), which is explicitly acknowledged with Lewis Carroll's diagram of the board as being "strictly in accordance with the laws of the game" (133). Humpty Dumpty, alluded to in Vonnegut's title, is a character in Carroll's sequel. Vonnegut's game is also true to the rules of chess, so much so that *Collier's* printed a diagram in the center of the last page to help readers follow the moves. This diagram was not reproduced for either *Canary in a Cat House* (1961) or *Welcome to the Monkey House* (1968), which both include "Horses."

Dan Wakefield, editor of Vonnegut's letters, brought forth correspondence preceding the story's publication: "It appears from the letter that someone at *Collier's* had objected to the ethnic identity of the villainous guerilla leader, named 'Pi Ying,' in the story 'White King' that was published as 'All the King's Horses'" (*Letters* 37). In a letter to the magazine's fiction editor, Knox Burger, dated 31 October 1950, Vonnegut defends the story:

> First off, leave me point out that nobody in the village or anywhere else would wince if the villain of my story were Baron Wolfgang von Steinhaus Kriegswald, scourge of the infamous S.S., ca. 1942.
>
> Second off, I am a registered Democrat, pro-Fair and New Deal, distressed by the new anti-subversive laws, hate McCarthy, enflamed by Communist smears on liberals – etc., etc. But, dammit, Knox, I don't like Communist Russia any more than I did Nazi Germany. There are some 3,000 Americans dead in Korea, killed in a chess game with Russia looking on. That is a lot of dead people and a plenty sickening situation. I have sixteen on my chessboard, which is peanuts. Them as may say I am insensitive to put an inflammatory thing like "White King" on the market are, perhaps, too insensitive to a casualty list as long as King Kong's arm. (37–38)

That said, Pi remains an Orientalized foe, complete with a speechless subaltern courtesan at his side. Before tackling those issues, historical context is necessary.

"Horses" appeared during the Korean War, fought from June 1950 to an armistice lasting July 1953 to November 1954. The conflict remains unresolved, with the Korean peninsula split North and South. During combat operations in the early nineteen-fifties, as Robertson points out, Americans confronted a set of expectations far different from those of WWII: "Total victory proved impossible, because the military objectives of the war were kept limited: America could not defeat the Russians or the Chinese in Korea, and the vision of atomic holocaust prevented most from playing with the idea of extending the limit of the war" (339). Sure enough, in Vonnegut's story we find a Russian official, Major Barzov, at Pi's ear. "Horses" is a fantasy depicting American anxieties in the early years of the Cold War and publication in one of the most popular magazines of its time underscores its significance as a product of and for the white middle class American psyche, which in 1951 was quite unsure of the Soviet Union's influence in the world, particularly in East Asia.

The Americans begin the story plane-wrecked in Pi's territory. Some of the specialists on board were bound for the Middle East, but Colonel Kelly, his wife, and twin sons were en route as military attaché to India. One recalls another Westerner who headed the long way around to India and came up short: Christopher Columbus, arch-usher of European imperialism in the Americas. Kelly's failed journey is an imagined international hiccup in post-war American imperialism, heading so far west it lands in the so-called Far East. Here there are "rice fields," "near-jungle," and Pi's "decaying palace" (91). That decay suggests an ailing seat of power in a foreign Waste Land, one even more beguiling than the Waste Land back home. Even use of the word "palace" is othering from the standpoint of American conceptions of normality: palaces are opulent Old World residences of command not found in the U.S.A., where the President rules from the modestly named White *House*.

Regarding whiteness, the story's original title, "White King," points to the color and chess piece Kelly assumes, as well as his race as a white American. The racial element is not subtle, though color is not used to describe the "Oriental" characters. This story operates, in part, through the myth of "The White Man's Burden." Rudyard Kipling brought the phrase into American and British consciousness with his poem of the same title, a poem written for Queen Victoria's Diamond Jubilee but rewritten to address the Spanish-American War (1898). The most common understanding of the myth is dependent upon the bigger myth of progress and places white Europeans and Americans above other people, their "influence" trickling down a hierarchy based on race and supported by biased sciences, bestowing them with the responsibility of "bringing up" those less fortunate races through civilizing (a.k.a. imperializing) means.

It is one of the most dangerous myths in the West and is not behind us. In 2007, Nobel Prize winner Dr. James Watson, who with Dr. Francis Crick discovered the double-helix structure of the DNA molecule, was forced to resign from his own institute for statements about the intelligence of black people:

> [Watson said] he is "inherently gloomy about the prospect of Africa," since "all our social policies are based on the fact that their intelligence is the same as ours – whereas testing says not really. [. . . And] people who have to deal with black employees find this not true."
>
> ("The Mortification of James Watson")

Vonnegut worried about being read as a racist, coming to his own defense in his letter. But even with the new title, this story presents white Americans falling prey to an uncivilized Orient and rising to the occasion of establishing dominance. Chess, developed from games from India and Persia but considered a game of medieval Europe, is used by an East Asian foe against white Americans, the effect being of one's own game used against him. And here, on the coattails of rebuilding Europe and Japan, is a newly anticipated burden of cleaning up the mess of red communism in "yellow" Asia. The emphasis on whiteness also relates to American military might, conjuring the image of President Theodore Roosevelt's Great White Fleet. In 1907, he sent the white-painted U.S. armada on a fourteen-month mission to sail the globe in a westerly direction. It was an unambiguously imperialistic strut, waving Teddy's proverbial Big Stick in a pageant that saw no action but spoke loudly. Vonnegut's story plays out a scenario of the white American military spreading into parts of the world lacking definition in U.S. consciousness and shows its individual members becoming entangled in unforeseen, deadly circumstances.

Pi Ying, whose name puns the act of urination in a culturally insulting way, has more in common with Raymond's Ming the Merciless from *Flash Gordon* or Rohmer's criminal mastermind Fu Manchu than he does with any East Asian military leader in 1951. Kim Il-sung, who became leader of the Democratic People's Republic of Korea, was the man to beat at the time, viewed as a puppet ventriloquized by the Russians and the Chinese. It is also worth noting that the same issue of *Collier's* contains "City Under a Dagger": sketches and an account by Howard Brodie, *Collier's* Combat Artist, from his visit to Hanoi, then undergoing the First Indochina War (32–3, 37). To be fair, Pi is not portrayed as a caricature of Kim, the U.S. is not at

Figure 2.3 Tran Mawicke's two-page spread illustration for "All the King's Horses." (© *Collier's* magazine, 1951)

war with him in the story, and specifics are avoided as to his nationality and locale in East Asia. He and his guerilla force are generalized, broadly labeled as communist and Oriental, underlining an undiagnosed American uneasiness with the unknown Far East.

Painter Tran Mawicke put terrific care into his two-page illustration for the story in *Collier's*. It depicts Pi and Kelly's game as it stands halfway through the story, nearly matching the diagram of the board reproduced in the magazine. The only deviation is a pawn absent from position 2c, likely a compositional decision, because from the chosen angle a grown man in that square would block our view of ten year old Jerry, greatly hampering the emotional tug produced by the boy's presence. Heightening that effect, Mawicke puts an armed guerilla over the child's shoulder. On the far left we see Pi's bishop, right hand held in an affected *mudra* – a symbolic gesture expressing Buddhist or Hindu values. The queen piece standing to his right is shown in Orientalized robes. Both pieces have East Asian facial features. Framed between them, at the far corner of the board, we see an American soldier, the pilot-cum-bishop, and Margaret as the white queen. The three, whose anxiety is expressed in worried postures, are dwarfed by the foregrounded pieces.

The right page is entirely illustrated. On this side of the board, Pi's knight dominates, standing between two of Kelly's pawns. The piece is a full-sized horse, its four hooves cramped together on a square base, an Orientalized knight upon its back. Ten-year-old Jerry stands on tiptoed-anticipation beyond the horse's rear end in striped shirt, looking at his father. From this angle, a trick of distance makes it look like the carved horse's face might bite off Kelly's face. He is shown at 1b, looking over his shoulder to his opponent standing in a balcony. Pi, cheerful in white military uniform with his hands on his waist, is flanked by a Stalinesque Barzov on the left and the unnamed "delicate young Oriental [. . .] motionless, ornamental girl" (94) on the right, her face painted something like a geisha's. A leafless, gnarled bonsai trunk stands in a pot beside them and a red banner with a golden Chinese dragon in ouroboric form drapes over the ledge.

So many of these elements, combined as they are, make the painting, inspired by the content of Vonnegut's story, a pictorial example of manifest Orientalism. The lack of specificity in an image pieced together from various East Asian cultures introduced this story to *Collier's* readers in a way, most likely unconscious, that appealed to their general ignorance. This isn't to say that middle class Americans were stupid. Rather, at the time of publication, mainstream America was at least a decade away from developing a widespread and open curiosity about the East (which would bring, with benefits, its own generalizing pitfalls). This was five years after the end of WWII, concurrent with the Korean War, and despite the scale of both, most Americans experienced those conflicts secondhand. Their ideas of East Asia had been largely shaped under the rhetoric of us vs. them, inflected by cartoon propaganda depicting slant-eyed and bucktoothed "Japs" by the likes of otherwise-great artists like Theodor Geisel. Someone at *Collier's* questioned the racial depiction of Pi, and yet his appearance in the magazine lifts the archetypal image of the "Oriental" foe from jingoistic cartoons and pulp modes and plops it into mainstream, middle class American discourse.

Critics Kevin Alexander Boon and David Pringle claim that, "there are no heroes in Vonnegut's 'All the King's Horses' [. . .] Colonel Kelly, the communist guerilla chief, Ying, and the Russian military 'observer,' Barzov are all military figures. It is their inhumane military logic that Vonnegut exposes, a 'logic' that women, to their credit, cannot fathom" (*At Millennium's End* 174). Apart from their doting sexism shoehorned in at the end, they approach this early Vonnegut story with an understanding of the author at a more mature stage. This might be a case of Vonnegut's persona getting in the way. To build upon a dictum from D. H. Lawrence: never trust *our idea of* the teller, trust the tale. One aspect of this story is that of its WWII veteran author, not six years on the other side of traumatic military service, flexing his ideological stance when it comes to exploring international relations through fiction. His defense of the story in the letter to Burger tells us that protagonist Kelly is, without a doubt, a hero in the sense that he symbolically stands up for and wins a victory for American values against Communist guerilla factions. Vonnegut is not your token subversive element; at times he is marvelously conventional in his convictions.

And yet Boon and Pringle are correct to say that the story exposes the inhumaneness of being put in the position of making tactical decisions that will kill not only one's enemies but also one's own soldiers. Repeatedly, the word "philosophically" is used, set apart by commas for emphasis, to describe the nature of the game. The warlord presents it as a metaphor for battle, which he acknowledges the wife and boys have not experienced but will come to appreciate. This idea of a philosophy of war in this story underlines, from a Western point of view, the notion of a psychological split between East and West. Pi is a pseudo-Sun Tzu in poor translation, offering the odd platitude about war, a convention common to pulp villains. Barzov supports this perceived split: "'He'll learn to be a pawn yet,' he roared. 'It's an Oriental skill Americans could do well to learn for the days ahead, eh?'" (99).

Campbell classified the world's dominant mythologies as Oriental and Occidental: "In their mythologies, religions, philosophies, and ideals, no less than in their styles of life and dress and in their arts, [. . .] they do group significantly in two orders of two: India and the Far East, on one hand; the Levant and Europe, on the other" (*Myths to Live By* 61–2). It is an old binary still popular in the West whether one believes it or not. The two overarching systems, as Campbell sees them, can enter into dialogue if engaged, neither superior to the other. This spirit does not come through in Vonnegut's story.

In time, he would challenge American views of other cultures – in *Man Without a Country* (2005) he went against the grain during the Afghanistan and second Iraq wars in thanking Arabs and central Asians for algebra and the concept of zero. But in "Horses," written at the beginning of his career, the East/West split is portrayed superficially, Kelly's opposing players little more than Vonnegut's game pieces representing Communist Russia and East Asians.

Accepting that caveat, the story does acknowledge the ethical complexity of decisions that military commanders must make. If Campbell is correct that "when you go to war with people, the problem of the newspapers is to turn those people into 'its'" (*POM* 78–9), then that ruthlessness is dictated by the war-making leaders when they send soldiers off to die. But Kelly experiences this "it-ness" in relation to his own troops: "He found himself thinking of the lieutenant in those terms – no longer human, but a piece" (97). When he loses his first soldier, the sergeant/pawn, and hears the gunshot in the next room, the Colonel suffers a crisis of conscience: "Kelly's calm was shattered, and with it went the illusion of the game. The pieces in his power were human beings again. The precious, brutal stuff of command was gone from Colonel Kelly. He was no more fit to make decisions of life and death than the rawest recruit" (99). Here we see the sanctity of life breaking through a man's condition as a seasoned career military officer.

Losing the sergeant shatters "the eerie calm" that Vonnegut calls "the essence of war" before the chess game begins: "Now [Kelly] recognized the eerie calm – an old wartime friend – that left only the cold machinery of his wits and senses alive. It was the narcotic of generalship. It was the essence of war" (95). This wartime stillness is present in countless accounts of war, historical, journalistic, and fictitious. World War I poets paid this stillness high respect, for instance Siegfried Sassoon in "Before the Battle" (1918) and Edmund Blunden in "Gouzeaucourt: The Deceitful Calm" (1928). This quiet "friend," a personified quality of atmosphere preceding combat, has deadened everything in Kelly but his wits and senses. As Vonnegut puts it, this "essence," "the narcotic of generalship," is a drug for those in command.

The watershed of humanity that floods his consciousness when the sergeant is killed inflicts a psychological wound on Kelly. He experiences it as a failure of his own command. Robert Emmet Meagher argues that, "Whether we have in mind a modern superpower like the United States or an ancient superhero like Herakles, both of which unleash irresistible force, we find that there is no such thing as killing without dying, no such thing as inflicting casualties without enduring them. Every wound inflicted on another is a wound suffered within" (13). Meagher refers chiefly to attacks on the enemy, the killing of a demonized stranger. The effect of seeing a subordinate killed due to one's orders invites a wound as great or greater.

Yet after Kelly has lost five servicemen to Pi, he suddenly steels his emotional core, invoking necessity of tactics. He switches from playing defensively to offensively, which realigns him under the "essence of war":

> Kelly didn't permit himself to think of the chessmen as anything but a cipher in a rigid mathematical proposition: if *x* is dead, the rest shall live. He perceived the tragedy of his decision only as a man who knew the definition of tragedy, not as one who felt it [. . .] The cold resolve deserted Kelly for an instant, and he saw the utter pathos of his position – a dilemma as old as mankind, as new as the struggle between East and West. When human beings are attacked, *x*, multiplied by hundreds or thousands, must die – sent to death by those who love them most. Kelly's profession was the choosing of *x*.
>
> (102)

He registers a need to embrace the situation's inhumaneness in order to save as many lives on his side as he can. Impersonalization, along with deliberate cruelty and coercion, is one of historian John Keegan's trinity of "the inhuman face of war" (320–31). Hillman comments: "It is not merely the industrialization of warfare and the large population involved, but the ontology of numerical thinking, of science itself, that produces the impersonalization which creates a new kind of deliberate cruelty in the precisely calculated bombing of the unnamed by the unnamed [. . .] War turns humans into parts, spare parts" (52).

The problem of naming is relevant. The sergeant, corporal, and pilot are all identified by these terms. These nameless characters are refurbished as two pawns and a bishop respectively, old parts becoming new parts for this miniaturized, stylized version of battle. The sergeant gives service as a pawn; the corporal offers his body to pawnship. But Kelly, too, surrenders his name, giving himself to coronation as the white king. Boon and Pringle remind us that the king is "the one piece that cannot die, that can only be captured" (174), so he is safe from everything – save command. In accepting this persona, Kelly makes the intellectual, programmatic choice to align with the ideological value that it is better to send some to slaughter in order to spare the majority than suffer a numerically higher loss of life.

The white king, in an Abraham and Isaac decision, moves the queen's knight forward. That knight is one of his ten-year-old twin sons, Jerry. Jerry was Allied slang during WWII for the Germans, as well as the name of MGM's cartoon mouse who perpetually outwits his predatory feline foe in *Tom and Jerry* shorts. Kelly's sacrificial offering outwits Pi – and sets the women into motion. When Pi takes Jerry with his bishop and orders the boy killed, the voiceless subaltern "girl" to his side, horrified by his cruelty, stabs him in the back. Pi dies a serpentine Humpty Dumpty, slithering over the balcony and falling to the floor. The "Chinese girl," the only East Asian character given a nationality, stabs herself in the chest and collapses against Barzov. Within this single instance of the word "Chinese" is all of America's notions of Red China, far less blatant than Barzov's status as a representative for Soviet Russia. The reality of the Korean War was that both Russia and China were backing the North Koreans.

The white queen, Kelly's wife Margaret, cannot accept the sacrifice of their son: "Death through a blunder she might be able to understand; but death as a product of cool reason, a step in logic, she could never accept. Rather than accept it, she would have had them all die" (105). This is what causes Boon and Pringle to carelessly espouse "that women, to their credit, cannot fathom" the so-called logic of war (174). Hillman disdains this as "the testosterone hypothesis":

> That is, everything to do with bellicosity and militarism is the expression of male physiology, both the cruelty and the courage – it's all reducible to glands of gender. The myths and legends tell it differently: the spirit of war and the rage of battle are archetypal, forced upon all animal life, all gender, all societies.
>
> (*TLW* 86)

Margaret rejects what Boon and Pringle call patriarchal rationalization, as does the Chinese girl. The focus on patriarchy, however, must not limit our reading to binaries. The opposite of patriarchal rationalization would be matriarchal irrationalization, but Hillman warns us of following that lead as a definitive answer. A quick consideration of chess in terms of binaries reveals plenty of cleavings: one side vs. the other, white vs. black (in pieces *and* alternating squares on the board), sixteen pieces vs. a mirrored sixteen pieces, and on each side a solid rank of pawns before a solid rank of specialized pieces, as well as each king and each queen having his or her own bishop, knight, and rook. The setup is hardly a model for the reality of war. As a simulation, it is intellectually contrived, rather than arising from the sublime realm of actuality. Vonnegut *almost* rejects the logic of war but ends up enacting it superficially to spare lives on Kelly's side.

The chief problem in "Horses" is respecting war only as a game played out by the frontal lobe of the brain. Cut off from the emotive and instinctual nerves, chemicals, and energies that course through all of us, people wage war from a place of psychological imbalance. Campbell pointed to cerebral intellectuality as a terrible danger for individuals:

> Consciousness thinks it's running the shop. But it's a secondary organ of a total human being, and it must not put itself in control. It must submit and serve the humanity of the body. [. . .] If the person insists on a certain program, and doesn't listen to the demands of his own heart, he's going to risk a schizophrenic crackup. Such a person has put himself off

center. He has aligned himself with a program for life, and it's not the one the body's interested in at all.

(*POM* 146, 147)

Kelly plays by the rules of the system of chess. Denied the rights of prisoners of war under the Geneva Convention, the Americans' alternative is death. It is with hope of saving some souls under his terribly limited protection that Kelly accepts the game. In a sense, this is a condition of generalship that we foist upon our military leaders when our political representatives send them to oversee battle. This is a paradox: they act on behalf of the collective and, in playing by a set of rules anathema to civilized life, risk losing their own humanity to protect it.

In a variation on British philosopher Philippa Foot's ethical "Trolley Problem," Smith posits a scenario in which a house is on fire and you only have time to rescue occupants of one of two occupied bedrooms. One room has three children unrelated to you in it and the other has your child: "[A] person who, being more altruistic, would let his child die to save the lives of the three others would probably be regarded by most people as a psychopathic monster" (138). Thus Margaret and the Chinese girl's disgust with the implications of Kelly's final move. His own duty is put to the test thanks to his presence on the line of battle, an uncharacteristic position for a military commander. Smith explains the significance of distance in psychological stability when issuing orders: "Distance also explains how it is possible for generals to condemn thousands of men, women, and children to death with a single order without suffering psychological harm, while a private who kills just one man in close combat may be haunted by the experience for the remainder of his life" (180). That buffer of physical distance most modern military commanders enjoy is taken away, as is the buffer that typically separates a citizen back home from the front lines for those who would have read the story from the comfortable, oversized pages of *Collier's*. This story aims to repersonalize those impersonalized to war.

While "Horses" gives us a man's world where men command the pieces on the board, we ought to know better than to end our reading there. Patriarchal rationalization is merely symptomatic of impersonalization. The women supersede not just patriarchy but its root cause, refusing to disassociate and revealing their individual humane capabilities for dignity and brutality. Margaret's courage is in her utter rejection of the game, seeing it as a horribly inhumane construct, a perversion of reality. The Chinese girl, an intervening anima, strikes out and kills Pi before sacrificing herself. The characterizations are not profoundly nuanced; most are bluntly allegorical. It is the process of war and the dynamism of individual reactions to it that are shown to be complex.

Vonnegut's story ends with Kelly achieving checkmate against Barzov, who finds little to do with the board he inherits from Pi. Kelly's family is spared and Barzov agrees to safe passage for the remaining troops through the territory. "Horses" ends in Saturday matinee serial style, with the promise of another skirmish down the road: "issue an invitation, Major, and I'll be there" (110). Reading the story today we sense prophecy, thinking of the Vietnam War. At the time though, "All the King's Horses" was expressing the collective anxiety that armed conflict with an East Asian, Russian-backed faction was inevitable.

Great war

"Great Day," published posthumously, is an account of boot camp gone wrong in a future where peace reigns and a time machine gives trainee soldiers a glimpse at a real battlefield: WWI's Battle of Château-Thierry. When the overeager, war-loving drill instructor, Captain Poritsky, ventures too far into the demonstration, he and the story's narrator are stranded in 1918. "I ain't no hero," the narrator insists, confronting the myth of the war hero, while Poritsky is portrayed as a pipsqueak Patton, his yearning for war overriding his faculties. The story pits the reluctance to war against the hunger to war and puts the reader in the position of listening to a veteran victim of combat. Hillman says, "War's inhumanity is captured best by poets and novelists, for their imaginations reach into the afflicted soul beyond the reporting of the facts" (*A Terrible Love of War*, 48). "Great Day," with its science fiction motif, takes us beyond the realm of fact to immerse us in wartime suffering.

Before delving, we need to consider critic Donald Morse's comments regarding recent collections of Vonnegut's unpublished short fiction[2] as "unfortunate posthumous publications bearing [Vonnegut's] name." He argues that these previously rejected works should have been available only to scholars, worrying that Vonnegut's standing is at stake: "Whether put together as an act of misplaced piety or out of greed, such books do a grave disservice to Vonnegut by damaging his reputation as well as disrespecting his clearly expressed wishes not to publish" ("Bringing Chaos to Order"). Morse's anxiety sounds like a flare-up from the early years of Vonnegut scholarship, when the case had to be made that this writer was worth studying. He compares these posthumous productions to those that followed Twain's death, but Twain's legacy as a canonized writer in American letters speaks to the insignificant damage wrought by such publications. Vonnegut fans, which his work produces beyond a "cult following," may appreciate these works because they measure his growth as a writer. Teeth were cut on these stories, so many of them simpler than – yet hinting at – the work to come. Several of the stories also stand to critical analysis. "Great Day" is one such story.

Great Day, we find out at the end, is the narrator's nickname granted by the nurses and wounded soldiers in the cathedral-turned-hospital where he is recuperating. For the majority of the story, the narrator is nameless, addressed only as "soldier" by his captain, giving the account as we encounter it as readers an archetypal quality. The individual relating his war story is "soldier," the grunt, the low-ranking unit that makes up one part of the collective Army. That is, until we find out the story title is his moniker, Great Day, for his insistence that he has come from a future with "the Army of the World, everybody like brothers everwhere, peace everlasting, nobody hungry, nobody ascared" (70). Here the story meets rationality: the reader is free to interpret Great Day's story of coming from a peaceful future as the ravings of a blinded "casualty" or a messenger speaking the truth. Like Cassandra, either way, he is hardly heeded by those caring for him.

Great Day's voice approximates that of an uneducated Midwesterner, descending from Huckleberry Finn. Vonnegut used first person narration in many of his stories and novels, often and increasingly in his signature, almost journalistic style. Great Day's voice is not to be found elsewhere in his output, however, making it a curiosity. It mimics the colloquial aspect of narration in *Adventures of Huckleberry Finn*. Twain was an early and persistent inspiration for Vonnegut, and here we see the latter flattering the former with imitation. Great Day's identity as a Hoosier is a projection of Vonnegut's. And while Minnesota, Alabama, and North Dakota have towns called Luverne, and Iowa has one called Lu Verne, none exists in Indiana. This gives Great Day a broader series of connections to the Midwest in general, Alabama being an outlier. Midwestern readers would recognize the towns with the same name in their own states or states nearby, and feel a neighborly kinship. It also suggests science fiction pioneer Jules Verne.

And yet his rustic vernacular hardly fits American notions of what his home year, 2037, would look like. In the fifties, when this story was written, Disney and the World's Fair made imaginings of the future into industries, inspiring the next generation's engineers into expectations of flying cars and moon cottages by the year 2000. Here we are confronted with a voice quite like Huck's Antebellum river-rat dialect. This speaks to Great Day's class, likely poor, white, and uneducated. When his mother warns him to steer clear of the Zulus he will meet when joining the Army of the World (which tells us racism is still alive in 2037), he insists it is a "high-class kind of army," to which she replies, "You just remember you *was* high-class [. . .] As long as I had you,' she said, 'you was'" (50). This tells us Great Day and his mother have been deemed or at least made to feel lower class. Like many recruits, Great Day's impetus for joining the Army of the World seems to involve the notion of class mobility and "climbing the ranks." While international conflict has been eradicated in 2037, class hierarchy, like racism, trundles onward. 2037 is not a Utopia.

The idea of a future where war has been wiped out creates a premise steeped in wishful thinking and pacifistic idealism. But Vonnegut does not simply build such a setting and leave the reader with its description. Actually, 2037 goes barely described, the details of its united Army of the World relayed mainly via context. The premise is actually that of mid-twentieth century human beings' reluctance to war and how they are made victims of war by those who desire it. "Although it is true that men have, from time to time, pursued carnage with bloodthirsty enthusiasm," writes Smith, "it is also true men have probably always tried to avoid it" (150). War, in 2037, is an action left to the past, which makes the use of a so-called time-screen to glimpse an actual battlefield a regressive act. The story then is one of collective regression into war and its blinding, impairing, psychological effects on the individual.

The time-screen itself is a variation on the time machine, a trope found in post-Industrial Revolution literatures. In the mid- to late nineteenth century, characters like Ebenezer Scrooge (1843) and Twain's Hank Morgan (1889) were transported through time, by spirits and a concussion, respectively; Vonnegut took Twain to task for this device in his introduction to *A Connecticut Yankee in King Arthur's Court*: "His explanation of how a Yankee gets back to the sixth century couldn't be more lame. He got hit on the head. Oh my, my, my . . . One remembers that Twain, in a funny and unforgiving essay, fricasseed poor James Fenimore Cooper for literary crimes not half that bad" (xxxii). As machines became more and more common, mechanical manipulations of time arose in literature. Enrique Gaspar y Rimbau's novel *El Anacronopete* (1887) holds the distinction of the first use of a time machine, and H. G. Wells's *The Time Machine* soon followed (1895). By the nineteen-fifties, time machines were a staple of fantastic fiction. The time-screen in "Great Day" presents a machine producing a projection that reveals the past. Captain Poritsky explains how it works with limited knowledge. Flares will be set out to mark the edges of the screen and between those it will simultaneously be their own time and the battle at Château-Thierry in 1918. He's been assured by scientists that no real harm can come between them and the vision: "We'll be ghosts to them, and they'll be ghosts to us. We'll be walking through them and they'll be walking through us like we was all smoke" (60).

This beam that shines back through time is not clumsily imagined. Projection is the unconscious act of seeing one's own shortcomings or graces manifested in the behavior of others. It is often a denial of the potential for such attitudes, qualities, and actions in oneself. When we moon over someone, we are seeing our own potential to love mapped onto that someone; when we loathe somebody, we are often witnessing our own consciously denied or unconsciously repressed capacities in full display. Named a time-screen, the device also carries significance attributed to various meanings of "screen": It screens the past for conflict, presents a screen upon which past events are watched, a sort of three-dimensional film screen, and even sifts time as an archaeologist's screen sifts soil to find easily-missed shards of bone.

In 2037, humanity unified has gone about creating a way to project the sins of its forefathers, believing this will "blood" its peacekeeping Army without any respect for the reality lurking beyond the beam's periphery. The machine bears a caveat that would tempt Bluebeard's latest wife: "All you got to do is cross one of them lines of flares, go through the edge of the beam. You'll disappear into nineteen-eighteen for real" (60–61). The scientists' invention, seemingly clever in its safety features, carries all of the real dangers of a battle fought 119 years earlier for reasons largely forgotten. Great Day's comrade Earl Sterling, of Salt Lake, demonstrates his ignorance of Château-Thierry the night before the demonstration: "Something big must of happened over there" (55). The demonstration carries with it the irreversible potential to feed lives to an unheeded history.

Captain Poritsky, who commands the time-screen company, the first of its kind, is one who has fallen in love with war, though he has never experienced it. Great Day introduces him, citing his sporty Midwestern Catholic education as a football player at Notre Dame and perverse fondness for his own physique, which he gropes when talking to his men. Poritsky's behavior is pathological. His penchant for masturbatory exhibitionism of his own muscles casts him as narcissistic at the very least. And his desire is entirely yoked to scientific progress. He has waited for the day the scientists would develop such a thing as their time-screen so that he might finally come close to experiencing a human event that has been rejected collectively, that of making war. Poritsky would gladly see peace undone because he seeks an outward manifestation of the war he feels within himself. "'I was born to *fight*!' he hollered. 'I'm rusting out inside!'" (65).

In taking classicist Victor Davis Hanson to task for his championing of the current war on terror, Meagher portrays him in a way that could very well apply to Captain Poritsky: "he has learned of war from books. His dreams of combat, if he has them, are secondhand, far from the nightmares of a veteran" (10). Meagher condemns the glorification of war by one who has not seen it, and so does Vonnegut in this story. But condemnation does not always pave the way to understanding where such an attitude arises. Campbell offered one explanation of the love of war as a desire, strange as it sounds, to live:

> Men sometimes confess they love war because it puts them in touch with the experience of being alive. In going to the office every day, you don't get that experience, but suddenly, in war, you are ripped back into being alive. Life is pain; life is suffering; and life is horror – but, by God, you are alive.
>
> (*POM* 114)

How are we to conduct ourselves humanely, if that is indeed our aim, in this life where certain others around us eagerly or unconsciously long to behave inhumanely? Despite Great Day's goal that we identify with him, the peace-seeking narrator, this story reminds us that there are war-lovers in the world.

All struggles in establishing and maintaining peace will be met by individuals who carry a yearning for war.

The story offers no solution to this conundrum. Short stories need not solve problems and few, if any, do. The form does, however, favor the warning, the drawing of consciousness to particular problems. This is not to reduce all of short fiction to the status of public service announcements; yet some stories do present human problems with a realized dynamism that refuses to simplify life-shaping forces. No moral is delivered, just a warning. Myths often act in the same way, not explaining the world, not solving it like a puzzle, but simply enfranchising aspects of experience within it, delivering the message that such-and-such is a feature, an event, a potentiality of being alive. "Fiction seeks out truth," writes John Gardner. "Granted, it seeks a poetic kind of truth, universals not easily translatable into moral codes. But part of our interest as we read is in learning how the world works" (79). "Great Day" presents soldiers struggling to metabolize the existence of war:

> "How come the folks just didn't go crazy in all them real wars – or quit?"
> "Folks are funny," I said.
> "Sometimes I don't think so," Earl said.
>
> (54)

In many ways, this is the experience of every halfway decent person who has not experienced battle him or herself. If Smith and others are correct that the vast majority of people are intrinsically reluctant to kill other people, disbelief or bewilderment must be typical when war happens.

Here Vonnegut's personal experiences as a Private First Class are clearly feeding the need to tell the story at hand. In his introduction to *A Connecticut Yankee*, Vonnegut identified his tendency as an aged novelist to read personal details in others' books: "Such autobiographical material is not *between* the lines. It is *in* the lines" (xxxi). As one who would eventually inject himself as a character into his fiction, Vonnegut was in every way present in his work from the beginning. "Great Day" offers two telling details that would emerge later in his fiction as deriving from his personal experiences in surviving the firebombing of Dresden. In *Slaughterhouse-Five*, Billy Pilgrim is given a Jack the Giant Killer quality as he waits out Allied bombing: "He was down in the meat locker on the night that Dresden was destroyed. There were sounds like giant footsteps above. Those were sticks of high-explosive bombs. The giants walked and walked" (*NS* 464). In "Great Day" the narrator says: "There was a barrage going on up above, like giants walking around, kicking the world apart" (53). Later Poritsky describes the approaching glimpse of Château-Thierry in terms evoking the meat locker that protected Vonnegut and his fellow P.O.W.s during the bombing of Dresden, calling it "a slaughterhouse in Hell" (59).

The depictions of the WWI battle then are fittingly infernal. WWI soldiers lining a muddy crater under them are "like snails crawling around in a fishbowl. There was a track leading from each one – the live ones *and* the dead ones" (66). When a 1918 shell hits this pit and explodes, a mortally wounded troop looks into the air and, on the point of death, sees the recruits in the future: "He wasn't surprised to see us hanging there in the air over him. Wasn't nothing could surprise him no more" (67). We do not often stop and realize that the field of history is in many ways a collective failure in time traveling into the past. The act of imagining an event with the trace materials we can gather after it has come to pass is a meditation aiming at reconstructing experiences that are gone. Cause for trying to piece together the past is entirely subjective and the desired goal of objective recreation can never be truly achieved in a living way. Facts provide clues but they cannot draw the past into happening again for the full experience of what it was like. One aspect worth noting in "Great Day" is the representation of men being shelled at the Battle of Château-Thierry, an actual event in our history that provides a setting in a fantasy that begins in the unknown future. The effect of wondering what the dying man thinks when seeing Great Day and Captain Poritsky standing over him is something we like to imagine when contemplating the lives and deaths of our ancestors: What would the dead make of us looking back at them?

"Great Day," going unpublished until its young author had died an old man, benefits from a familiarity with what Kurt Vonnegut had experienced as a soldier. It is an attempt, unsuccessful, to exorcise *miasma* from its writer's life. Great Day himself, only nicknamed, archetypally cast as a Soldier, tells his story to us and anyone else who will listen to his own attempt to overcome the pollution war has left in his soul. "They should ought to have special hospitals for heroes, so heroes wouldn't have to lay next to the likes of me," he says.

> "I never done a thing to make the world safe for democracy," I tell 'em. "When I got hit, I was crying like a baby and trying to kill my own captain. If a bullet hadn't of killed him, I would of, and he was a fellow American." [. . .] But all these heroes here, they don't seem to care. "That's all right, Buddy," they say, "You just go right on talking."
>
> (69)

One problem with heroism is the perpetuation of what are typically identified as heroic circumstances and emerging, initiated, without feeling the anticipated sensation of having become a hero. Many veterans find themselves derided or unappreciated for their service by those who disagreed with the justness of the conflict their community sent them to fight, an experience that deepens their disillusionment into an abyss. This is why stories that represent the horrible dynamics of battle are integral to our collective psyche: they place us briefly within the experience of war-making without bodily danger of killing or being killed. For the veteran who does not feel like a hero, who feels its opposite, "Great Day" is a story where he or she will find a voice expressing the same feeling. Vonnegut, always trying to be a useful member of society, was unable to express his own wartime trauma to his own satisfaction, for lack of a better word, until he was nearly fifty years old. *Slaughterhouse-Five* was not his final word on WWII or war itself, but with the publication of "Great Day," it is clear that his cathartic novel was also not his first.

Looking back on Armageddon

Another 1950s story Vonnegut failed to place for publication in his lifetime is "Armageddon in Retrospect." An epistolary narrative, the story's form is that of a generic form letter asking for money to fund a dubiously supernatural enterprise: capture of the Devil. It stands apart in Vonnegut's canon for the way it engages the Judeo-Christian myth of evil. Nowhere else did Vonnegut so directly play with the binary, religiously inflected, that pits the concept of good in a war with the concept of evil. Play provides the means in this story to reconsider not only faith but also science, which stand today as another binary many accept at face value as being irreconcilable opposites in constant conflict; Vonnegut's Dr. Gorman Tarbell explains "if you'll investigate the history of science, my dear boy, I think you'll find that most of the really big ideas have come from intelligent playfulness. All the sober, thin-lipped concentration is really just a matter of tidying up around the fringes of the big ideas" (216). The letter writer's goal, as he explains it, is to defeat the Devil by scientific means and rid the world of evil. Instead of focusing on war between nations, this story delves into metaphysical war, sizing up a major Western spiritual/metaphorical (depending on your persuasion) explanation for the root cause of conflicts, both inner and communal.

Addressed "Dear Friend" and signed by "Dr. Lucifer J. Mephisto, Chairman of the Board" (209, 232), the letter unspools the history of the Pine Institute and UNDICO, the United Nations Demonological Investigating Committee. Given the purported author's name – "as you might expect," he writes, "I was subjected to a lot of poor jokes about my being the perfect man for the job because of my name" (220) – there is reasonable cause to weigh him on the scales of reliable narration. Lucifer, of course, is one of the many names of the Devil, though it initially referred to the planet Venus, which shines brightly in the sky at dawn and dusk. In Latin, *lux* means "light" and *ferre* is "to bring." Later Lucifer became associated with the chief angel who rebelled against God in the Old Testament (*Isaiah* 14:12). Lucifer points to the light-bringing, Promethean attractiveness of the Devil, his ability to disguise himself in brightness as a means of deception, hiding his nefarious nature. The pairing of light with good and darkness with evil may be primordial, but it has certainly existed in Western conscious expression at least since belief in Zoroastrianism, a 6th century BCE Persian religion that influenced the Judeo-Christian traditions.

The middle initial J. could stand for any number of names, but the surname of Mephisto is specific. It is a shortening of Mephistopheles, the name of a demon in German folklore and attributed to the Faust legend in the sixteenth century as a minion of Lucifer. Christopher Marlowe used Mephistopheles in *The Tragical History of the Life and Death of Doctor Faustus* (1604) but Johann Wolfgang von Goethe stole his thunder in his two-part tragedy titled *Faust* (1808 and 1832). In a spin on the competition between God and Satan for Job's devotion, Mephistopheles wagers that he will lure Faust, an intellectual pursuing enlightenment, away from truth. Faust makes a pact with Mephistopheles for greater access to knowledge. Fully intending to claim Faust's soul, Mephistopheles puts him through a series of labors but loses him to the angels of heaven. Reed and Rackstraw have written on Vonnegut's intertextuality with Goethe's *Faust* in *Mother Night* (where its title originates) and *Slaughterhouse-Five*, with Rackstraw noting: "Vonnegut's whimsical recapitulations of honored literatures like *Faust* affirm the continuity as well as the transforming cultural powers such archetypal figures have had and will continue to have" ("Paradox" 60–61). This Pan-American tendency of re-presenting European archetypes is also expressed, we recall from Chapter 1, by Canadians and Latin American writers like Roberto Fernández Retamar and Oswald de Andrade.

In the prologue to Goethe's *Part One*, Mephistopheles introduces himself:

> I am the spirit that seeks to do evil
> But always turns out to be good.
>
> (1.1335)

Rollo May reads the play as an expression of the hope and failure of Westerners from the Enlightenment onward who place faith in the bright-shining notion of progress: "Goethe's *Faust* is a poignant and powerful expression of the myth of our modern age in which people yearn to believe that the God of progress [. . .] will have a beneficent effect upon us and will bring vast gains to humanity" (*Cry for Myth* 235). Campbell similarly drew a line between technology and Satan's little helper: "Mephistopheles, the machine man, can provide us with all the means, and is thus likely to determine the aims of life as well. But of course the characteristic of Faust, which makes him eligible to be saved, is that he seeks aims that are not those of the machine" (*POM* 18). In this sense, Mephistopheles is the metaphysical mouthpiece for materialism, throwing seekers off the transcendent path and grounding them in an understanding of existence that allows only for the machinations of concrete matter. Reading Sir Isaac Newton's explanation of light, modern Irish mystic

John Moriarty pinpointed what he felt to be a juncture in the collective rejection of the metaphysical function:

> Now I think modern scientists have led us into a 'nothing but' universe that is without colour, that is without taste, without touch, without all of these things. And I'm not denying that Newton isn't right here. I mean, what Newton's saying, it's so far, so good. But, like, in the hands of lesser persons. And by the time we reach the eighteenth century we are straight into the 'nothing but' universe. Now add that to *Genesis*, chapter one, verses twenty-six and twenty-eight, and we have the formula for the modern world.
>
> (*Seeking to Walk*)

In those verses, God decides to make human beings and grants them dominion over all the earth. Moriarty saw moderners as having granted ourselves dominion over a "nothing but" universe,[3] which is precisely what Mephistopheles wants to inspire in Faust. That positivistic belief system, which denies the force of unconscious energies, is his trick, which is succinctly expressed in the saying that *the greatest trick the Devil ever pulled was convincing people he doesn't exist.* This masterly deception certainly might be Lucifer J. Mephisto's game, if that is how we choose to read "Armageddon in Retrospect."

Armageddon comes down to us from *Revelation* (16:16), given as the place where the final battle between good and evil will take place. In Vonnegut's story, that location is Verdigris – not oxidized copper but a town in Oklahoma located on Route 66, the interstate highway that holds a mythic place in people's imaginations around the world. Mephisto, in his letter, outlines the history of the Pine Institute, set up by Jessie L. Pine, an oil magnate who bought 200 feet of books for his library. Included were the collected works of Dr. Selig Schildknecht, holder of five degrees and native to Dresden, Germany (grabbing the attention of any reader of Vonnegut), who "believed that the mentally ill were possessed by the Devil" (210). Selig means "blessed, happy" in Yiddish and Schildknecht means "shield boy," or squire, in Middle High German. Pine feels this happy armor-bearer's philosophy harmonizes with his own: "Onliest thing in the world that's wrong with folks is that the Devil's got aholt of 'em" (211). Mephisto tells us that the Pine Institute, its aim being to eradicate the Devil, is soon filled with quacks and shysters seeking free money: "Their experiments, usually awfully expensive, were principally satires on the ignorance and credulity of their benefactor" (211–12). And then a retired physicist approaches the institute with new ideas.

Dr. Gorman Tarbell is a Tarbell in the tradition of Ida Tarbell (1857–1944), a "muckracker" whose *History of the Standard Oil Company* (1904) is a feat in investigative journalism admired to this day. Her reputation for undermining John D. Rockefeller is echoed in this character's exasperation with his oil tycoon boss. Gorman leads in several directions but may point directly to the Irish surname Gorman, which in Irish is a diminutive for *gorm*, or "blue," a color of mood and nobility.[4] Of the story's cast, he is certainly the most noble, possessing an iconoclastic view of the "nothing but" universal perspective of the physical sciences: "We have some ideas that are little more than matters of faith. Perhaps they're laughable, but it's ignorant and unscientific to laugh until we've had some time to experiment" (214–15). Considering that electro-shock therapy "cures" many cases of mental illness, he hypothesizes that the Devil may have an aversion to electricity and starts experimenting across nine counties in Oklahoma to see if the Devil can be driven away.

When Pine blabs what Mephisto calls *Operation Rat-hole* to the press, the world takes notice. Blame shifts from Othered peoples to the Devil:

> The trouble with the world wasn't the Russians or the Americans or the Chinese or the British or the scientists or the generals or the financiers or the politicians, or, praise be to God, human beings anywhere, poor things. People were all right, and decent and innocent and smart, and it was the Devil who was making their good-hearted enterprises go sour. Every human being's self-respect increased a thousand-fold, and no one, save the Devil, lost face.
>
> (218–19)

With this mass psychological inflation, UNDICO is formed, with the Pine Institute's very own Lucifer J. Mephisto elected Chairman. They calculate the economic cost of equipping every man, woman, and child in the world with electric headsets and batteries to $90,000,000,000: "As modern wars go, the price was about right. But we soon found that people weren't inclined to go that high for anything less than killing each other" (221). The Committee starts working on a talking cure to fight the Devil but talking soon puts an end to the whole endeavor; an American delegate, not realizing his mic is live, makes a comment about bombing the Devil where he works in the Kremlin. The Soviets release a statement in response, stating their view of the Satanic "problem as being uniquely American" (223). The bottom falls out from under UNDICO and the Pine Institute. "Frankly," Mephisto devilishly admits, "I was relieved and delighted" (223).

Tarbell, however, is persistent. In a last ditch effort, he decides to summon the Devil by reenacting the Black Mass, as laid out in *The Golden Bough* by Sir James George Frazer, to catch him in an electrified copper drum. Mephisto's letter claims Tarbell was demonically possessed in the act and unfortunately trapped himself in the electrified drum, the upkeep of which requires money. Donations are encouraged from the reader and the suspicious feeling evoked leads us to think Tarbell has been imprisoned in his own trap – that Mephisto is, despite denial, the Devil himself. This reading relies on the intuitive sense that evil is insidious, that it lurks within our own institutions and can even sit at the head of the table on committees and boards of trustees. Vonnegut likely encountered *The Golden Bough* while studying Anthropology at the University of Chicago and his direct quotation of Frazer's description of the Black Mass is thematically irreverent: "'And many other things ["the bad priest"] does which no good Christian could look upon without being struck blind and deaf and dumb for the rest of his life'" (225). It is a bold statement coming from a Scottish social scientist remembered as a rationalist.

"Armageddon in Retrospect" riffs thematically and historically off Twain's *The Mysterious Stranger* (1916), the story of Austrian boys encountering Satan, who criticizes what he deems the Moral Sense, or binary of good and evil, that the West claims as its foundation. It is a complicated text, as William M. Gibson laid out in 1969: "Mark Twain's *The Mysterious Stranger, A Romance*, as published in 1916 and reprinted since that date, is an editorial fraud perpetrated by Twain's official biographer and literary executor, Albert Bigelow Paine, and Frederick A. Duneka of Harper & Brothers publishing company" (1). Gibson discovered that Paine and Duneka scrubbed provocative passages from Twain's unfinished manuscript of *The Chronicle of Young Satan*, tacked on the last chapter of another unfinished manuscript, *No. 44, The Mysterious Stranger*, and packaged it as a Christmas gift book for children. Morse may be appalled at the publication of Vonnegut's manuscripts, but they have not received treatment anything like the disingenuousness shown Twain's unfinished works. Gibson's publication of *The Mysterious Stranger Manuscripts*, however, came in 1969, many years after Vonnegut wrote "Armageddon in Retrospect." Therefore, if he did draw in any way from Twain's Satan, it was through the edition cobbled by Paine and Duneka. As engrossing as the unfinished manuscripts are, our task calls for an appraisal of what Gibson deemed "an editorial fraud."

Satan in *The Mysterious Stranger* appears in 1590 Austria to Theodor and friends. Taking the form of a youth, Satan wows the boys with supernatural feats and blunt criticisms of humanity. What they perceive to be indifferent cruelty at his hand he sees as a matter of fact – or is it dream? Prior to the esoteric final chapter, in which Satan decrees life is but a dream, he pushes past the boys' concepts of good and evil, what he calls the Moral Sense. At one point, he entertains Theodor's desire to see the local jail, revealing a scene of graphic torture he uses to rail against the Moral Sense:

> A sense whose function is to distinguish between right and wrong, with liberty to choose which of them [man] will do. Now what advantage can he get out of that? He is always choosing, and in nine cases out of ten he prefers the wrong. There shouldn't be any wrong; and without the Moral Sense there couldn't be any. And yet he is such an unreasoning

> creature that he is not able to perceive that the Moral Sense degrades him to the bottom layer of animated beings and is a shameful possession. (78)

Rackstraw identifies this binary split as symptomatic of our condition: "[O]nce consciousness evolved out of the cosmic chaos and became self-aware, it inevitably invented distinctions with language – differentiations between self and other, night and day, life and death, good and evil – which, with its enlightened ego, it took to be absolute" ("Paradox" 60). And Smith makes the same point about brutality: "Like it or not, war is distinctively human" (6).

Twain was a staunch moralist who grew increasingly pessimistic as he aged (Vonnegut, too); the *Mysterious Stranger* manuscripts were written at the end of his life and express profound abhorrence of humanity. Satan's sentiment may be read as immoral, but that would miss the point. Satan, in this imagining, is amoral. His disgust with the concepts of good and evil challenges the reader to think about his or her own understanding of morality. The mythological objective is not to reject morality but to exercise one's consciousness into recognizing how the binary functions, its ramifications and consequences. There is a danger in conceiving of oneself or one's group as humane, as if it has already been achieved individually or collectively. Humane conduct is a struggle, not a destination. There is no merit badge for it and those pinning such badges to their lapels suffer from denial. Cultural, communal, even national values are all too often held to be self-evident and believed to be unalienable while the barometer on one's own cultural, communal, and national behavior goes unchecked and off balance. This ambivalence, according to Smith, Hillman, Twain, and Vonnegut, engenders war.

War, from these points of view, is human but not excused. All the writers mentioned agree that there is such a thing as war with a just cause – even Vonnegut, scarred as he was, said that WWII was the last just war while criticizing the ways it was carried out. Twain did not live to see the World Wars, though Paine and Duneka's *Mysterious Stranger*, containing passages about the future mechanization of war, would be published during World War I (perhaps the only time a children's Christmas gift book starring Satan could appear). One of Satan's most damning tirades historicizes the myth of progress as applied to war, from Cain's murder of Abel long ago into the unseen future. Given our own place in time today, we are aware of Pfc. K. Vonnegut, Jr., hunkered in Schlachthof-fünf under Dresden on 13 February 1945, aged twenty-two, one of Twain's literary descendants directly surviving the effects of this anticipated weaponry.

Lucifer J. Mephisto is not *The Mysterious Stranger*'s Satan, who seeks to educate the boys about human nature. Dr. Gorman Tarbell, duped, fails to see the demon beside him. In aiming to eradicate the Devil, Tarbell neglects the insidiousness of his chosen opponent. He is no Faust, opting for battle over dialogue, suffering capture in the end. He loses because the unconscious processes Mephisto represents sneak past the limits of his awareness. In winning, the masked Devil lies to us, insisting that he has been captured in the electrified drum with Tarbell, that Armageddon has come to pass. Readers of the letter who would accept these weak arguments are oblivious to the continued presence of darkness in their community, and thereby complicit. Those who would answer Mephisto's request and send money are even worse: compliant.

This story is an early iteration of what Rackstraw classifies as a technique Vonnegut honed later: "Through irony and satire he came to excel in making language reveal its inherent paradox: to function simultaneously with *daemonic* creativity or *demonic* destructiveness" ("Paradox" 54). By telling the story through a generic form letter, he plays on what Smith and Hillman argue is the greatest force behind the occurrence of war: ambivalence. Most people receiving form letters are inclined to toss them out after a skim. Editors were ambivalent toward "Armageddon in Retrospect," declining to publish it, and response to the collection it titles has been lukewarm at best. One cannot help wondering if the largely apathetic reaction to the story has anything at all to do with the unpleasantness of the sentiment that frames it: that we are, in our lack of care, all responsible for what we deem as evil's mobility throughout the world and in our own communities.

War myths

The idea of responsibility in postwar U.S. culture saw the formation and implementation of the United Nations, and its first great test in handling international crisis was the Korean War. The 2 September 1950 issue of *Collier's* contains an editorial titled "United We Stand." Its final paragraph presents common views arising from this sense of responsibility for regulating war around the world:

> [The U.N. soldiers] need help which will refute the Soviet charges of "American imperialism." And they need help which will give the world "for the first time since the Crusades," as the *New York Times* has put it, "a great international army fighting for a common ideal."
>
> (74)

A few national anxieties are given away in this editorial: confusion as to whose war this was, uncertainty about its scale, insecurity about the U.S.A. being viewed as imperialistic, hyperbolic conflation with holy wars of the Middle Ages, and ultimately the legitimacy of the U.S.-backed United Nations. And Donald F. Moss's accompanying artwork operates like propaganda, showing a gargantuan U.N. flag flying high above flags of member nations carried by soldiers.

This was a mainstream American attitude to war, the cultural climate in which Vonnegut produced these stories. Traumatized by experiences as an American infantryman and P.O.W. in WWII, he would grow in adulthood into a wounded healer through his fiction. His stories of war are sorrowful testimonials and grave warnings from one of its living victims and survivors. While the early short stories have often been overlooked, we see now that his bid for artistic *katharsis* began in the pages of *Collier's* magazine with his very first publication. "Report on the Barnhouse Effect" is a fantasy for those Americans dismayed by weapons development in the nuclear age and the ethics of proliferation. "All the King's Horses" offers up the fantasy of war as a game – with a pro-American outcome and a fine-print forewarning of the inevitability of conflicts with Communist nations and warlords in the near future. "Great Day" warns against regression into war as we imagine ourselves building a united humanity, and "Armageddon in Retrospect" warns us that the Devil we deny in ourselves is free and probably mailing us form letters. The first two stories placed successfully in one of the leading middle class American weekly magazines of its day; the last two went unread until after their author's death.

As products of the early nineteen-fifties, they all reveal a score of tensions emerging from the U.S.A.'s newfound prominence as a superpower, a super *war* power. As myths, they both challenge and toe the line, scrutinizing new problems, such as proliferation of weapons of mass destruction, and old problems, entered into through a time-screen, without the conceit of solution. Archetypal situations are universally human and can be charted throughout world myth. Individual mythmakers express these universals always with the unique timestamps of their own place, culture, and individuality. While this study is not focused on world myth, we recognize that War, though often fought over borders, does not know them itself. In these stories Vonnegut courts universal concerns with the tools he has as a white Midwestern American man who suffered in the nation's largest international conflagration. Caution is an aim in the various narrators' tellings – caution of the might behind one's own capacity for war, let alone that of the collective American capacity – giving them the mysterious quality of prophecy, or something like it.

Notes

1 See Jonathan Shay's *Achilles in Vietnam: Combat Trauma and the Undoing of Character* (New York: Simon and Schuster, 1995) and *Odysseus in America: Combat Trauma and the Trials of Homecoming* (New York: Scribner, 2002); Keith Armstrong, Suzanne Best, and Paula Domenici's *Courage After Fire: Coping Strategies for Troops Returning from Iraq and Afghanistan and Their Families* (Berkeley, CA: Ulysses Press, 2009); Erin P. Finley's *Fields of Combat: Understanding PTSD among Veterans of Iraq and Afghanistan* (New York: ILR Press, 2011); and the National Center for PTSD's publication: *PTSD Research Quarterly*.

2 *Armageddon in Retrospect* (New York: G.P. Putnam's Sons, 2008); *Look at the Birdie* (New York: Delacorte Press, 2009); *While Mortals Sleep* (New York: Delacorte Press, 2011); and *We Are What We Pretend To Be* (New York: Vanguard Press, 2012).

3 Vonnegut later imagined himself meeting Newton in Heaven in his collection of vignettes, *God Bless You, Dr. Kevorkian* (2001): "[The] late Sir Isaac Newton [. . .] got to make only a single one-way trip down the tunnel. He wants to know what it seems to be made of, fabric or metal or wood or what. I tell him that it's made of whatever dreams are made of, which leaves him monumentally unsatisfied. | Saint Peter quoted Shakespeare to him: There are more things in Heaven and Earth, Horatio, than are dreamt of in your philosophy" (52). Like Moriarty, Vonnegut rejects Newton's positivism as a reductive denial of universal complexity transcending our capacity for understanding.

4 In Irish *fear gorm*, translating to "blue man," is the term for a black man. This is because *an fear dubh*, translating to "black man," is taken to mean the Devil. Vonnegut's Gorman, even if Vonnegut did not realize it, stands in purposeful differentiation from the Devil.

Chapter 3

Fragmented independence

Vonnegut's critiques of the American trinity

When Vonnegut wrote commercial short fiction in the years spanning the Truman, Eisenhower, and Kennedy presidencies, he did so under the demands of providing for a family that grew to eight. He carried himself through these stresses with convictions about the role of a writer in his or her society. In 1973 he expressed as much in a *Playboy* interview: "Writers are specialized cells in the social organism. They are evolutionary cells. Mankind is trying to become something else; it's experimenting with new ideas all the time. And writers are a means of introducing new ideas into the society, and also a means of responding symbolically to life. I don't think we're in control of what we do" (Allen 76). When he introduces anti-aging products or state-run ethical Suicide Parlors or compulsory handicappings for the better-than-able in his stories, Vonnegut engages with topical issues of the era – the growing emphasis on youth, overpopulation, civil rights – but he also takes on supposedly exceptional American ideals. The trinity of life, liberty, and the pursuit of happiness, the nation's poetic foundation for independence, is the wellspring for American entitlement that repeatedly comes under scrutiny in Vonnegut's improbable stories. Reed iterates the playfulness that adjoins this sacred role in a profane age:

> The Cassandra in Vonnegut that always wants to warn, to alert his readership to what he sees as "real" issues confronting society, can speak out, but so can the comedian, the entertainer, who enjoys comic situations and childlike deconstructions of traditional assumptions about life. He finds a comfortable narrative voice in these pieces, and he can use science-fictional terms and futuristic settings with a comic hyperbole that banishes resistance to their implausibility.
>
> (*SFKV* 67)

"Where do I get my ideas from?" one of Vonnegut's screen prints asks, "I was goofing around like everybody else in Indiana, and all of a sudden stuff came gushing out. It was disgust with civilization" (*Armageddon In Retrospect* 233). "Certainly in most instances," writes Reed, "Vonnegut's motivation in the use of the science fictional is sociological. It comes not from a fascination with speculations about technology but from a desire to show the moral and practical consequences of patterns of behavior" (*SFKV* 5). It is also, as we shall see, mythological.

Life

Vonnegut's second published story was "Thanasphere," appearing in *Collier's* (2 Sep. 1950) at a time when Stalin ordered the development of the S-25 Berkut anti-aircraft missile system in anticipation of an American attack. "Something was terribly wrong with this rocket flight 2,000 miles above the earth," reads the teaser, "The pilot flew into the heart of a mystery that upset all the calculations of the scientist listening below" (18). Mawicke provided two pieces of art for the story, the dominant one being Earth from space, painted before a photo of Earth from space existed. Just beyond the atmosphere, a rocket arcs upward, and, across the page fold, white smudges in the dark emptiness suggest heads, torsos, outstretched arms. Only later, in reading the story, does one return to this image and see the ghosts. The effect harmonizes with the story in that only Major Rice can see the dead while the others must be convinced of their reality. Those characters, a scientist, a Lieutenant General, and a radio operator, are painted in the lower right page in front of a radio. This smaller image's paint-stroke borders contrast against the sharp rectangular frame of the larger, roughing in Vonnegut's protagonist: not the man who touches the afterlife in the heavens but the myopic man on the ground, who has conceived of Project Cyclops, a mythological name evoking captivity, pride, and odyssey.

Dr. Bernard Groszinger is a "youthful rocket consultant for the Air Forces" (18). Bernard was the name of Vonnegut's older brother, who would become a chemist respected for his discoveries in cloud seeding. "Thanasphere" can certainly be read as the work of a youngest sibling ribbing the eldest, but here it is merely noted. Bernard derives from Germanic elements: "*bern* 'bear' combined with *hard* 'brave, hardy'" (*BTN*). If this Bernard is in any way a bear, his strength may be expressed in his ingenuity as architect of the experiment described. Bears are noted in ARAS's *Book of Symbols* as "often functioning as a 'tutelary figure' or spirit helper to mythic heroes" (272), worth considering given Bernard's supportive role for the astronaut. There are also those known as St. Bernard, eight men canonized by the Roman Catholic Church and, of course, the dog breed bred for mountain rescues in the Alps. Bernard's surname is a variation on Grossinger – the change to Groszinger, however, turns the name into a pun. The "gross zinger" that awaits this scientist is the revelation of mysteries in the universe that transcend human capacity for understanding.

Major Allen Rice, on the other hand, the "sullen" widower astronaut whose mission is "To report weather conditions over enemy territory, and to

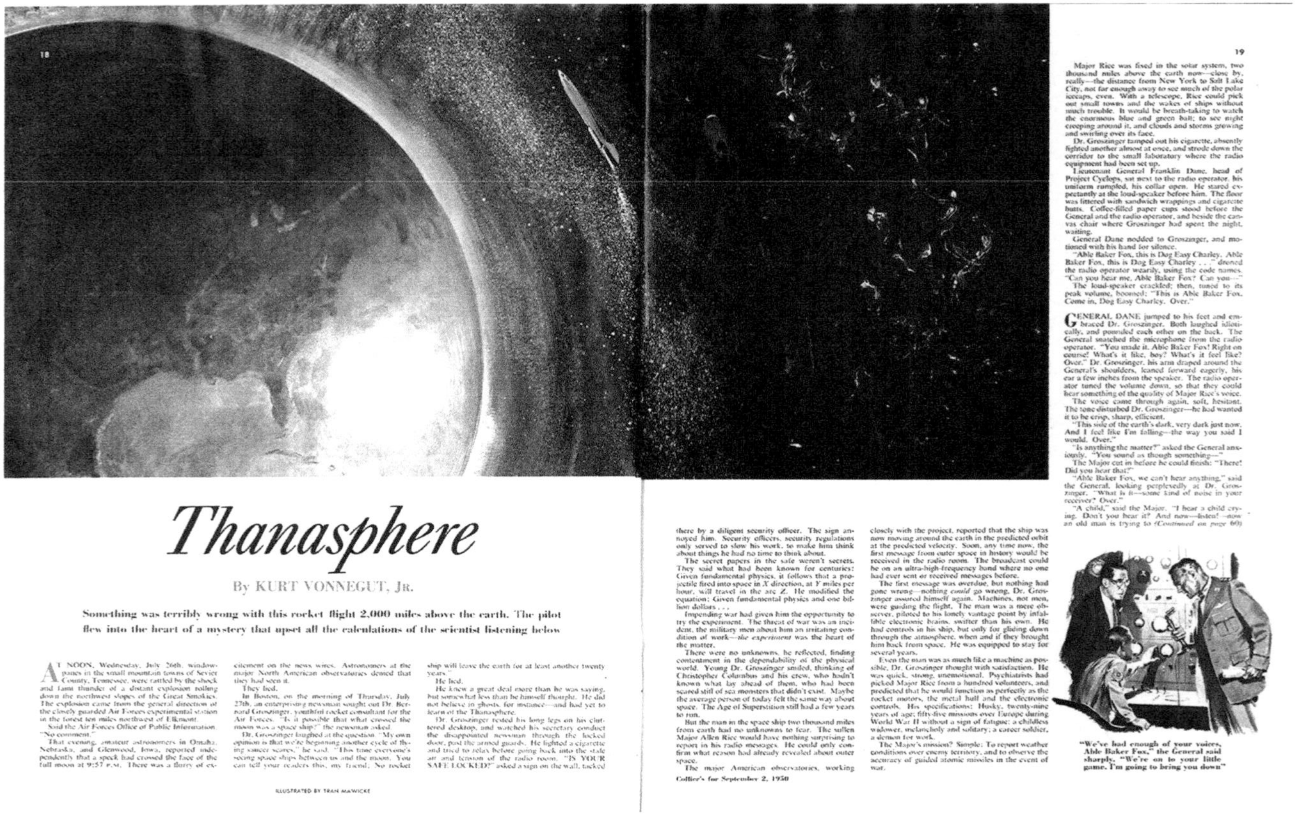

18

Thanasphere

By KURT VONNEGUT, Jr.

Something was terribly wrong with this rocket flight 2,000 miles above the earth. The pilot flew into the heart of a mystery that upset all the calculations of the scientist listening below

AT NOON, Wednesday, July 26th, windowpanes in the small mountain towns of Sevier County, Tennessee, were rattled by the shock and faint thunder of a distant explosion rolling down the northwest slopes of the Great Smokies. The explosion came from the general direction of the closely guarded Air Forces experimental station in the forest ten miles northwest of Elkmont.

Said the Air Forces Office of Public Information, "No comment."

That evening, amateur astronomers in Omaha, Nebraska, and Glenwood, Iowa, reported independently that a speck had crossed the face of the full moon at 9:57 P.M. There was a flurry of excitement on the news wires. Astronomers at the major North American observatories denied that they had seen it.

They lied.

In Boston, on the morning of Thursday, July 27th, an enterprising newsman sought out Dr. Bernard Groszinger, youthful rocket consultant for the Air Forces. "Is it possible that what crossed the moon was a space ship?" the newsman asked.

Dr. Groszinger laughed at the question. "My own opinion is that we're beginning another cycle of flying saucer scares," he said. "This time everyone's seeing space ships between us and the moon. You can tell your readers this, my friend: No rocket ship will leave the earth for at least another twenty years."

He lied.

He knew a great deal more than he was saying, but somewhat less than he himself thought. He did not believe in ghosts, for instance—and had yet to learn of the Thanasphere.

Dr. Groszinger rested his long legs on his cluttered desktop, and watched his secretary conduct the disappointed newsman through the locked door, past the armed guards. He lighted a cigarette and tried to relax before going back into the stale air and tension of the radio room. "IS YOUR SAFE LOCKED?" asked a sign on the wall, tacked there by a diligent security officer. The sign annoyed him. Security officers, security regulations only served to slow his work, to make him think about things he had no time to think about.

The secret papers in the safe weren't secrets. They said what had been known for centuries: Given fundamental physics, it follows that a projectile fired into space in *X* direction, at *Y* miles per hour, will travel in the arc *Z*. He modified the equation: Given fundamental physics and one billion dollars . . .

Impending war had given him the opportunity to try the experiment. The threat of war was an incident, the military men about him an irritating condition of work—*the experiment* was the heart of the matter.

There were no unknowns, he reflected, finding contentment in the dependability of the physical world. Young Dr. Groszinger smiled, thinking of Christopher Columbus and his crew, who hadn't known what lay ahead of them, who had been scared stiff of sea monsters that didn't exist. Maybe the average person of today felt the same way about space. The Age of Superstition still had a few years to run.

But the man in the space ship two thousand miles from earth had no unknowns to fear. The sullen Major Allen Rice would have nothing surprising to report in his radio messages. He could only confirm what reason had already revealed about outer space.

The major American observatories, working closely with the project, reported that the ship was now moving around the earth in the predicted orbit at the predicted velocity. Soon, any time now, the first message from outer space in history would be received in the radio room. The broadcast could be on an ultra-high-frequency band where no one had ever sent or received messages before.

The first message was overdue, but nothing had gone wrong—nothing *could* go wrong, Dr. Groszinger assured himself again. Machines, not men, were guiding the flight. The man was a mere observer, piloted to his lonely vantage point by infallible electronic brains, swifter than his own. He had controls in his ship, but only for gliding down through the atmosphere, when and if they brought him back from space. He was equipped to stay for several years.

Even the man was as much like a machine as possible, Dr. Groszinger thought with satisfaction. He was quick, strong, unemotional. Psychiatrists had picked Major Rice from a hundred volunteers, and predicted that he would function as perfectly as the rocket motors, the metal hull and the electronic controls. His specifications: Husky, twenty-nine years of age; fifty-five missions over Europe during World War II without a sign of fatigue; a childless widower, melancholy and solitary; a career soldier, a demon for work.

The Major's mission? Simple: To report weather conditions over enemy territory, and to observe the accuracy of guided atomic missiles in the event of war.

ILLUSTRATED BY TRAN MAWICKE

Collier's for September 2, 1950

19

Major Rice was fixed in the solar system, two thousand miles above the earth now—close by, really—the distance from New York to Salt Lake City, not far enough away to see much of the polar icecaps, even. With a telescope, Rice could pick out small towns and the wakes of ships without much trouble. It would be breath-taking to watch the enormous blue and green ball; to see night creeping around it, and clouds and storms growing and swirling over its face.

Dr. Groszinger tamped out his cigarette, absently lighted another almost at once, and strode down the corridor to the small laboratory where the radio equipment had been set up.

Lieutenant General Franklin Dane, head of Project Cyclops, sat next to the radio operator, his uniform rumpled, his collar open. He stared expectantly at the loud-speaker before him. The floor was littered with sandwich wrappings and cigarette butts. Coffee-filled paper cups stood before the General and the radio operator, and beside the canvas chair where Groszinger had spent the night, waiting.

General Dane nodded to Groszinger, and motioned with his hand for silence.

"Able Baker Fox, this is Dog Easy Charley. Able Baker Fox, this is Dog Easy Charley . . ." droned the radio operator wearily, using the code names. "Can you hear me, Able Baker Fox? Can you—"

The loud-speaker crackled; then, tuned to its peak volume, boomed: "This is Able Baker Fox. Come in, Dog Easy Charley. Over."

GENERAL DANE jumped to his feet and embraced Dr. Groszinger. Both laughed idiotically, and pounded each other on the back. The General snatched the microphone from the radio operator. "You made it, Able Baker Fox! Right on course! What's it like, boy? What's it feel like? Over." Dr. Groszinger, his arm draped around the General's shoulders, leaned forward eagerly, his ear a few inches from the speaker. The radio operator tuned the volume down, so that they could hear something of the quality of Major Rice's voice.

The voice came through again, soft, hesitant. The tone disturbed Dr. Groszinger—he had wanted it to be crisp, sharp, efficient.

"This side of the earth's dark, very dark just now. And I feel like I'm falling—the way you said I would. Over."

"Is anything the matter?" asked the General anxiously. "You sound as though something—"

The Major cut in before he could finish: "There! Did you hear that?"

"Able Baker Fox, we can't hear anything," said the General, looking perplexedly at Dr. Groszinger. "What is it—some kind of noise in your receiver? Over."

"A child," said the Major. "I hear a child crying. Don't you hear it? And now—listen!—now an old man is trying to *(Continued on page 60)*

"We've had enough of your voices, Able Baker Fox," the General said sharply. "We're on to your little game. I'm going to bring you down"

Figure 3.1 Art for "Thanasphere" by Tran Mawicke. (© *Collier's* magazine, 1950)

observe the accuracy of guided atomic missiles in the event of war" (19), carries an appropriately indistinct name. This supports Groszinger's estimation that he is "as much like a machine as possible": "His specifications: Husky, twenty-nine years of age; fifty-five missions over Europe during World War II without a sign of fatigue; a childless widower, melancholy and solitary; a career soldier, a demon for work" (19). The description skims over his wife's death, a detail attentive readers will congratulate themselves for remembering when her spirit later appears. Allen/Alan has an ambiguous etymology: "little rock" or "handsome" to sixth century Bretons, "harmony" to the Celts (Thornbury xxiii), a fourth and fifth century Persian tribe (*BTN*). Rice is a nutritious but otherwise bland grain. By the end of the story, Rice, like that tossed at a wedding, falls back to Earth, signaling his re-union with his wife. He is an Orpheus who, finding Eurydice in orbit, sacrifices his life to join her on the other side. His wife is another of Vonnegut's "pearls," Margaret, from Greek μαργαριτης (*BTN*).[1]

Their designated radio names work like Homeric epithets. Ground Control is Dog Easy Charley – Charles being Germanic for "man" or "warrior" (*BTN*) – DEC in the old U.S. Army/Navy Radio Alphabet.[2] Rice is Able Baker Fox, or ABF. Communications from Dog Easy Charley are relayed by the nameless radio operator, the designation making him and those in the control room *men* or *soldiers* with *canine* loyalty who have it *easy*. Able Baker Fox, however, casts Rice, floating in the satellite, as one who can *ably* transform basic ingredients into *bread* with *vulpine* ability. Our relationship to the fox is complicated, some people showing the crafty animal admiration for its wiles while others victimize it with the hunt. Martin Wallen sees in "the ubiquitous, mercurial fox" one who crosses "between wild forest and cultivated farmland, between unconventional, intuitive intelligence and collective social norms, and between animal, human and spirit worlds, both beneficent and demonic" (*Book of Symbols* 278). In this story, it is Able Baker Fox Major Allen Rice who meets the threshold of the afterlife and crosses into it.

Yet we follow Groszinger, a materialistic rationalist who deflects questions from the press about spaceship sightings: "He knew a great deal more than he was saying, but somewhat less than he himself thought. He did not believe in ghosts, for instance – and had yet to learn of the Thanasphere" (18). Possessed with science, he has no trouble accepting the possibility of war as an outcome of conducting his work, for his is a programmatic life, one determined not by empathy but by intellect: "There were no unknowns, he reflected, finding contentment in the dependability of the physical world. [. . . The] man in the space ship two thousand miles from earth had no unknowns to fear" (19). "No unknowns" calls to mind a statement made by U.S. Defense Secretary Donald Rumsfeld in the 2002 lead up to the second Iraq War: "[A]s we know, there are known knowns; there are things we know we know. We also know there are known unknowns; that is to say we know there are some things we do not know. But there are also unknown unknowns – the ones we don't know we don't know" ("Defense.gov News Transcript").[3] Polonius could not convolute knowledge of the world much better while managing to leave out, as Slavoj Žižek points out, "the 'unknown knowns,' the things we don't know that we know – which is precisely, the Freudian unconscious, the 'knowledge which doesn't know itself,' as Lacan used to say" ("What Rumsfeld Doesn't Know"). From a post-Jungian perspective, it is the collective unconscious, the biological dimension of archetypal energies. Vonnegut goes so far here as to describe the "*experiment*," italicized, as "the heart of the matter" (19). It is a common metaphor employed coyly, for this story is about accepting unknown aspects of existence, an "unknown known," something the protagonist cannot at first conceive as a possibility.

At some point, a metaphor breaks down: an experiment does not actually have a heart. Not all metaphors cross the bridges they build – some metaphors fail – and this one, a cliché, fails on purpose. Groszinger is a glib young man, easily patronizing America's most controversial explorer from the comfort of his own thoughts. Columbus's fear of sea monsters can be read as a healthy awareness of the dangerous animating forces rising within the unconscious. Groszinger has yet to acknowledge those archetypal forces and that territory populated by the dead, here called the Thanasphere, an aspect of existence that transcends all human capabilities to know or understand. He is one of Moriarty's pitiable scientists living in a "nothing but" universe.[4]

The scientist's mechanistic view of life itself breaks down as soon as the astronaut parlays with the dead. This breakthrough is rationalized as a malfunction in "the lunatic who peered down at earth from his tiny steel moon and heard voices" (60). Groszinger blames a mechanically construed fault in Rice's psychology, assuming the man has a screw loose, which itself is one of our mechanistic metaphors for the broad spectrum of mental illness: "The one thing he had not designed, the damn' [sic] man in it, had failed, had destroyed the whole experiment" (60). Throughout his career Vonnegut explored the dangerous metaphor, all too often taken literally, that people are machines, most extensively in his novel *Breakfast of Champions* (1973). How easy it is to forget that our bodies are not machines, that we are not machines; bodies are bodies and we are people. Saying that bodies are machines disenfranchises them of what machines lack: life.

The mechanistic attitude prevails in the West, illustrated in biologist Richard Dawkins's first preface to his book *The Selfish Gene*: "We are survival machines – robot vehicles blindly programmed to preserve the selfish molecules known as genes. This is a truth which still fills me with astonishment" (xxi). That Dawkins confuses metaphor for "truth" is all the more ridiculous given his public crusade against those who find "truth" in religious metaphors. David Abram takes Stephen Jay Gould to task for his criticism of the Gaia Hypothesis, the idea that Earth is a self-regulating entity: "[It] offers no new mechanisms. It just changes the metaphor. But metaphor is not mechanism!" "What Gould failed to state is that 'mechanism,' itself," Abram writes, "is nothing more than a metaphor" (66). The emperor has no clothes, society plays along, and, as in Andersen's fable, it takes a child, someone unlikely to be taken seriously – in this case, Vonnegut – to come along and remind us that it is valuable to see through a metaphor that misses its mark.

But Rice is not ill. The voices are real and they belong to the dead, a population Jung would heed: "turn to the dead, listen to their lament and accept them with love" (*Red Book* 344). Just as the living characters cannot speak to the spirits, the spirits are unable to speak to the living – save Rice. Afterlife strangers pester him with messages for loved ones: Andrew Tobin, a twentieth-century American Abel, "claims his brother murdered him," and "Mrs. Pamela Ritter wants her husband Harvey to marry again for the sake of the children" (60). Rice becomes a psychopomp, in Jungian terms the "go-between connecting EGO and UNCONSCIOUS" (*CDJA* 123). Bridging the binary, life and death start a discourse. When the names Rice provides check out, Groszinger's dead mother, asking for him, relays a poem in German which carries great significance for the scientist. It is his mother's favorite Goethe quote. Michael Hamburger translated the poem into English in 1958:

> All things the gods bestow, the infinite ones,
> On their darlings, completely,
> All the joys, the infinite ones,
> All the pains, the infinite ones, completely.
> (*Great Writings of Goethe* 278)

The poem comes from a letter Goethe wrote to Auguste Stolberg in 1777, consisting of those four lines. In this exchange between the living and the dead, a poem expressing the breadth of being's joys and sorrows is recited; hierophantic totality is more palatable coming from Groszinger's departed mother. This is mere speculation, but one senses Vonnegut's mother, a suicide, a failed short story writer, the daughter of wealthy German-Americans, in the Goethe-quoting ghost of Rice's mother. And what about the presence of German poetry in a postwar American magazine? German-Americans make up the largest segment of United States citizens, and yet their ancestry, since WWI, has gone largely denied.

Once Groszinger accepts Rice is speaking with the dead, he faces a dilemma: "Did the world have a right to know, or didn't it?" (62). In discovering this unknown, he inherits the responsibility that comes with privileged knowledge. As he weighs options, Dane and the radio operator discuss the influence of Rice's wife's spirit, which has appeared to him. Here we see compassion from the General, who imagines the effect of seeing Margaret:

"Guess that's enough to throw anybody, wouldn't you say?" (62). All are aware that Rice has means of safe landing but doubt he will take it, presented as he is with the chance of marital reunion. Groszinger, however, intellectualizes the situation:

> Maybe that was the spirit of this world of the atom bomb, H-bomb, God-knows-what-next-bomb – to be amazed at nothing. Science had given humanity forces enough to destroy the earth; and politics had given humanity a fair assurance that the forces would be used. There could be no cause for awe to top *that* one. But proof of a spirit world might at least equal it. Maybe that was the shock the world needed; maybe word from the spirits could change the suicidal course of history. (62)

His line of thought wanders from the possibility that verification of the afterlife might bring the empirically armed world into balance to the overwhelming anxiety that the dead, led by the spirits of emperors from Caesar to Roosevelt – and Jesus Christ – might return and conquer the living. All of history presents itself; he is terrified of what the dead want to say. It is telling that the scientist, a representative of U.S. interests in spying on Russia, should suffer imperial insecurities: dead empires – Roman, Holy Roman, Russian, French, German, and American – loom as if they might renew themselves. And just as Groszinger's private logic approaches Christianity, it is interrupted by Rice's transcendence. The Major reports seeing thousands upon thousands of souls glowing like the Aurora Borealis on the meniscus of the atmosphere. Among them is his departed wife, who welcomes him on the verge of this heaven with a wave and a smile. His voice is cut off, jammed from the ground, and Dane orders Groszinger to never speak about the spirits out there to anybody. The scientist is forbidden from holding the channel open, an act that would vitalize the life in him and his society. Forced forfeit comes as anxious relief: "He didn't want to be the one to tell the world" (62).

If Groszinger is a witness to Rice's connection and absolute assimilation with the funereal plane, readers are witnesses to Groszinger's inability to metabolize it. Vonnegut presents the modern day alchemist, a rocket consultant, achieving unexpected mythological outcomes while experimenting with base matter – and then suppressing the discovery. All he can muster in letting it go is an oblique comment made to a reporter after the fact, explaining that beyond the atmosphere lies "dead space" (62). Off the cuff, he coins Thanasphere from *Thanatos*, Ancient Greek for *death*, to identify this region. Categorized and labeled in a private joke with himself, Groszinger, in a parody of the scientific method, has reduced the significance of that unconscious zone, filed it away. At the same time, fear holds him from sharing it, fear of its forces, which are beyond his control. This denial of powers capable of superseding intellectuality, with its gifts of weapons of mass destruction, is a condition apropos for American life at the dawn of the Cold War.

Liberty

When *The Magazine of Fantasy and Science Fiction* published "Harrison Bergeron" in October 1961, the page header billed it as "a mordant little tale with rather more to say than its size would indicate . . ." (5). Ten years earlier, Vonnegut sold stories for higher pay to mainstream magazines; the ability to make a living writing short stories was increasingly difficult, thanks, in part, to the spread of television. "Bergeron," published two years later and set in the future – "The year was 2081, and everybody was finally equal" (5) – is about a married couple watching television. There is no description of setting until the very end, when the television tube burns out and George goes to the kitchen for a beer; all we need to know about where the protagonists are as events unfold is that "George and Hazel Bergeron were watching television. There were tears on Hazel's cheeks, but she'd forgotten for the moment what they were about" (5). The lack of orientation, amplified by Hazel's, compels us to find out what is happening to these people sitting in front of their TV.

What transpires is their witnessing, from home, the murders of a ballerina and their son. Harrison, aged fourteen, was taken from the home earlier in the month – April, the cruelest – by the H-G men, agents under the command of the United States Handicapper General, a satire on the office of the U.S. Attorney General, who oversees the Department of Justice, and the U.S. Surgeon General, who oversees the Public Health Service Commissioned Corps. He is considered "extremely dangerous" by the powers that be, who suspect him of trying to overthrow the government. When he escapes jail they interrupt a televised ballet to alert viewers, describing him as "a genius and an athlete" and "under-handicapped" (7). Making a grand entrance, Harrison crashes the ballet, entering the live televised dance looking "like a walking junkyard" (8); to hamper his unique, seemingly superhuman qualities – for instance, he stands seven feet tall – they have saddled him with three hundred pounds of weights, cuffed his ears with headphones blasting noise, covered his eyes with thick spectacles holding wavy lenses, shaved his eyebrows, covered "his even white teeth with black caps at snaggle-tooth random" (8), and forced upon him the red rubber ball nose of a clown. Denuding himself of these crosses, he rises up and declares himself Emperor:

> "Do you hear? I am the Emperor! Everybody must do what I say at once!" He stamped his foot and the studio shook.
>
> "Even as I stand here," he bellowed, "crippled, hobbled, sickened – I am a greater ruler than any man who ever lived! Now watch me become what I can become."[5]
>
> (8–9)

Next he selects an Empress from the ballerinas on stage, honoring the one brave enough to step forward. Together they dance like superheroes, leaping to the thirty-foot ceiling and kissing it:

> And then, neutralizing gravity with love and pure will,[6] they remained suspended in air inches below the ceiling, and they kissed each other for a long, long time.
>
> It was then that Diana Moon Glampers, the Handicapper General, came into the studio with a double-barreled ten-gauge shotgun. She fired twice, and the Emperor and the Empress were dead before they hit the floor.
>
> (10)

After she reloads and threatens the studio musicians, the Bergerons' television burns out – and both succumb to a demential disorientation:

> "You been crying?" he said to Hazel, watching her wipe her tears.
>
> "Yup," she said.
>
> "What about?" he said.
>
> "I forget," she said. "Something real sad on television."
>
> "What was it?" he said.
>
> "It's all kind of mixed up in my mind," said Hazel.
>
> "Forget sad things," said George.
>
> "I always do," said Hazel.
>
> "That's my girl," said George. He winced. There was the sound of a riveting gun in his head.
>
> "Gee – I could tell that one was a doozy," said Hazel.
>
> "You can say that again," said George.
>
> "Gee – " said Hazel – "I could tell that one was a doozy."
>
> (10)

It is a devastating ending that, whimpering with that last repetition, echoes a legendary exchange – legendary because they never used it – between early TV comedy duo George Burns and Gracie Allen. "Say goodnight, Gracie," George is imagined saying, with Gracie responding, "Goodnight, Gracie." Mr. Bergeron is even named George.

The name George is Greek and means "earth worker" or "farmer" (*BTN*), which comes across in the character's down-to-earth manner. The family surname, Bergeron, is of French extraction, deriving from a German word, *berg*, and originally identifying "someone who lived beside a hill or mountain" (*House of Names*). George and Hazel, handicapped by the 211th, 212th, and 213th Amendments to the Constitution, don't so much live next to a hill or mountain as they seem to live under it. Hazel comes from the Old English word *hæsel* for the species of nut-bearing tree, as well as a light shade of brown (*BTN*). Chevalier and Gheerbrant traced the hazel through European traditions, finding it often represented fertility but became associated with lust and the Devil after medieval times. "Germanic mythology," they note, "makes the hazel an attribute of the god Thor" (476). Hazel's son is described as "a man that would have awed Thor, the god of thunder" (9).

As for that son's name, which titles the story, Harrison derives from an English surname which means "Harry's son," Harry being a Medieval English form of Henry. Henry comes from German *Heimrich*, or "home ruler" (*BTN*). Harrison Bergeron is the *son of the home ruler* who *lives by a hill or mountain*. As far as home rule goes, George and Hazel are both divested of their civil liberties; life in their house is infringed upon to an alarming extent – George's above-average intelligence requires him to wear an ear radio that blasts breaking noises. And while the boy is set up to be a hero, a super-teen, usurper of a clearly oppressive America gone wrong, he goes down easily with a gun blast. The shooter, the Handicapper General, Diana Moon Glampers, bears a blatantly mythological name. Diana is the Roman goddess of hunting, the beasts, and the moon. The middle name here is even Moon, the celestial night sphere that waxes and wanes with reflected sunlight, that draws tides of ocean and menstruation. "Glamp" is a verb: "To grope, as in the dark. *to glamp at*: to make snatches at" (*OED*). If Diana Moon glampers, Diana Moon is snatching at things in the dark, a rather terrifying constellation of characteristics for someone holding the office of Handicapper General.[7] She represents feminine energies, suppressed by patriarchy, lashing out from the darkness of collective denial. In *Metamorphoses*, Ovid tells of Actaeon, the youth who stumbles upon Diana bathing in her grotto. As punishment she transforms him into a stag and delights in his death at the teeth of his hunting dogs:

> [. . .] Diana was not satisfied
> until, so mangled, young Actaeon died;
> for – so they say – that was the destiny
> the quiver-bearing goddess wished to see.
>
> (86)

Diana Moon Glampers appears in "Bergeron" like a perversion of the *deus ex machina*, wielding not a bow but a double-barreled shotgun – weapon of the American duck hunter – to murder the godlike boy and his Empress. Note how Glampers is *not* handicapped, as if she is society's benchmark average member – and is left bare when it comes to her physical description, although we are informed that "Hazel, as a matter of fact, bore a strong resemblance to the Handicapper General" (6). This transmits a maternal aspect to Diana Moon, who to the Romans was a virgin, and casts her as the archetypal Terrible Mother, a destroyer of her own young.

George and Hazel, traumatized, only manage small talk. The government's handicapping torture keeps them in a constant state of anxiety as it is, but after seeing their son murdered they cannot orient themselves beyond an inhumane dictum: "Forget sad things" (10). Rollo May's perspective on anxiety incorporates orientation: "if the person can reorient himself [. . .] and again relate himself to the world directly, experientially, with his senses alive, he overcomes the anxiety" (*Love and Will* 152). Reorientation is not a possibility for the Bergerons. The burned-out television tube will be replaced and their suffering will continue. Reed has said "Having the dramatic events be on television within a story puts 'reality' at two removes, giving emphasis to Vonnegut's technique" (81). This is fine, but we must not forget George and Hazel. We witness everything over their shoulders – even though they are lost we have to keep track of them. Just as Dr. Groszinger is the unlikely protagonist of "Thanasphere," George and Hazel Bergeron are the central characters in "Bergeron."

It is hard to understand what Boon and Pringle mean when they declare that, "Although brief and primitive, 'Harrison Bergeron' is one of Vonnegut's better short stories" (*At Millennium's End* 187). What constitutes its primitiveness is never defined, and while they are right to point out its aura of futility, they trip over the symbol of handicapping. Reading the handicappings as "a metaphor for ideological systems, such as religion," they take up one that is not even used. When Hazel suggests chimes as a possible handicapping, they claim, "The critique is obvious: if religion is chimed in our ears long enough, we will lose the ability to think, and we will all become the same" (*At Millennium's End* 189). First, the government isn't using chimes, so it isn't the example to use. Second, Hazel is "a little envious" when she makes her suggestion (6), for with her average intelligence (as judged by the government) she does not wear a handicapping radio like her husband. She is one of the oppressed imagining what it would be like to be in power. Lacking the wickedness required for the job, the worst she can imagine is chimes, whose sound evokes for religious people any number of things; perhaps we could agree to say an atmosphere of spirituality. George rejects the idea without hesitation because many would *not* be handicapped by those sounds. The actual handicappings, not those conceived of by good-natured Hazel, are rather a spoof, a jibe, a satire on fear of the long reach of government.

Reed comes closer to the mark when he describes the story's focus as equality. The U.S.A. at the time was embroiled in a debate over civil rights for African Americans – a connection he fails to make, asking, "The achievement of a truly egalitarian society has occupied politicians and philosophers for centuries, but was there a particular social context giving it relevance in 1961?" (*SFKV* 81). The story throws a punch to the kidneys of American exceptionalism, imagining a United States that has turned from celebration of the individual toward an attack on him or her. Ironically, "Bergeron" was reprinted by conservative commentator William F. Buckley, Jr.'s *National Review* in 1965.[8] According to biographer Sam Tanenhaus, Buckley later called it a mistake that *National Review* did not support the civil rights legislation of 1964–65 ("Q&A on William F. Buckley"), but at the time he and his magazine opposed it. In 1957, Buckley even expressed approval of white supremacy in the South:

> . . . for the time being, [the white community] is the advanced race. It is not easy, and it is unpleasant, to adduce statistics evidencing the median cultural superiority of White over Negro: but it is fact that obtrudes, one that cannot be hidden by ever-so-busy egalitarians and anthropologists.
> ("Why the South Must Prevail")

This pseudo-intellectual attitude, we must remember – and be on the lookout for ourselves – is what those working in the Civil Rights Movement were up against.

One wonders if Vonnegut's satire was lost on conservative readers of the day, the joke being the ludicrousness of the anxiety dictating that extending rights to others will amputate the rights of those who already have them. There is no comfort here for the myth of the Great White Hope, Harrison Bergeron, who is simply obliterated when it looks like he might, as expected, save the day. The story works the way R. Crumb's comics "When the Niggers Take Over America!" and "When the Goddamn Jews Take Over America!" (1993) do – that is, by expressing with hyperbole the absurdity of irrational fears that hold back equal rights – albeit without the underground cartoonist's focus on race or his overblown sensationalism. Interestingly, just as neoconservatives have embraced "Bergeron," white supremacists have appropriated Crumb's comics and used them as propaganda toward their own ends. What happens when satire gets a seal of approval from those it attacks? Has it failed? Such readings must be considered valid, as they are considered to be valid by those putting them forth. In a way, this appropriation confirms the existence of those values the satire amplifies, and yes, this phenomenon ought to make us uncomfortable.

Obviously, "handicapping," which Vonnegut also uses in *The Sirens of Titan* (1958) and *Between Time and Timbuktu* (1972), is not the answer to leveling the playing field, so to speak. Intelligence, beauty, physical prowess: all are valued through subjective means; there can be no objective measurement of any of these qualities. One question that goes unanswered: how is life different for those deemed disabled in the future America imagined in "Bergeron"? Are they somehow unburdened of their imagined shortcomings? The story does not say. It is concerned only with worries about rights plaguing the white American middle class family, whose exceptional children turn out to be privileged and, above all, mortal. "Bergeron," with its slapstick sound effects and grotesque exaggerations, is a false warning. It is not a dire vision like those put forth in Orwell's *1984* (1948) and Bradbury's *Fahrenheit 451* (1953).

Rather, it is "a mordant little tale" that exposes the average American's insecurities with his or her own equality as it relates to the equality of others, reflecting views held by large segments of American society and iterated historically by Virginia Congressman John Randolph of Roanoke (1773–1833): "I love liberty; I hate equality" (Woodard 55). While vicious and oppressive, instead of a government that is frightful for its realistic potential, the federal government is here reduced to sitcom. Godhead Big Brother is swapped for the comically demonic Diana Moon Glampers – and what is more frightening to and parodic of American patriarchy than rearing feminine energies? The story is not "about" rights being taken away; it depicts the *fear* of rights being taken away in the process of extending them to all members of society, a fine distinction that has been lost on many. "We hold these truths to be self-evident, that all men are created equal, that they are endowed by their Creator with certain unalienable Rights" is a collective commandment in constant conflict with the American myth of individual freedoms, a tension we see playing out in the U.S.A. today with the fights for marriage equality and the Affordable Care Act, as well as the Supreme Court's decision in 2013 to strike down Section 4(b) (thereby nullifying Section 5) of the Voting Rights Act of 1965, a key piece of Civil Rights legislation. "Harrison Bergeron" coyly draws attention to this distinctly American paradox.

"2BR02B" is another imagining of a future United States so orderly that its citizens' rights are impinged. Rejected by *Playboy* and *Esquire*, it was published in January 1962 in the pulp digest *If: Worlds of Science Fiction*. By this time, Vonnegut was near the end of his run as a short story writer. He only sold two more stories in 1962, "The Lie" to *Saturday Evening Post* and "Go Back to Your Precious Wife and Son" in *Ladies Home Journal*. In 1963 he sold two: "Lovers Anonymous" to *Redbook* and "Hyannis Port Story" to *Saturday Evening Post* – a story about the Kennedys which, due to the President's assassination, was not published until it appeared in the 1968 collection *Welcome to the Monkey House*. As discussed later in this chapter, that collection's title story, published in *Playboy*, features Ethical Suicide Parlors and virgin purple-clad Suicide Hostesses, echoing the Ethical Suicide Studios and defeminized purple-clad gas chamber hostesses in "2BR02B," which *Playboy* rejected six years earlier.

The title and basic premise of "2BR02B" also appears in Vonnegut's 1965 novel *God Bless You, Mr. Rosewater*, described as a novel by Kilgore Trout: "Trout's favorite formula was to describe a perfectly hideous society, not unlike his own, and then, toward the end, to suggest ways in which it could be improved" (*NS* 203). Vonnegut had not yet put himself into his fiction as a character, but here he gives the title and setting of one of his own stories to his character Kilgore Trout. In so doing, he teases himself over his own storytelling preferences, speaking of his "favorite formula." However, while Trout supposedly offers possible solutions to society's ills, Vonnegut typically lets discord hang in the air. His first iteration of a suicide parlor future, "2BR02B," much like "Bergeron," erupts with violence and then whimpers to a close without suggestions for improvement.

Like "Bergeron," "2BR02B" opens with an ironically idyllic declaration, describing a future America without prisons, economically depressed neighborhoods, mental institutions, disabilities, or war. In addition, "The population of the United States was stabilized at forty-million souls" (59). This sense of order muddles once we realize the burden is on Edward K. Wehling, Jr., a father-to-be of triplets, to bring forward three willing suicides: "The law said that no newborn child could survive unless the parents of the child could find someone who would volunteer to die. Triplets, if they were all to live, called for three volunteers" (63). The orderliness set up around this system, underscored by the brief presence of an *orderly* working in the Lying-In Hospital, is maintained by the Federal Bureau of Termination. The obstetrician who brings Wehling's triplets into the world is also the man who set up Chicago's very first gas chamber.

This future U.S.A. is a scientocracy, legislated by scientists responding to unfavorable conditions arising from limited resources and starvation. Advances in feeding people and keeping them alive to unfathomable ages (the average age being 129) brought about a population explosion, responded to with what we must assume was a regulated cull that remains ongoing. At the time of the story's publication, according to the 1960 United States Census, the total U.S. population was 183,285,000 people. The country's population in "2BR02B" is much lower, 40,000,000, which was roughly the U.S.A.'s aggregate population in 1870 (38,925,598).

Vonnegut's relationship to suicide is complicated, perpetually appearing in his fiction. At the turn of the millennium, he penned a series of vignettes published as *God Bless You, Dr. Kevorkian* (2001), in which Jack Kevorkian brings him to the brink of death so he may interview the dead. But suicide iterates itself as early in his career as "Thanasphere," where Rice crashes his satellite into the ocean and history is described as "the suicidal course" (62). Vonnegut deemed his mother's death from sleeping pills in 1941 a suicide. Writing to José and Maria Donoso after finishing *Breakfast of Champions* (1973), he identifies her death as a key element of the "formless anger" that plagued him: "Well – if I had to guess, I would say that it was caused by a combination of bad chemicals in my bloodstream and the fact that my mother committed suicide. I have finally dealt with that suicide, by the way, in the book I just finished. My mother appears in it briefly at the end, but keeps her distance – because she is embarrassed by the suicide. And so she should be" (*Letters* 191). "I *saw* my mother in the void," he writes in *Champions*, "My mother stayed far, far away, because she had left me a legacy of suicide" (*NS* 732–733). Such a tragedy cannot be dealt with once and for all in a rite of active imagination and set aside from then on; Vonnegut made an attempt on his own life with alcohol, antidepressants, and sleeping pills in 1984, on the thirty-ninth anniversary of the Dresden firebombing he survived.

Edward K. Wehling, Jr., the desperate father of "2BR02B," carries a name of resonances. Edward comes down from Old English and means "rich guard" (*BTN*), appropriate for one set on protecting the lives of his newborn triplets. Wehling imbues him with the quality of *welling*, that deep filling that carries him to the story's climax. The middle initial of K. and suffix of Jr. point tantalizingly back to the author's name, who we recall had to make room in his family for three of his sister's sons, just four years earlier in 1958, when she and her husband died days apart. Described as a "mere stripling" at fifty-six (59), as "red-eyed and frowzy" (63), Wehling will kill two and die by his own hand by the end of the story.

When it seems the father-to-be is the story's central character, Vonnegut again shifts the focus to another character in the room: "A sardonic old man, about two hundred years old, sat on a stepladder painting a mural he did not like" (60). Though so old, he looks to be about thirty-five because that is how old he was when the cure to aging was discovered; Vonnegut will return to this so-called aging cure in "The Big Trip Up Yonder" and "Monkey House." This character, who oversees everything that takes place, is never named, referred to only as the muralist and the painter. "Mural" comes from Latin *murus* for "wall"; the *OED* traces the word "paint" back to the Indo-European base of "faw": "Coloured, stained, streaked; particoloured, variegated." He is almost a part of the wall he so grudgingly paints, marked within and without by the inhumanity American society has reached. The etymology of "sardonic," from Sardinian, reveals black humor that will eventually claim him: "the word had primary reference to the effects of eating a 'Sardinian plant' [. . .], which was said to produce facial convulsions resembling horrible laughter, usually followed by death" (*OED*).

Like Michelangelo did in the Sistine Chapel's *Last Judgment*, the muralist paints in specific people, though many of the faces are currently left blank as he awaits their models to come by appointment to be added. The chosen subjects were "important people on either the hospital staff or from the Chicago Office of the Federal Bureau of Termination" (60). The fresco is titled *The Happy Garden of Life* and depicts doctors and nurses tending a controlled plot of land. Weeds, fallen leaves, and sick plants are being carried to furnaces so as to maintain the balance of the garden: "Never, never, never – not even in medieval Holland nor old Japan – had a garden been more formal, been better tended" (60). The work is heavy-handed allegory for the system of state-enforced voluntary suicide. The mention of medieval Holland points to the phantasmagorical triptych by Early Netherlandish painter Hieronymus Bosch, *The Garden of Earthly Delights* (1490–1510). That painting's center panel, full of naked people, humongous fruit, birds, and stone towers, has inspired and perplexed probably since it was unveiled.

This work, on the other hand, lacks mystery, boring its own painter. When an orderly compliments his skill, he grumbles and gestures to a paint-splattered dropcloth on the floor: "Frame that, and you'll have a picture a damn sight more honest than this one" (60–61). "His vision may resemble that of 'Jack the Dripper,' Jackson Pollock," writes Reed, "the abstract expressionist painter about whom Vonnegut has written" (85). Of Pollock, Vonnegut said, "this man was capable of depicting in photographic detail the crossing of the Delaware by the Father of our Country, if such a tableau had been demanded by the passions of himself and his century" (*Fates Worse Than Death* 42). The mature muralist, trapped in a future America demanding the inanity of a dictated metaphor, is not free to portray society as he sees it. This archetypally identified character, called Grandpa by the orderly, displays qualities of the *senex*, Latin for "old man," an archetype which depth psychology recognizes as bearing "balance, generosity towards others, wisdom, far-sightedness [. . .] *Senex* pathology may be characterized as excessively conservative, authoritarian, over-grounded, melancholic and lacking in imagination" (*CDJA* 137). From his stepladder, the muralist certainly over-grounds the scene below with wisdom and melancholy. If he lacks the will to imagine and express finer work, that fault points to his society.

Another character, Chief Obstetrician Dr. Benjamin Hitz, is named for one of Vonnegut's high school friends, "Ben Hitz, who was later best man at his wedding" (*SFKV* 85). The name is not simply an inside joke. In the Old Testament Benjamin is the twelfth and youngest son of Jacob and Rachel, the founder of one of the southern tribes of the Hebrews. We might think of this Benjamin, the good-looking, "tanned, white-haired, omnipotent Zeus, two hundred and forty years old," seven feet tall[9] and booming with authority and *joie de vivre*, as a son of the system he upholds. We recall Zeus as a patricidal son who carries on recklessly as chief god of the Olympians. Hitz, as a name, packs a punch, smacks of slapstick, strikes with violence, sharing also a first syllable with Hitler. If the muralist carries qualities of the *senex*, this life-and-death wheeler-dealer holds those of the *puer aeternus*, archetype of the eternal youth: "Jung [. . .] speculated that its recurring fascination springs from man's projection of his inability to renew himself" (*CDJA* 125). Depth psychology recognizes the *puer* as an animating daimon in immaturity and narcissism, pathologies we see exhibited in this character and the society's anti-aging dictum.

The second victim is gas-chamber hostess Leora Duncan: Leora is a Hebrew name for "my light"; Duncan is the name of the king murdered in *Macbeth*, also Isadora Duncan (1877–1927), famous for dancing and death: her neck broke when her scarf tangled in the wheel-spokes of an Amilcar. As a suicide hostess, this light-bound-for-death wears a uniform something like that of an airline stewardess of the early sixties, consisting of a trench coat and overseas cap colored "the purple the painter called 'the color of grapes on Judgment Day'" (61). Purple is the color designated to the Ethical Suicide

Parlors and their Hostesses here, in the summary from *God Bless You, Mr. Rosewater*, and in "Monkey House" – perhaps because purple "lies directly opposite GREEN [on the color wheel]. Thus it stands, not for the springtime passage from death into life, but for the autumnal passage from life into death" – noted also for its elementary colors, blue and red, brought into balance (Chevalier and Gheerbrant 1069). The hostesses' sexualities are also suppressed, as those of bishops are, who wear purple vestments.

The muralist in "2BR02B" does not paint himself into *The Happy Garden of Life*, as Michelangelo is believed to have painted himself into *The Last Judgment*,[10] but *is* tasked with painting Leora's mustachioed face into it. Vonnegut calls it "A curious thing about gas-chamber hostesses" (61), the way they all develop mustaches after a few years of serving as gas-chamber hostesses. Most American women, in the middle of the twentieth century and now, opt for epilation when facial hair appears, a natural occurrence so common that products and services for its removal are easily found. There is no explanation for suicide hostesses embracing the phenomenon, but a masculine pubescence arising through their role in euthanizing people in gas-chambers is assumed. Described as a "coarse, formidable woman" (61), Leora bears associations stereotypical of male warriors. In a time when fewer blinked at the notion of "men's work" and "women's work," carrying out so-called ethical suicides is cast as a career that displaces a woman's femininity. And yet, "She was demure [. . . when making] people comfortable while she killed them" (62).

Duncan carries a bag bearing "the seal of the Service Division of the Federal Bureau of Termination, an eagle perched on a turnstile" (61). This detail melds the eagle emblems of the United States and Nazi Germany, whose swastika resembled a turnstile. Vonnegut's vision here presents a United States that has incorporated the gas-chambers synonymous with the Holocaust. Two characters in "2BR02B" react against the inhumanity, albeit in very different ways. Wehling faces something akin to *Sophie's Choice*: "All I have to do is pick out which one of the triplets is going to live, then deliver my maternal grandfather to the Happy Hooligan,[11] and come back here with a receipt" (63). But of course he wants his kids and he does not want his grandfather to die. When Dr. Hitz fails to placate him with an idiotic simile, likening overpopulation to the drupelets of a blackberry,[12] he spiels what Reed calls their "regulated paradise" (85). Wehling responds by producing a revolver and killing Dr. Hitz and Leora Duncan. "'There's Room [sic] for two,'" he calculates just before shooting himself, "making room for all three of his children" (65). His weapon, a revolver, keeps the society revolving, making the act not so much a revolutionary murder-suicide as a tragic perpetuation of the system.

The muralist, witnessing the slaughter atop his stepladder, becomes reflective: "The painter pondered the mournful puzzle of life demanding to be born and, once born, demanding to be fruitful . . . to multiply and to live as long as possible – to do all that on a very small planet that would have to last forever" (65). Schopenhauer, in what Campbell called his "dreadful phrase" (*MGOM* 262), declared "the world and man is something that had better not have been" ("On the Sufferings"). We sense this misery in the muralist's thoughts, horror at the constant and ceaseless feeding of life on life, justified and propagated in the Occident by Biblical scripture despite pain wrought through the entitlement of dominion, with no end in sight. The bloody climax is too much for him: "He knew that he would never paint again" (65). Earlier, the orderly chides the muralist's statement that he would prefer to kill himself over going to a suicide studio, calling him a "do-it-yourselfer" (61). The painter, unflagged by the discouragement, expresses what he sees as a necessity for disorder in life: "The world could do with a good deal more mess, if you ask me" (61). When he decides he has had it and descends from his perch, he picks up Wehling's gun intending suicide, "But he didn't have the nerve" (65).

He does, however, have the phone number of the municipal gas chambers of the Federal Bureau of Termination memorized: 2 B R 0 2 B, or "to be or not to be." Hamlet's question has been repackaged as a phone number to dial when someone decides to end his or her life. He goes to the telephone booth in the corner of the waiting room and schedules an appointment that afternoon. The hostess on the line thanks him on behalf of his city, his country, his planet, and all future generations. Thus ends the tale, with a pending state-assisted suicide. There is no liberty in this imagined future, where the right to life in the U.S.A. is "stabilized at forty-million souls" and suicide is venerated in state-sponsored art. The muralist is unwilling – he has not the will – to add "a good deal more mess" to the world.

Thc pursuit of . . .

The third ingredient in American independence is also its most subjective. "The Euphio Question" (*Collier's* 12 May 1951) asks if unqualified happiness is safe for society. It plays out as a transcript of one man's testimony to the Federal Communications Commission, warning them about the destructive effects and consequences of a new invention: the euphoriaphone, or euphio (à la radio) for short. The device amplifies a frequency from deep space that incapacitates listeners with joy, rendering them prone to deathly dangers.[13] When Lew expresses reservations, another is incredulous: "'People ought to be happy,' Fred said" (53).

Ought we? "Ought" suggests obligation and, if we are so obliged, the fact that happiness eludes many people despite the ardent pursuit of it can become a cause for despair. Happiness is but one of the uncountable feelings, experienced in our own individual ways, that happen to us. While establishing that people have an unalienable right to its pursuit, what makes some of us happy causes the opposite in others, not to mention that too great an emphasis on one emotional quality courts psychological imbalance. How many Americans, in 1951 and now, have internalized the narrative that something is wrong with them because they do not feel happy, or at least happy *enough* – when in fact they are something far more dynamic in being alive? The problem does not affect Americans alone, but a distinct strain infects plenty of U.S. citizens who have accepted their nationality as exceptional and undergo crisis when they cannot "live up" to its subjective promises/premises. Some may argue the nation's founders merely pledged the pursuit, not the arrival. To plenty of human beings, the pursuit alone is a hell of a yoke. "The Euphio Question" is a fable built on the premise that easy happiness, the kind that can be exploited, packaged, and sold, is not the variety encountered naturally, which is not and cannot be a constant.[14]

A more nuanced story exploring obstacles obstructing the pursuit of happiness was published as "The Big Trip Up Yonder" in the January 1954 issue of *Galaxy: Science Fiction*. It follows the extended Ford family, twenty-three of them cramped into a one-bedroom apartment, for in 2185 the world is this overpopulated, forcing people to eat "egg-type processed seaweed" (106) and "buckwheat-type processed sawdust cakes" (107). Science fiction writer Harlan Ellison "thought it was the very best Malthusian pastiche I'd ever read" (228). Four generations crammed together, twenty-two of them vie for the patriarch's favor, dreading the common occurrence of getting in his way and being written out of his last will and testament. With mattresses and sleeping bags in the hallway, the most coveted place is Gramps's bedroom, which he keeps to himself. His bed, which everybody wants, is not a luxurious king; it is a standard double.

When grandson Louis decides to replace Gramps's age-defying medicine with water, and in the process breaks the glass bottle, he is written out of the will and replaced by his father, Willy (his name is a playfully adjectival form of "will"). After Gramps pulls a disappearing act, the descendants erupt in a massive fight that draws cops and news media, sending the Fords to jail where they gleefully bask in the privacy of their own cells. Living conditions are so rotten that prison is a step up in the world. The illustration accompanying the story is a line drawing of Gramps thinking over his two-page will while the shadow figures of his warring children, grandchildren, great-grandson, nephew, grandnephew, great-grandnephew, great-grandniece, and assorted spouses storm around his head.

When included in *Canary in a Cat House* (1961) and *Welcome to the Monkey House* (1968), this story was titled "Tomorrow and Tomorrow and Tomorrow"; Vonnegut's drafts collected at the Lilly Library indicate this was the original title.[15] It comes from Shakespeare's *Macbeth*, spoken in the main character's final soliloquy (V.v. 19), which also renders up the declaration that life "is a tale | Told by an idiot, full of sound and fury | Signifying nothing" (V.v. 26–28); William Faulkner found the title for his novel *The Sound and the Fury* (1928) here, as did David Foster Wallace in titling one

Figure 3.2 Illustration by Kossin of Gramps in *Galaxy Science Fiction*. (© Galaxy Publishing Corp., 1954)

of the stories in *Brief Interviews with Hideous Men* (1999). Upon word that Lady Macbeth is dead, he laments the drag of time:

> Tomorrow, and tomorrow, and tomorrow,
> Creeps in this petty pace from day to day,
> To the last syllable of recorded time
>
> (V.v. 19–21)

In Vonnegut's story, human time has been strung to ridiculous lengths thanks to anti-gerasone, an elixir and highly marketed product that stops the aging process. The eldest character is a startling 172 years old due to regular ingestion of this chemical compound, which we are told has an "almost imperceptible smell [. . .] like Worcestershire sauce" (105). "Anti-gerasone" and the implied "gerasone" are fictional, the former apparently blocking or inhibiting the latter. The etymology of "gerasone" combines the Ancient *Greek* γῆρας (geras) for "old age" and the suffix "-one," used in chemistry to form "unsystematically the names of organic compounds derived from other compounds" (*OED*). This suggests that in the fictional future of "Big Trip," as well as the stories "2BR02B" and "Monkey House," aging is caused by a chemical or hormone common to all people, and, thanks to a potion, it can be arrested.

Reports of waters of longevity in the West harken back to Classical Greek historian Herodotus (*The Histories*, III:23), while the myth of the fountain of youth became an obsession in the American Hemisphere during the early years of colonization by Europeans. In *Historia General y Natural de las Indias* (1535), explorer Ponce de León was said to have sought the youth-restoring waters of Bimini. Originally imagined to be in the Caribbean, these waters were later re-imagined to the Florida peninsula. Three centuries later, Nathaniel Hawthorne's story "Dr. Heidegger's Experiment" (1837) presents men repeating youthful mistakes after imbibing the rejuvenating water and, when the effect wears off, leaving for Florida to "quaff at morning, noon and night from the Fountain of Youth" (167). The year before "Big Trip" was published, Disney released a theatrical short cartoon titled "Don's Fountain of Youth," in which Donald Duck tricks his nephews into believing the waters regress him back to the egg. The wish for waters that will restore youth is ancient, occurring long before the U.S. existed, and so we again find a "cannibalized" European myth. When Vonnegut, at the end of "Big Trip," introduces "safe, tested *Super*-anti-gerasone" (110), the new-and-improved medicine that will *reverse* aging, he dresses the old myth in the cloak of American television advertising, then arising in the early nineteen-fifties.

Aging is one of the inevitables of living for an extended period of time. All mammals that live through adulthood experience it. Despite its universality, the process, which plays out differently for every individual, is a common source of anxiety. The changing of one's energies, the shifting of abilities, appetites, and enzymes is often enough bemoaned and denigrated as a cause for shame. Psychologically, it is possible to accept the tilt and rebalance oneself in whatever phase of life one is unfolding into, but this is easier said than done. Philip Coleman and Stephen Matterson acknowledge the "larger cultural sense of the United States *as* youth: the young nation among older nations, the nation that enshrines promise and potential, where youth is listened to and nurtured" (*'Forever Young'* 5). A culture so focused on youth that its members will do whatever they can to reverse the aging process is one in which individuation marches in a procession of regression. Discussing Jung's esoteric *Red Book*, Hillman and Sonu Shamdasani grapple with calling individuation a process for the fact that it implies progress. Shamdasani, who spent five years translating *The Red Book*, says Jung first conceived individuation as a sequence but over the years began viewing it as a process. "He's implying that there is a natural urge to fulfill, that there's an entelechy in there, in our lives," says Hillman (*Lament of the Dead* 137). This understanding of individuation casts it as an openness to the movement of experience within as it participates with experience without. But life is full of hindrances and impediments to simply this. In "Big Trip," something as stultifying as a euphio device has been mass-produced, bottled, and sold as advertised: "Wouldn't you pay $5,000 to be indistinguishable from everybody else?" asks the ad for *Super*-anti-gerasone (110). Anti-aging wipes away possibility for individuality, rendering everybody unidentifiable. Maturity is denied manifestation, the result being this story about immature characters we can hardly tell apart.

Behind the collective dis-ease with aging is, of course, fear of the ultimate universal: death. Hillman identifies this: "[The] biggest of all collective problems [. . .] is the suppression of the dead. Not hearing the voices of history. Not hearing what we've lost. And the fear of the dead, the fear of death, in our culture" (*Lament for the Dead* 151). We think back to Groszinger's struggle in "Thanasphere." Jung's *Red Book*, the illuminated fantasy he invested more time in than any of his other works, challenges us to recognize the dead in the characters arising from our imaginations:

> These figures are the dead, not just your dead, that is, all the images of the shapes you took in the past, which your ongoing life has left behind, but also the thronging dead of human history, the ghostly procession of the past, which is an ocean compared to the drops of your own life span. (340)

Vonnegut met the dead, had direct experience moving the corpses of families, pulled them out of firebombed homes with his hands, carried them in his arms to pyres, as a P.O.W. after the aerial massacre of Dresden. That isolated experience was an atypical initiation for Americans of his generation. When the dead are denied access to the awareness of the living in Vonnegut's work, it is because he, having encountered them, sees them ignored in his culture. This future America pursues happiness at the expense of death, its citizens snubbing the dead with the attitude that joining their ranks should be avoided at all costs. The story unfurls the mystery of American fears of the mystery of death, death being the threat in Gramps's first utterance: "'Next one shoots off his big bazoo while the TV's on is gonna find hisself cut off without a dollar – ' his voice suddenly sweetened – 'when they wave that checkered flag at the Indianapolis Speedway, and old Gramps gets ready for the Big Trip Up Yonder'" (101). The story title extracted for the *Galaxy* publication is this euphemism for death.

Gramps's theatrics hinge upon his wills, both the document and his determination.

Rollo May, harmonizing Hillman and Shamdasani's discussion of individuation, writes, "*Will is the capacity to organize one's self* so that movement in a certain direction or toward a certain goal may take place" (*Love and Will* 218; italics in original). In one sense, Gramps divests himself of his family so that he might attain solitude, but this privacy merely opens him, in the final lines of the story, to the passivity of being entertained: "Life was good. He could hardly wait to see what was going to happen next" (110). He and his descendants engross themselves in *The McGarvey Family*, "a television serial that Gramps had been following since he was 60, or for a total of 112 years. 'I can't wait to see what's going to happen next,' he said'" (104). The sly old grouch, in sending off for age-reversing *Super*-anti-gerasone and re-uttering his line of anticipation, surrenders to the episodic melodrama of soap opera. His yearned-for enjoyment leaves him alone in a seemingly endless existence, a solitary audience member willingly watching life. This is not the wise old man, the balanced *senex* who has accepted aging and grown mature; Gramps is the pathological *senex*, who inconsistently lords and denies his station as an elder. And where has Granny gone? There must have been a woman in order for there to be descendants. The maternal and matriarchal feminine powers are fully denied in the Ford (à la Henry?) apartment, his missing spouse never even mentioned.

When Gramps pulls his disappearing trick, and the reader doesn't know he is still alive, it seems he might have actually died in sacred fashion:

> The door swung open before her fist. In the middle of the room, the soft, deep, wide, canopied bed, the symbol of the sweet by-and-by to every Ford, was empty.
>
> A sense of death, as unfamiliar to the Fords as Zoroastrianism or the causes of the Sepoy Mutiny, stilled every voice, slowed every heart. Awed, the heirs began to search gingerly, under the furniture and behind the drapes, for all that was mortal of Gramps, father of the clan.
>
> (107)

"But Gramps had left not his Earthly husk but a note" (107), the narrator tells us. This event riffs off the rolling back of the stone from Christ's tomb in the New Testament, when the myrrh bearers discover Jesus' body has vanished. Instead of encountering an angel, however, the Fords find what reads like a suicide note. The ensuing argument over inheritance escalates into familial war, drawing police and news cameras – a situation prescient of the American documentary television series *COPS*. The Fords' infighting strife becomes entertainment for "500,000,000 delighted viewers on the Eastern Seaboard" (109). Suffering as entertainment. We might hope witnessing violence and pain would evoke compassion, but that is not always the case; often enough it brings out delight, even happiness. A haunting touch reveals the emptied apartment subjected to the calamity all over again: "In the stillness of the three-room Ford apartment on the 76th floor of Building 257, the television set had been left on. Once more the air was filled with the cries and grunts and crashes of the fray, coming harmlessly now from the loudspeaker" (109). The apartment, however, is not empty. Having returned from his hideout, the Idle Hour Tavern, "which commanded a view of Building 257 from across the square of asphalt known as Alden Village Green" (110), Gramps Ford scratches down the address for *Super*-anti-gerasone and settles into his own passive regression.

In January 1968, more than four years since a Vonnegut short story had been published, "Welcome to the Monkey House" appeared in *Playboy*. All of the Vonnegut stories examined thus far were written between 1949 and 1962, making this one, sold in 1967, an outlier. I intended to limit the scope to stories written up to the assassination of President John F. Kennedy – a historical demarcation in the American psyche – but this work would be incomplete without addressing this story, particularly given its connections to "Big Trip" and "2BR02B" – and, peculiarly enough, the Kennedys. The social and political soul of the U.S.A. had changed, and some of the differences stand out in the issue of *Playboy* at hand. Essays and ideas unimaginable in the years between WWII and the end of "Camelot" are printed alongside the magazine's standard fare: Harvey Cox explores contemporary Christianity in relation to the youth movement in "God and the Hippies"; John Clellon Holmes prematurely announces the arrival of Postfeminism; and novelist Norman Mailer, in the extended interview, imagines what the U.S.A. might be like if Kennedy hadn't been murdered. The issue also features an essay by Bradbury on the collective need for imagining death, in which he iterates an attitude that would please Jung, Hillman, and Shamdasani: "To fantasize is to remain sane" (252).

Charles Slackman's illustration for "Monkey House" shows a redheaded woman in a purple nightgown standing hip-deep in the grip of a giant chimpanzee's foot. Perched in the cousin of Kong's hand idles a redheaded man in spectacles reading a book. The chimp, red-eyed, grins a row of yellow teeth, sitting in the starry night on a field of green. From the neck down his

WELCOME TO THE MONKEY HOUSE

fiction By KURT VONNEGUT, JR. *hidden in that future world where all that was pleasurable in sex had been destroyed was an outlaw poet with revolutionary ideas*

SO PETE CROCKER, the sheriff of Barnstable County, which was the whole of Cape Cod, came into the Federal Ethical Suicide Parlor in Hyannis one May afternoon—and he told the two six-foot Hostesses there that they weren't to be alarmed, but that a notorious nothinghead named Billy the Poet was believed headed for the Cape.

A nothinghead was a person who refused to take his ethical birth-control pills three times a day. The penalty for that was $10,000 and ten years in jail.

This was at a time when the population of Earth was 17 billion human beings. That was far too many mammals that big for a planet that small. The people were virtually packed together like drupelets.

Drupelets are the pulpy little knobs that compose the outside of a raspberry.

So the World Government was making a two-pronged attack on overpopulation. One pronging was the encouragement of ethical suicide, which consisted of going to the nearest Suicide Parlor and asking a Hostess to kill you painlessly while you lay on a Barcalounger. The other pronging was compulsory ethical birth control.

The sheriff told the Hostesses, who were pretty, tough-minded, highly intelligent girls, that roadblocks were being set up and house-to-house searches were being conducted to catch Billy the Poet. The main difficulty was that the police didn't know what he looked like. The few people who had seen him and known him for what he was were women—and they disagreed fantastically as to his height, his hair color, his voice, his weight, the color of his skin.

"I don't need to remind you girls," the sheriff went on, "that a nothinghead is very sensitive from the waist down. If Billy the Poet somehow slips in here and starts making trouble, one good kick in *(continued on page 156)* 95

ILLUSTRATION BY CHARLES SLACKMAN

Figure 3.3 Charles Slackman's title illustration for "Welcome to the Monkey House." (Archival material from Playboy magazine. Copyright © 1968 by Playboy. Reprinted with permission. All rights reserved.)

body holds the forms of a multitude of outward-staring primates. The man held and woman grabbed by the towering primate-composite chimpanzee calls to mind Nietzsche's post-Darwinian discovery: "I have *discovered* for myself that the old human and animal world, indeed the entire prehistory and past of all sentient being, works on, loves on, hates on, thinks on in me" (Hollingdale 146). Moriarty picks up on this, calling "[our inner psychological ancient condition the] regime of cravings, hungers, impulses, energies, which, for the most part, were biologically instituted in the Palaeozoic. The ancient regime we innately are" (*TGLT2* 91).

Darwinism does not claim we evolved from chimps or monkeys, but rather that we and the great apes and monkeys share a common ancestor. Here we see people in the clutches of an ape, which is itself made up of simians, illustrating the commonly held – and unscientific – myth of our evolutionary lineage from monkey to man. There are no gargantuan chimpanzees in the coming narrative, so where the image succeeds is in this sense, integral to Vonnegut's story, that primal aspects, inherited from our genetic ancestry, live on within us. Unsurprisingly for *Playboy*, patriarchy is at play as well, for the woman is gripped to inaction by a foot while the intellectually stimulated man lolls in a bestial hand. This is appropriate, for the monkey house in question is located in the zoo of human sexuality as dictated by white American heterosexual men of the forties and fifties, who were trying to maintain their authority over women in the late sixties.

Again we find an overpopulated future with 17 billion human beings on Earth, where anti-aging is bought and consumed and citizens are encouraged to undergo euthanasia at Federal Ethical Suicide Parlors. This time, however, Americans fall under the jurisdiction of a World Government and "compulsory ethical birth control" (95):

> The pills were ethical because they didn't interfere with a person's ability to reproduce, which would have been unnatural and immoral. All the pills did was take every bit of pleasure out of sex.
>
> Thus did science and morals go hand in hand.
>
> (156)

Again we are presented with life in an oppressive scientocracy where Vonnegut has taken an aspect of American culture – the combined oral contraceptive pill – and amplified it to the *n*th degree. The Pill, granted caps for its perceived godlike revolution of women's sexuality, met FDA approval in 1960 and by 1968 its use was widespread. Consider Holmes's three points on its liberation of American women in "The New Girl: an appreciative appraisal of the emergent modern female . . ." published in the same issue: "[The Pill] freed women from their own biology, putting into their hands (rather than men's) an inexpensive, simple-to-use, foolproof method of preventing conception and even controlling menstruation [. . .] It freed her to [the body's] desires [. . .] It freed [women] from men as well and from men's wishful images of them" (186). The final point alone appearing in the pages of a magazine famous for publishing men's wishful images of nude women is a contradiction, to say the least – these points show men were trying to figure out what the Pill meant to *them*.

What unfolds in "Monkey House" is abduction culminating in rape. The victim is Nancy McLuhan, a Hostess in the Ethical Suicide Service. Unlike those in "2BR02B," these Hostesses do not sprout mustaches. Actually, they receive the sort of sexualized attention one might stereotypically expect from *Playboy*, wearing white lipstick, boots, and purple leotards without underwear. They are required to be virgins, to have studied nursing and psychology at a postgraduate level, to be six feet tall at minimum, and be trained in martial arts. Their uniform is said to be powerfully arousing to the Nothingheads. "A nothinghead," as it goes, "was a person who refused to take his ethical birth-control pills three times a day. The penalty for that was $10,000 and ten years in jail" (95).

The name Nancy was a medieval diminutive of Annis, deriving from Greek ἁγνος for "chaste" (*BTN*); McLuhan conjures Marshall McLuhan, the Canadian communications theorist who authored *Understanding Media* (1964), in which he coined the phrase "the medium is the message." The character's name then triggers awareness of chastity amid the manner in which the story is presented and received: on pages interspersed throughout a so-called "gentlemen's magazine." She may also be read as a literary jibe at "Little Annie Fanny," the comic creation of Harvey Kurtzman and Will Elder under heavy editorial control by publisher Hugh Hefner. Little Annie Fanny, a cartooned and hyper-sexualized young blond woman, intertextually refers back to "Little Orphan Annie," sharing its red font for the title. She is a Barbie for an adult male audience, an innocent surviving picaresque episodes in which her character never develops beyond being objectified in two-to-eight-page comics running in *Playboy* from 1962 to 1988. Vonnegut's Nancy is just as wide-eyed, vapid, and sexually exploited for narrative purposes. Nancy's co-Hostess and friend, Mary Kraft, bears both the name of the Occident's venerated Virgin and Kraft Foods, manufacturer of boxed macaroni and cheese – an American staple.

Though not mentioned, anti-gerasone or something like it is being ingested, for, despite her youthful appearance, Nancy is sixty-three years old, another arrested youth. She is also sarcastically referred to twice by the story's notorious nothinghead as Juno, the Roman fertility and marriage goddess: "Young, but fully mature, at the height of her powers, commanding, aggressive and fertile, she symbolizes the female principle" (Chevalier and Gheerbrant 560–561). Indeed, Nancy and Mary begin the story utterly defiant of the sheriff's warning, delivered in person, about the serial rapist who has come to Hyannis to prey on Hostesses. The patriarchal narrative they perpetuate casts blame for the crime on the victims: "I'm not as mad at *him* as I am at the women who let him do it to them without a struggle" (156).

It is worth addressing Vonnegut's relationship with women, acknowledged in his *New York Times* obituary as "a lifelong difficulty." He first became aware of vitriolic conflict between men and women through his mother's verbal abuse of his father:

> I have heard and seen hatred that pure coming from women maybe ten times since she died on Mother's Day in 1944 (about a month before D Day). I don't think the hatred has much to do with the particular man who gets it. Father surely didn't deserve it. Most likely, it seems to me, it is a response to aeons of subjugation, although my mother and all the other women who have displayed it for my supposed benefit were about as enslaved as Queen Elizabeth or Cleopatra.
>
> My theory is that all women have hydrofluoric acid bottled up inside, but my mother had too much of it. When the clock struck midnight (and we really did have a grandfather clock which struck the hours with authority), out it came. For her it was like throwing up. She had to do it. Poor soul! Poor soul!
>
> This is a self-serving theory, insinuating that Father and I did not deserve to be so hated. Forget it.
>
> (*Fates Worse Than Death* 36–37)

Vonnegut's awareness of women's historical subjugation and his allowance for its influence in women's behavior of his day has something to do with W. H. Auden's sense that, "We are lived by powers we pretend to understand" (97). Hillman claims the concept in the service of depth psychology: "The only axiomatic basis I have is that we are lived by powers we pretend to understand, so the axiomatic basis are these powers. They're our mysteries, they're our figures, they are occasions of invasion and they are our lives, or at least determine our lives in strong ways" (*Lament* 201). Vonnegut's shame is not merely personal; it is collective. Notice the generations of maleness he presents, with the son, the father, and the authoritative clock known and coveted as a grandfather, pointing backward through time with minute and hour hands to a long-accepted ancestry of patriarchy, as well as forward with guilt and doubt to the possibility of shedding it. To throw the hydrofluoric acid back in Vonnegut's face and brand him a misogynist would miss the complexity of the problem as he experienced it. Woodman picks up on it, too, when she says, "The rage in both sexes comes out of centuries of abuse" (48).

A brief letter in response to Marianne Brown, a thirty-six-year-old widow with three children who wrote to Vonnegut, shows his compassion toward women:

> It can't be said often enough, "It is the woman who pays." The miracle is that so many can and do somehow. I was in love (still am) with a

> widow with four kids (two not her own). She somehow raised them all on a teeny weeny salary. I told her one time, "I worry about women." She said, "Don't."
>
> ("It is the woman who pays")

The widow he refers to with love is Loree Rackstraw, his former student in the Iowa Writers' Workshop and a scholar. What is most telling is his acknowledgment that this relationship allowed him to abandon his outworn savior complex. Rackstraw taught him that he and all men, by extension, are not responsible for rescuing women; respect and appreciate women, yes, but the projection of damselhood on all women is narcissistic, a narrative that inflates men's notions of their own greatness. The letter and the previous passage were written in 1990, more than twenty years after "Monkey House," which, after all, we are reading in the context of its own history. Vonnegut's attitudes were not the same in 1968.

Long after Wild West outlaw Billy the Kid's death and a year before Billy (the?) Pilgrim made his author famous, Vonnegut issued forth Billy the Poet, the nothinghead serial rapist of this story. Could this character be a satire of the contemporary image of the philandering U.S. poet, embodied by John Berryman and James Dickey? His title comes from his penchant for harassing Suicide Hostesses, his chosen prey, with salacious poems. A master of disguise, no one can identify him, imbuing him with boogeyman virility. But this phantom of the parlor is not the disfigured, unloved, lovelorn Phantom of the Opera, who transforms after receiving his first kiss when his own act of abduction fails. He is a revolutionary, a fundamentalist activist whose cause rebels against the government's regulation through compulsory ethical birth-control pills. His acts of terrorism involve "deflowering" the women who oversee the voluntary suicide of citizens – thus do sex and death go hand in hand, as Billy will later say.

While the government has not inhibited reproduction, it has vanquished pleasure from the act itself: natural desire unnaturally suppressed. Disguised as a Foxy Grandpa named Mr. Howard – a Foxy Grandpa being a flirtatious old man who comes to a parlor to be euthanized – Billy conflates the history of the pills' invention by a druggist from Grand Rapids and a television play set at a zoo that is broadcast every Easter. "There is nothing like an Easter morning to make a man feel clean and reborn and at one with God's intentions," he says, claiming he was there – and spiritually tainted by what they found at the monkey house: "We saw a monkey playing with his private parts! [. . .] And J. Edgar Nation was so upset he went straight home and he started developing a pill that would make monkeys in the springtime fit things for a Christian family to see" (196). Nothing shatters some people's at-one-ment like a masturbating monkey. In blending the holiday celebrating Christ's resurrection with repulsion at animal sexuality, which lives on in us, Billy packages the legend of the pills' creation as a new mythic narrative. American readers, as Reed discusses, would recognize actual people in the druggist's name: "The druggist's name is a portmanteau derivation from J. Edgar Hoover and Carrie Nation. Hoover, as the FBI Director of the time, was vigorous in his rigid moral judgments, despite some peculiar proclivities of his own, while Carrie Nation sought to purge the society of alcohol-induced sin" (*SFKV* 100). The spectres of Prohibition and federal surveillance combine.

Once Billy reveals himself, armed with a "snub-nosed" revolver, he bombards Nancy with another sophomoric poem, this one admitting a high opinion of himself. The confessed narcissist takes her out the window and through the sewers of Hyannis to his gang's hideout: the Kennedy Compound, which is a summertime museum preserved under a geodesic dome.[16] Here the statues of all fourteen Kennedys to have been Presidents are frozen in a game of touch football. "Monkey House" was published six months before Robert F. Kennedy, a presidential hopeful, was assassinated; a dynasty of Kennedys in the White House, while exaggerated, is topical – Berryman wrote "Formal Elegy" for Kennedy and, in "Dream Song 105," refers to "dynasty K" (122). There is even, we discover, a Kennedy leading the World Government: 'Ma' Kennedy, who was a Suicide Hostess and is derided for not being a true Kennedy though she is.[17] This is like a Vestal Virgin becoming Emperor of Rome, but the fact she is regarded as unworthy of the Kennedy name indicates that a patriarchal attitude thrives.

Billy's gang of at least eight, split equally as men and women, hold her down in a servant's bedroom, while a former Suicide Hostess subdues her with an injection of truth serum. When asked how it feels to be a virgin at sixty-three, she surprises herself with her own foggy answer: "Pointless" (200). Nancy does not live a life devoid of sex by choice; she lives so because her culture dictates that sexual desire must be numbed away at threat of imprisonment. She has never experienced arousal, so when she later awakens and the ethical birth-control pills have worn off, Nancy experiences feelings likened to being swarmed below the waist by mosquitoes and bees, which are described along with birds as extinct. She has become a nothinghead, awakening to the birds and the bees, to those sexual urges that motivate living beings, even the insects, who are as mysteriously alive as we are.

Nancy is shuttled to the cabin of the *Marlin*, a yacht that belonged to Ambassador Joseph P. Kennedy, progenitor of the Kennedy clan. There, amid antique furnishings and leaded glass, she encounters Billy, dressed in the silk pajamas of a throwback playboy – as stylized, by *Playboy* publisher Hefner, with pipe and smoking jacket. And "writhing across Billy's silken breast was a golden dragon. It was belching fire" (200). Dragons, we recall from Campbell, are stockpilers of gold and captors of virgins, selfish monsters that have no purpose beyond hoarding life's potentials and bounties: "The problem of the psychiatrist is to disintegrate that dragon, break him up, so that you may expand to a larger field of relationships" (*POM* 149–150). Instead of being freed from state-dictated sexual oppression, Nancy is trapped by a new dragon. When he suggests she make him happy by throwing herself into his arms, she delivers the story's big question: "And what about *my* happiness?" (201). When this puzzles him, she clarifies: "What if my idea of happiness doesn't coincide with yours?" (201). Nancy bravely defies him, saying that if he wants his happiness he will have to rape her with his minions holding her down and a loaded gun to her head.

Billy, in one of the most disturbing turns in Vonnegut's canon, does precisely this. It is not narrated, other than to tell the reader it happened. We return to the pursuit of happiness and the fact that any two happinesses may not accord. In this case one's happiness subjugates the other's. For all the stories we read of people who connect beyond their individual concepts of self, we need other stories that acknowledge violence wrought across the interpersonal chasm. Of this rape: "[Billy] didn't hurt her. He deflowered her with a clinical skill she found ghastly" and emerges depressed by his own actions (201). The notion of rape without hurt is false, denying culpability by insisting the victim must have enjoyed the violation. Using "deflower" as a floral euphemism to potpourri the event of a woman's virginity being "taken" is another such construct. If Nancy is not hurt physically, she certainly is psychologically – as narration indicates when she is revealed in the next sentence as having "a face like stone – and silent tears of humiliation" (201).

Reed raises questions, admitting that "the fact of Billy's rape of Mary [actually, it's Nancy] remains hard to dismiss. [. . .] Even in comedy, there may be a little too much to laugh off here" (*SFKV* 102). This story's place in the pages of *Playboy* plays a role in how we read it and how it was read. Coleman has noted the dichotomy between the magazine's ethos and a Chuck Palahniuk story "where eroticism yields to violent self-abasement and dangerous abuse": "The publication of 'Guts' in *Playboy* is particularly interesting [. . .] because of the way that the story interrogates ideas of the sexualised body and embodiment" ("Hauntedness" 8). In a similar way, after one has flipped through the January 1968 issue and seen the nude photographs, reading "Monkey House," in which a woman reacts with disgust to a man's sexuality being forced upon and within her, might dampen the sense of sophistication and carefree sexuality editors tried to assemble; men did not buy *Playboy* for the opportunity of being told they were revolting creatures in the eyes of women. At one level, this story subverts the very nature of *Playboy* by depicting a character wearing its publisher's iconic uniform as a rapist. Nancy, hiding her face under a war-surplus blanket – the sort Vonnegut was surely wrapped in when repatriated at Le Havre – chastises Billy's masculinity when he chokes on post-coital cigar smoke. Billy's tactic, faced with her pain, is more manipulative rhetoric, likening her to all the others. When she asks why they haven't killed him, he tells her, "They're *grateful*" (201).

Billy emphasizes his aided-and-abetted superiority over her by saying she will eventually be grateful, too, because it was no worse than what brides typically experienced on their wedding night one hundred years earlier. In a disturbing twist, he reveals that his silk dragon pajamas are the same his great-great-grandfather wore on his wedding night. Citing his diary, he says his great-great-grandmother cried and vomited twice upon consummating their marriage but eventually came to crave sex. Billy wears the uniform of his own ancestral patriarchy. His is an inherited abusive reign that he sheepishly attempts to downplay with self-depreciatory magniloquence. In telling her that she is furious with him not because of the rape but because he is an unfulfilling lover, Billy reveals himself to be truly pathetic.

But something upsetting happens, something I am struggling with in this analysis: Nancy begins to accept his narrative. "She understood the tale. It frightened her to understand so easily that, from gruesome beginnings, sexual enthusiasm could grow and grow" (201). The similarities between a painful or humiliating wedding night loss of virginity and one where the woman is held down and raped with a gun to her head are incongruous. Sexual initiation may very well hurt in any number of ways, and in time this eventually passes on to enjoyment for most people. But even with a just-victimized Nancy being "frightened" by the realization, I do not see Vonnegut earning this moment. One thinks of the controversy over the rape in Sam Peckinpah's film *Straw Dogs* (1971), in which Amy may seem to take pleasure as she is attacked, a depiction Melanie Williams claims "purposely catered to entrenched appetites for desired victim behavior and reinforces rape myths" (71).

Is this a case of chauvinistic storytelling? Might a person who has just been raped "with a clinical skill" anticipate a fulfilling sexual appetite in the future? One of David Foster Wallace's briefly interviewed hideous men asks, "Alls I'm saying is who are we to say getting incested or abused or violated or whatever or any of those things can't also have their positive aspects for a human being in the long run. Not that it necessarily does all the time, but who are we to say it *never* does, in a knee-jerk way?" (99). Sexuality refuses universal manifestation. It is fired and tempered by fantasies, experiences, cultures, relations, hormones, organs: a constellation of powers we are lived by that we pretend to understand. The American sexual climate in the late 1960s was undergoing significant changes. Perhaps, as with Holmes's essay, what we see here is the difficulty WWII generation men had in trying to figure out where shifting attitudes relating to a phenomenon as old as life itself led. Kathy J. Phillips, critiquing reductive binary understandings projected upon mid-twentieth-century American sexuality, argues "The false notion of women as the 'passive' partner reinforces an odd, recurrent myth that women do not really have any sexuality" (179). Billy's tale of his great-great-grandmother, which causes Nancy to "understand so easily" the mystery of her own sexuality, falls short of hierophany. Yet there seems to be a point pushing through the story: The Pill has not freed women at all.

Billy the Poet rounds out his spiel like a Bond villain, railing against the agreeably oppressive government and its sexualized Suicide Hostesses: "The only sexual beauty that an ordinary human being can see today is in the woman who will kill him. Sex is death. There's a short and nasty equation for you: 'Sex is death, Q.E.D.'" (201). He describes himself in savior terms and, explaining he'd like to read a poem to her, "to have you know I've loved you" (201), gives her, against her wishes, the first four lines of Elizabeth Barrett Browning's "How Do I Love Thee?" It is the same poem his grandfather read to his wife at dawn after their wedding night. Before leaving her, he also gives Nancy a bottle of birth control pills to be taken once a month that will preserve all sexual desires and urges without numbing; its label, the story's ending detail, reads "WELCOME TO THE MONKEY HOUSE" (201).

Gregory D. Sumner, who carelessly misses the connections to "2BR02B" and *God Bless You, Mr. Rosewater* in his long essay on Vonnegut's process of writing "Monkey House," finds an "ultimately redemptive message" in the story, claiming "it alerts us to the costs that come with suppressing our animal nature, and it urges us to accept and love ourselves as we are, to celebrate our capacity for pleasure and joy" (342). But the pill bottle does not read "WELCOME TO THE AUSTRALOPITHECINE SAVANNAH" or "WELCOME TO THE OLIGOCENE TREES" or "WELCOME TO THE TROGLODYTE CAVE" – whatever image we might seize in our evolutionary understanding of human beings' primal prehistory. It reads "WELCOME TO THE MONKEY HOUSE." These Monkey House pills do not restore natural sexuality. What they do is take people back to the monkey house, an enclosure within a zoo, a controlled environment, some would say a prison for animals.[18] Billy's libertinism is not a path to liberty. We do not know Nancy's next move, but clearly Billy has attempted to replace the existing system with the deeply flawed antique system of his forefathers. The inhumanity of compulsory birth-control pills is attacked not by a luminous liberator, but a pathetic fellow who would happily reinstate outworn patriarchal power. The return to the monkey house is a grim prognosis for humans, a damnation to our inherited, unpredictable, masturbatory, manipulative, power-brokering, and at times violent sexual urges as they play out in caged conditions. It also renders null and void Holmes's assumption that The Pill had brought an end to the "man's world" – Americans, it dreams, will suffer in pursuing happiness under monolithic reductions of sexuality for generations to come.

Independence myths

In 1972, Harlan Ellison published a new Vonnegut short story in *Again, Dangerous Visions*. Titled "The Big Space Fuck," Ellison introduces it with the understanding that Vonnegut might be ending his run as an artist of the form, saying, "to think that even a story as hilarious and incisive and deadly as this one is to be his last, is a sad-making thing" (229). It proved to be the last he wrote. If the stories we have unpacked unfurl the fragility of the egalitarian trinity of American independence, this one, brief as it is, sallies forth as if its plot wants to fall apart. Set in 1979, a future much nearer than most of the others Vonnegut created in his short fiction, two cultural shifts have taken place: twenty-one year olds can sue their parents for the way they were raised, and the nation has thrown itself into a space program initiative to shoot a rocket carrying 800 pounds of the freeze-dried "jizzum" of intelligent, athletic, or artistic Americans toward the Andromeda Galaxy. This latter event is called the Big Space Fuck. When the rocket, named the *Arthur C. Clarke*, passes through one of Andromeda's chronosynclastic infundibulae, or time warps, the ship will be multiplied a trillionfold, appearing everywhere in space and time, increasing chances that the seed will encounter fecundity and multiply. Never mind, of course, that freeze-dried sperm do not spring to life like Sea Monkeys, that no eggs are sent along, that the entire phallic act of shooting a rocket full of semen into space constitutes jingoistic onanism – Americans are behind this patriarchal idiocy with great enthusiasm.

As in "Bergeron," we meet a married couple watching television. As in "Monkey House," the local sheriff comes to the door with bad news. Reed has noted numerous intertextual links to Vonnegut's other fiction, mostly in recurring character names, and the effect, for one who consumes his body of work, is that of a series of shout-outs. He even borrows Flem Snopes from Faulkner, casting him as a Mississippi Senator and Chairman of the Senate Space Committee who wears a codpiece emblazoned with the Confederate flag. The bad news Dwayne and Grace Hoobler receive from the County Sheriff is that their daughter is suing them for her upbringing in a bid to get herself out of jail for leading a shoplifting ring. As the television broadcasts coverage of the Big Space Fuck launch, the Sheriff and the Hooblers are overcome with grief.

Where does Vonnegut take it from here? Visionary puppeteer Jim Henson had a rule for ending a skit that seems to be going nowhere: "It all ends in one of two ways: either someone gets eaten or something blows up." Early in the story, thirty-eight foot long "man-eating lampreys," as innocuously placed as Chekhov's rifle on the wall, are said to live nearby in the sewage of "what used to be Lake Erie" (230). Here is what happens: "[The Sheriff] left sobbing, and stumbled right into the mouth of a lamprey. The lamprey ate him immediately, but not before he screamed. Dwayne and Grace Hoobler rushed outside to see what the screaming was about, and the lamprey ate them, too" (234). As in "Big Trip," the television broadcasts to an empty room. The story is over before we know it. Each story in Ellison's collection bears an afterword written by its own author. Laconically cheeky, we might take Vonnegut's to be the epitaph to his entire career in writing short stories, merely repeating, as it does, the refrain following every instance of death in *Slaughterhouse-Five*: "And so it goes" (234).

Notes

1 We recall that Colonel Kelly's wife in "All the King's Horses," the white queen, is also named Margaret.
2 The International English Phonetic Alphabet would be standardized later, in 1955.
3 Regarding Donald Rumsfeld, in 2005 Vonnegut contributed the following noun to *The Future Dictionary of America*:

> rumsfeld *[ruhmz'-feld] n. one who can stomach casualties.*
>
> (117)

4 As introduced in Chapter 2.5 ARMAGEDDON IN RETROSPECT
5 The typesetter at *The Magazine of Fantasy and Science Fiction* goofed the final four lines of the right column on page 8: "lowed, 'crippled, hobbled, sick- | ened – I am a greater ruler than | any man who ever lived! Now | 'Even as I stand here,' he bel-". I corrected this above.
6 "Harrison Bergeron" predates psychoanalyst Rollo May's bestselling book *Love and Will* by about eight years (1969), though these characters seem to have, in their final moments, attained its revitalizing aims.
7 Another character named Diana Moon Glampers appears four years later in *God Bless You, Mr. Rosewater* (1965). In that iteration, she is an illiterate domestic servant for Senator Rosewater:

> [A] sixty-eight-year-old virgin who, by almost anybody's standards, was too dumb to live. Her name was Diana Moon Glampers. No one had ever loved her. There was no reason why anyone should. She was ugly, stupid, and boring. On the rare occasions when she had to introduce herself, she always said her full name, and followed that with the mystifying equation that had thrust her into life so pointlessly:
>
> "My mother was a Moon. My father was a Glampers."
>
> (*NS* 231)

This Diana Moon Glampers is portrayed as lonely, powerless, and suffering – an about-face from the character in "Harrison Bergeron." If we seek evidence of broad valence in archetypal figures, here it is.
8 *National Review* 16 Nov. 1965: 1020–1021, 1041.
Vonnegut's papers at the Lilly Library indicate he sold the reprint rights for $50 on 26 Dec. 1961, meaning *National Review* sat on the story for nearly four years before reprinting it (Box 13).
9 The same towering height as Harrison Bergeron.
10 See John W. Dixon, Jr.'s "Terror of Salvation: The Last Judgment." *Crucifixion Fine Art*, n.d. Web.
11 Happy Hooligan is one of many euphemisms for the Suicide Studios, "whose fanciful sobriquets included: 'Automat,' 'Birdland,' 'Cannery,' 'Catbox,' 'De-louser,' 'Easy-go,' 'Good-by, Mother,' 'Happy Hooligan,' 'Kiss-me-quick,' 'Lucky Pierre,' 'Sheepdip,' 'Waring Blender,' 'Weep-no-more' and 'Why Worry?'" (61).
12 This detail is repeated by the narrator of "Welcome to the Monkey House": "The people were virtually packed together like drupelets. | Drupelets are the pulpy little knobs that compose the outside of a raspberry" (95). This repetition may account for the exclusion of "2BR02B" from *Welcome to the Monkey House* (1968), remaining uncollected until *Bagombo Snuff Box* (1999).
13 A similar effect erupts from the master tape in David Foster Wallace's *Infinite Jest*, not to mention the lotus in *The Odyssey*'s land of the Lotus-eaters.

14 We also sense in this story's device, the euphio, more anxiety over the rising technology of television, mentioned earlier in the discussion of "Harrison Bergeron." NBC Hollywood contacted Vonnegut about "The Euphio Question" in November 1963 to say Rod Serling wanted to write a script from it (*Letters* 93), likely for his TV show *The Twilight Zone* (1959–1964). The episode never precipitated.

15 Bradbury wrote a story called "Tomorrow and Tomorrow" in 1943, but any link to *Macbeth* seems tenuous.

16 As Billy Pilgrim will be when transported to the planet Tralfamadore in *Slaughterhouse-Five.*

17 In the same issue's "Little Annie Fanny" comic, Annie enters the office of Dr. Masters (of sexologists Masters and Johnson fame), where she passes a book titled *Ethel Kennedy and The Pill* (269). Ethel was Robert Kennedy's wife and, as a Catholic, might be assumed to have opposed contraception, although in 1965 she sat in the Supreme Court gallery to hear arguments in *Connecticut vs. Griswold*, which ruled in favor of privacy with contraceptive use, suggesting a complicated position on the issue. The visual gags in "Little Annie Fanny," despite Elder's brilliance, can fall flat and all too often make little sense. In any case, we see another Kennedy woman teased in the same magazine.

18 Which, of course, is where Billy Pilgrim ends up, en-zooed on planet Tralfamadore, in *Slaughterhouse-Five.*

Part II

Ray Bradbury

A polychromatic Pollyanna

Figure 4.1 "Ray," reproduced with permission from the artist. (© 2014 Kevin Storrar)

Chapter 4

Dynamic domesticities

Bradbury splits the nuclear family

"If you have a family to bring up," Joseph Campbell said, "you're concerned for the family" (POM 14). Food, clothing, and a roof overhead are all crucial to the rearing of children but so are the stories we tell them—and about them:

> These are all very important concerns, but they have to do with physical conditions, mostly. But how are you going to communicate spiritual consciousness to the children if you don't have it yourself? How do you get that? What the myhs are for is to bring us into a level of consciousness that is spiritual.
>
> (*POM* 14)

After the Great Depression, Ray Bradbury was rejected for military service in WWII (poor eyesight) and soon found himself happily married with children, a professional writer riding the current of postwar prosperity, participating in the Baby Boom proliferation of the mythologically labeled nuclear family. We ought not to think of a monolithic American Family – for such a conception reduces an archetype, which exists in valence, to a dogma – but rather of American families. The following stories analyzed depict white middle class American families in ways that defy a reductive understanding of them as representative of all white middle class American families. The cookie cutter shape of the patriarchal narrative will not render these characters flat on Betty Crocker's baking tray. Bradbury's gift is humanizing and individualizing characters the statisticians happily lump together demographically. Our role is in exploring how these families relate to, represent, buck, and toe our inherited and all-too-often easy conceptions of mainstream American families between WWII and the Kennedy assassination. Bradbury wrote endlessly of families; they appear in nearly everything he produced, but space and focus call for a shrewd selection of his stories depicting families, from origin to dissolution.

Father death

Heinrich Zimmer maintains, "Birth and death and rebirth in unending cycle is the permanent character of the process of life" (85), and that we find in "The Scythe," first published in *Weird Tales* (July 1943). In analyzing

Bradbury's treatment of American families in short fiction, this one's setting historically bridges the Great Depression and WWII. Though he went on to revise it a number of times,[1] our focus rests on its initial publication. Fred Humiston's title page illustration draws from Grim Reaper imagery dating at least to the fifteenth century and recognizable through the West: Death personified, carrying a scythe with which it harvests life. In Humiston's drawing, an ordinary man, looking a lot like Al Capp's comic strip hillbilly Li'l Abner, wields the scythe, spooked by outreaching, hooded wraiths. These spectres do not appear in the tale, but the disembodied head sitting atop the handle is likely the scythe's previous user, the farmer found dead in his house at the beginning of the story. A skull on already-mown ground shows what is about to happen to six figures in the wheat. The field stretches on with dark hills and dark sky above, a huge moon or sun either rising or setting – an ambiguous and disorienting detail thanks to the simplicity of the art. The drawing, the title, the hook – "*Can you oppose the forces that see that people die just when they are supposed to die – not too soon, not too late?*" (46) – confront the reader up front with death.

"When Bradbury had trouble starting his idea for this story," write Eller and Touponce, "the more experienced [Leigh] Brackett wrote the first five or six hundred words" (*Ray Bradbury: The Life of Fiction* 73). Brackett, who went from pulp writing to sharing screenwriting credit with William Faulkner and Jules Furthman for *The Big Sleep* (1946), was Bradbury's most significant mentor, criticizing his juvenilia until his work sold. Her contribution to this story, essentially beginning it for him, is acknowledged. In this version, the year is 1939, the season is spring, and the Kansas farmer traveling west with his family is Tom Joerg. Tom as a diminutive of Thomas, the doubting apostle, is also the Greek form of an Aramaic name meaning "twin," fitting for a man who inherits a role twinning him to the farmer he finds dead in his farmhouse. Tom Joerg also evokes Tom Joad, Steinbeck's protagonist in *The Grapes of Wrath* (1939), who travels west to California with his family in search of a better life; this naming was Brackett's and may explain why in future versions, from the collection *Dark Carnival* (1947) onward, Bradbury names him Drew Erickson, making him his own. Joerg also looks to be an Americanized Jörg, a German form of George, meaning "farmer" or "earthworker" (*BTN*). Aptly named, we meet the "twin farmer" just as the family car runs out of gas and into a metaphysical realm – or *field* – where "Quite suddenly there was no more road" (46). The road comes to its ambiguous end beside a house "that belonged to the wheat field" (47).

The road, the path, the way that has led this family into the valley is an agent of inevitability, drawing them into the undefined and expansive frontier. A mention of the hoped-for destination of California and mountains would put this location somewhere from Colorado to Nevada, though a precise place is never given because this valley, with its possessive wheat field (the house "belonged" to it), is the supernatural Land of No Return.

Can you oppose the forces that see that people die just when they are supposed to die—not too soon, not too late?

The Scythe

By RAY BRADBURY

QUITE suddenly there was no more road. It ran down the valley like any other road, between slopes of barren stony ground and live oak trees, and then past a broad field of wheat standing alone in the wilderness. It came up beside

46

Figure 4.2 Title page of "The Scythe" with Fred Humiston's illustration. (© *Weird Tales*, 1943)

It exists beyond the physical frontier so prominent in American consciousness, where it is believed that strength, courage, and ingenuity can conquer all. This is the mortal frontier, feared by most of us because all who live will enter it and be conquered by death. A most ideologically un-American place: the fact that this family follows a road that could only take them to the Valley of Death, suggesting predestination, is disquieting to American belief in Opportunity. Perhaps this is because one of the only universals is the guarantee that everybody dies.

In the house, Joerg finds an old man dead in a bed, wearing a suit for the grave. Against the wall is propped an old fashioned scythe and in the dead man's hands a single stalk of fresh wheat: "A ripe blade, golden and heavy in the tassel" (47). A note on the pillow, dated April 3, 1939, introduces the corpse as John Buhr, "*only the giver, not the ordainer*" (47–8), and bequeaths the farm in antiquated language to whichever man finds his body. He signs it with a postscript of "*Kyrie eleison*!" (48), Ancient Greek for "Lord have mercy," an acclamation kept alive in Christian worship even though the phrase antedates it: "It was used in various forms of pagan worship including the imperial cult in which the emperor was called *kyrios* (lord)" ("Definitions"). Why April third in 1939? On that day Adolf Hitler ordered his military to prepare for Fall Weiss, the strategic plan to invade Poland, which later figures in the story's climax.

Joerg takes to the scythe and the mysterious wheat field because of Depression-Era American stresses. As a farmer fleeing the droughted Midwest for hope of work on the west coast, a move Bradbury's own family made in the thirties, Joerg is urged by his wife to work the field even though he senses it may be too good to be true. His initial doubts, which become enduring anxieties, are a credit to his intuition: "How it was too big for one man to tend, and yet one man had tended it. How it ripened only in separate clusters, each set off far from others. And, most important how when he cut the wheat it rotted within a few hours, and the next day dug in and come up with roots with green sprouts, born again" (48). But Joerg works on and the verb we anticipate arises: "reaping" (48). The scythe, "[gleaming] like a half moon," is "scratched" with words, expanding its numinosity: "*Who wields me – wields the world*" (48).

The tool is a step back for Joerg, who, like the half moon, is halfway through life. In the twenties and thirties, mechanized wheat farming using binders and combines was practiced; as far back as the mid-nineteenth century, the scythe and cradle were replaced with a horse-drawn machine tantalizingly called a grain reaper. To take so readily to a long outmoded method of harvest speaks to Joerg's desperation to feed his family and the power this valley has of stripping all notions of advancement from a human being, reorienting him to the primordial conditions of life and death. Zimmer, in his analysis of the fourteenth-century poem *Sir Gawain and the Green Knight*, identifies the Green Knight as personified death and comments upon his weapon of choice, an archaic axe: "Death, caring absolutely nothing about progress and the developments of human invention, remains unalterable, and, despite everything man can do to change him, sticks to his tradition" (85). This is the motif at work in the inherited scythe.

The responsibility Joerg now wields is that of ending human lives around the world through the abstraction of cutting wheat, unwittingly making him the Grim Reaper. He begins hearing pleading voices in the grain, and the sun, when he neglects the threshing, hounds him from within to fulfill his task of maintaining the cycle of death. Dying has been heaped with any number of death-vanquishing traditions and beliefs, from spiritual immortality to reincarnation to simple acceptance. No matter one's grounding, death is not a moralist. Death is and was and will be. Joerg's dilemma then is that of the individual's conscience in relation to his inadvertent role in this unending cycle. The consequences strike with horror when he realizes he has committed matricide: "I just killed my mother! [. . .] I did it by cutting down the stalk of wheat that was her! I killed her. I felt her dying" (50). His devout wife, Molly, will not let them leave the farm, insisting upon living there. And so life joins hands with death.

With no empirical way of historicizing the field, Joerg turns to his own imagination: "The valley seemed ancient, mummified, secretive, dried and bent and powerful. When the Indians danced on the prairie it had been here. The same sky, the same wind, the same wheat. And before the Indians? Some Cro-Magnon, gnarled and shag-haired, wielding a crude wooden scythe, perhaps, prowling down through the living wheat . . ." (51).[2] Joerg is limited by his own frame of reference, which, if held to literal scrutiny, fails to provide an acceptable explanation of the field's history. In taking the field as an enduring geographical feature of the American West, he passes the baton of its tending back to the Indians, that generic amalgamating construct pinned over the diverse peoples indigenous to North America. He takes it one step further though, bestowing the agricultural tradition on Cro-Magnon, a distinctly European prehistoric modern human, today believed to have first existed some 43,000 years ago. Current scientific data about human presence in the Americas place people there around 14,000 years ago. Bradbury and, more importantly, his character Joerg were not privy to facts as assembled today.

This is a field of supernormal experience, which a literal, historicizing interpretation cannot support. And yet the impulse behind the archetypal images Joerg's imagination brings forth is correct: the ceaselessness of living and dying and rebirth is ancestral to all living things. Reframed, his notions stretch back in an attempt to narrativize the dawning of our awareness of personal implication in the perpetual cycle. A child of patriarchy, he imagines it being a "man's job"; a westward-headed American a generation or two on from the Indian Wars, he imagines Death's responsibility as having passed to his culture from the romanticized and mistakenly vanished Indians.

Immortality presents itself as a possibility when Joerg realizes he could spare the stalks that are him and his family: "Trembling, he knelt down and looked at the three strands of life. The energy of them struck at him" (51). He is struck by a sense of unfairness, of the absurdity of the family's suffering leading to this moment. His duty in his new role is to cut down his wife and two children, but he cannot do it. Grabbing the scythe, he retreats to the house. Over a supper of pork, white bread, and milk, Molly urges Joerg to consult with the Agricultural Bureau about entirely plowing the field. When he asks if she believes him about the scythe's power, she shuts him down. Made to feel more alone in his duty, he harvests after dinner, cutting down six of his "old, loved friends" (52). Ashamed, he locks the scythe in the cellar but later finds himself back in the field at midnight, unconscious of having returned, out of control, compelled to be there again with the scythe.

An explosion at the house interrupts his work and running back he finds it ablaze, his wife and children inside. When the flames settle, Molly and the kids sleep in the smoldering ashes of their beds, their flesh "perfectly intact" (53). Or so it seems at first. All three sleep in a coma: "She wasn't dead. She wasn't alive" (54). Joerg discerns this unconscious nullification of their lives has occurred because of his refusal to cut their stalks: "They *should* have died in the fire. That's the way Fate wrote it" (54). As it is, they have no purpose and are suspended, "Simply – waiting" (54). Driven by an awful mercy, Joerg goes to the field and cuts his family down. We see this motif, of death violently befalling an American family, in works published later in this same era: Steinbeck's *East of Eden* (1952) has Cathy Ames killing her parents in a house fire, O'Connor's "A Good Man is Hard to Find" (1953) shows a family gunned down on their drive to Florida, *The Bad Seed* (1954) by William March presents Christine, who tries to poison Rhoda, her murdering daughter, before shooting herself dead. Familicide is the antithesis of family values, upsetting the narrative of family as a stabilizing unit of civilization. And yet headlines then and now tell us so often that people are often murdered by family members.

Hereafter Joerg is consumed by the office he holds, slaying the wheat "with a fierce unrelenting insanity of vengeance against Fate in every muscle" (54). With each swing of the blade "singing and whistling" in the sun (55), an international catastrophe occurs: Hitler invades Austria, Czechoslovakia, Poland, and bombs fall on London and Moscow. "And the blade went on rising, crashing, scarring with the hot fury of a man who has fought and lost his loved ones and does not know or care what he does to the world" (55). His scything is not the cause of geopolitical catastrophe any more than his earlier refusal to scythe was the cause of the fire that should have killed his family; Joerg merely acts to maintain the cosmic system of death determined by Fate. By this reckoning, individual lives are scheduled to die thanks to an algorithm calculated beyond human understanding, bucking the concept of free will in favor of predestination. Hillman argues that "fate causes only events that are unusual, that oddly don't fit in. Not each and every thing is laid out in a superior divine plan. That sort of comprehensive explanation is fatal*ism*, which makes for paranoia, occultist Ouija board prognostics, and passive-aggressive behavior combining meek submission to fate with bitter anger against it" (193). Fate in "The Scythe" is fatalism and both Joerg and the story succumb to it.

Post-Jungian psychology proposes that the individual experiences the life of the collective within. If we approach the story in this way, "The Scythe" renders itself as a fever dream of American anxieties born out of the U.S.A.'s rise as an intervening power on the world stage. Like Joerg, who resists the job he has wandered into, the nation avoided military involvement in WWII for three years. Published in the middle of the war, a time of intense nationalism, doubting the burden of responsibility was anathema. Fatalism is a surrendering to this burden, the assumption being that because of warring events beyond American borders, the U.S.A. had no choice but to unleash itself. Hillman explains this in an American context: "Fatalism is the seductive other side to the heroic ego, which shoulders so much in a do-it-yourself, winner-take-all civilization. The bigger the load, the more you want to put it down or pass it off to a larger, stronger carrier, like Fate" (*SC* 192).

The story ends not on a decisive note but a slow fade, shifting to present tense, explaining that Joerg continues to reap the unripe wheat, not even pausing to give directions to California-bound motorists, no end to his fury in sight. In 1943 no one could guess how much longer the war would last, but most Americans accepted the idea that it had to continue until it was done. That attitude is present in "The Scythe," as is the anxiety that in surprising the world by becoming a superpower, the U.S.A. would inevitably cause unseen and far-reaching death the world over. The price of America's full-scale international military intervention is blood on the hands of those family men astute enough to conceive of ramification – while those who can't, the jalopy drivers pulling over to ask for directions, continued to head west.

Be my baby

"A third element has come in. Before, it was just you and me. We protected each other, and now we protect the baby, but get no protection from it. Do you understand?" (69). So confides new mother Alice Leiber to her husband David in "The Small Assassin," one of Bradbury's most anthologized stories. Eller contextualizes the tale, which first appeared in pulp digest *Dime Mystery* (Nov. 1946): "'The Small Assassin' emerged from Bradbury's abiding conviction that he retains neonatal memories, including recollections of the birth trauma itself. His extrapolation was pure fantasy, but horrifyingly simple: can this trauma, as psychologists such as Melanie Klein have argued, manifest as infant hatred toward the parents? And is such a child capable of using the nursery environment to kill?" (*CSRB* 463). Though Bradbury and his wife would become parents to four daughters, this story was published the year before they wed and three years before the birth of their first child. It was not written under the duress of early parenthood, though that situation's stresses are the story's basis. And while Bradbury remembered his birth, or at least claimed to, this story is situated from the parents' and Dr. Jeffers's points of view, not the baby's.

Infants transform people into parents and the psychological shift required for their care is profound. The arrival of a child is the creation of family, an archetypal unit of human relations that has a vast array of configurations determined by innumerable factors in America, let alone the history of the world. The mid-century notion of the nuclear family – of a mother and a father and two and a half children – is a cliché we collectively project onto postwar American culture. Families (and cultures) of many kinds existed then, as they do today, as they always have. Yet certain master narratives, such as that of the unconditionally loving mother, persist. As "The Small Assassin" begins, Alice is giving birth in the care of doctors and nurses, but she is convinced she is being murdered. Her amorphous dread was foreshadowed the previous month by "things as deep as sea tides in her" (66), what depth psychology recognizes as fluctuations in the unconscious. When her child is born, a boy, she wants nothing to do with him because she identifies him as the entity that wants to kill her. The same year this story appeared, Dr. Benjamin Spock's bestseller *The Common Sense Book of Baby and Child Care* was published and sold over 500,000 copies. Its opening sentences prove a bit dire for Alice Leiber's situation: "Trust yourself. You know more than you think you do" (1).

A mother's inability to connect with her infant was and remains taboo, high treason against the patriarchal American understanding of motherhood. Today there is recognition of postpartum depression in the mainstream, but Bradbury's Dr. Jeffers expresses a sense of it himself, taking David aside and telling the new father, "It's been a hard thing for her. The whole thing. She'll need a lot of love in this next year" (68). His prescription for tenderness is accompanied with instructions that the trio come back if "things don't get along" (68). Calling mother-infant bonding a "scientific fiction," psychologist Diane E. Eyer "would like to urge the impossible – that we discard the word [bonding] entirely [. . . which] would force us to notice that children are not merely putty in our hands. They are born with vastly different personalities and capabilities" (2, 199). Hillman draws comparison between her assertion and his own regarding what he calls "parental fallacy," which holds that "the primary instrument of our fate is the behavior of your mother and father" (*SC* 63) while reducing the individual to "a mere effect myself, a result of their causes" (*SC* 77). Such a narrative denies the myriad influences, forces, accidents, serendipities, fates, myths, and incalculable factors beyond parental control that affect how our individual lives unfold in time and stand at any given moment. Alice's fearful intuition, butting heads with David's expectations that she exhibit innate attentiveness to the baby, honors the infant's unknowable potential. She tells him, "a baby is so new, so amoral, so free of conscience" (69). He is undeniably their own offspring, but he is also, already, a distinct individual and there is no telling how his calling will coalesce.

The illustrated spread by an uncredited artist shows in comic book pen and ink two images. The panel over the title and bleeding onto the next page shows Alice dead at the base of the stairs, the patchwork doll placed so she would slip and fall. This depicts the scene David returns to at the end of chapter two, the editor at *Dime Mystery* having split the tale into three chapters. The other drawing shows David and Alice cowering under a towering baby, big as the Incredible Hulk.[3] He wears a diaper like a sumo wrestler's *mawashi* and capes a blanket over one shoulder, his stance imperious. Something in the lower right corner, a lampshade or scribbled-over coloring book – hard to tell what – bears a crude drawing of Disney's iconic hothead, Donald Duck, and David seems about to fall backward on a rubber

THE SMALL ASSASSIN

By RAY BRADBURY

CHAPTER ONE

The Third Element

JUST when the idea occurred to her that she was being murdered she could not tell. There had been little subtle signs, little suspicions for the past month; things as deep as sea tides in her, like looking at a perfectly calm stretch of cerulean water and liking it and wanting to bathe in it, and finding, just as the tide takes your body into it, that monsters dwell just under the surface, things unseen, bloated, many-armed, sharp-finned, malignant and inescapable.

A room floated around her in an effluvium of hysteria. Sharp instruments hovered and there were voices and people in severe sterile white masks.

My name, she thought. My name, what is it?

Alice Leiber. It came to her. David Leiber's wife. But it gave her no comfort. She was alone with these silent whispering white people and there was great pain and nausea and death-fear in her.

I am being murdered before their eyes. These doctors, these nurses don't realize what hidden thing has happened to me. David doesn't know. Nobody knows except me and—

Here is a story, so unusual and yet so compelling in its strange power, that, like it or not, we guarantee that you will experience the arctic chilling tingle along the spine which comes only once in a red moon, when reading a classic of eerie, sinister mystery fiction. . . . WARNING: If you suffer from a weak heart—don't *read this story!*

"I'm going to have him christened next Sunday. Know what name I'm giving him? I'm going to call him—Lucifer!"

66

Figure 4.3 Uncredited illustrated spread for "The Small Assassin." (Interior images from *Dime Mystery* courtesy of Steeger Properties, LLC. Copyright © 2015 Steeger Properties, LLC. All rights reserved.)

ducky. At no point in Bradbury's story does the baby grow like Gargantua; this is artistic license, a stylization of the parents' despair under their baby's sinister nature. *L'enfant terrible* is not only unconventional and iconoclastic; in this instance he actually is terrible, successfully outwitting and murdering his parents.

After failing to kill David with the patchwork doll on the stairs, the baby succeeds in dropping the mother down them with the same trap. Later, when David expresses his desire to kill the baby, finally believing his wife's worries, Dr. Jeffers sedates him with sleeping pills. The baby presumably takes his father's incapacitation as an opportunity and releases a gas jet at floor level, poisoning him dead as he sleeps. The baby also, we might say, murdered their married-life home of two by being born to begin with. In any case, the story ends with Dr. Jeffers discovering David's corpse and becoming convinced of the infant's parricidal feats. In a sensational and desperate act, the doctor announces, "I had to operate to bring you into this world. Now I guess I can operate to take you out of it . . ." (75). He draws the baby's attention with something shiny; the final paragraph is a grim two-word sentence: "A scalpel" (75).

It is a stock pulp ending, leaving the reader hanging with his or her own uncomfortable freedom to imagine what happens next. Like the adult characters, we have been restricted to the realm of adult consciousness in this story, which further divides us from the baby's inner life. At no point are we privileged with seeing the baby creeping around, setting up the murders. We are left to wonder. The condition of wondering what goes on inside others ought to be familiar to us in our encounters with anybody and everybody, though we often take people's presented selves for granted. But there is something special about babies that makes us want to know who they are within their small bodies, as new parents and people entrusted with their care will attest.

Between the deaths of the mother and father, David and Dr. Jeffers enter into a brief Socratic dialogue, speculating upon the nature of babies and their effects on parents. Bradbury runs free, unspooling raw questions, inquiries anathema to standards of the mainstream that could never be comfortably answered. David's suspicions of the baby he wants to name Lucifer take him to the unknowable, though once experienced and since forgotten, recesses of infant consciousness:

> "How many [mothers] have suckled strange little improbabilities who cause death in one way or another? Strange, red little creatures with brains that function in a scarlet darkness we can't even guess at. Elemental little brains, aswarm with racial memory and hatred and raw cruelty, with no more thought than self-preservation. [. . .] I ask you, doctor, what is there in the world more selfish than a baby? Nothing!"
>
> (74)

When Jeffers challenges him to name the baby's motive, a cornerstone of the mystery genre – this story, remember, is published in *Dime Mystery* – David falls back on notions of infant separation anxiety:

> "What is more at peace, more dreamfully happy, content, at ease, at rest, fed, comforted, unbothered than an unborn child? Nothing. It floats in a sleepy dark effluvium of timeless wonder and warm nourishment and silence. All is an enclosed dream. Then, suddenly, it is asked to give up its berth, is forced to vacate, propelled out into a noisy, uncaring, selfish, swift and merciless world where it is asked to shift for itself, to hunt, to feed from the hunting, to seek after a vanishing love that once was its unquestioned right, to meet confusion instead of inner silence and conservative slumber! And the newborn resents it! Resents it with all the soft, small fibres of its miniature body."
>
> (74)

David supposes that the family is a self-contained unit sitting apart from the greater world, not amid it. Existence is reduced to relationships among three individuals bound by reproduction without space for outside influences. Though thinking of himself as bucking "a thousand years of accepted medical belief" (74), David manages to project a heavy load of gendered parenting ideology onto the baby. If the baby in this story is a murderer, he is also a victim of the assumptions postwar white American parents made – and continue to make – about babies' fears, comforts, loyalties, grudges, and resentments. Hillman mentions that psychologist Mary Watkins has observed how the twentieth-century psychological theorists who stressed "the mother-child relation as *the* determinant of life ever after worked out their ideas while bombs were falling and buildings burning in England, or just before and just after World War II" (*SC* 79).[4] That is, they essentialized the mother-infant bond at the expense of acknowledging the developmental effects of the geopolitical turmoil surrounding them. "The Small Assassin" defies the mainstream narrative of an innate loving connection between every mother and baby. It takes us to the uncomfortable reality that all relationships are complex and babies, with all of their unknowable capacities, can arrive accompanied by profound fears.

Bradbury offers another inflection of fear in "The Shape of Things," which would be titled "Tomorrow's Child" after its initial publication in *Thrilling Wonder Stories* (Feb. 1948). First drafted in 1943, again we have a story expressing anxieties surrounding childbirth and infant care written by a man in the years preceding his induction into fatherhood. Perhaps it is inappropriate to make such a point; returning to parental fallacy, parenting belongs not only to two human beings who create a child together. As Hillman puts it: "We are parented by everything around us – if 'parenting' means watching, instructing, encouraging, and admonishing" (*SC* 86). If we are involved in life and happenings, we are also, by that logic, called upon to parent. In "The Shape of Things," Peter and Polly Ann Horn find themselves called upon to raise their small, newborn *pyramid*: "The blue pyramid had six blue snakelike appendages, and three eyes that blinked from the tips of projecting structures" (48).

Set in the then-far-off year of 1969, where people travel by 'copter or beetle (these characters fly "'copters" the way postwar Americans drove cars) and faith in technology is high, the Horns' inauguration to the shared office of parenthood is sullied by a glitch in new birthing gadgetry at a place called the Institute. As Dr. Wolcott explains, "'There was a dimensional distructure caused by the simultaneous short-circuitings and malfunctionings of the new birth-mechs and the hypnosis machines. Well, anyway,' the doctor ended lamely, 'your baby was born into – another dimension'" (48). As a result, their newborn appears as it would in that dimension – fourth, fifth, or sixth, the doctors aren't sure – while it is simultaneously stranded in that dimension in human form. Py – his temporary name, as shortened from pyramid and evocative of π, the mathematical ratio of a circle's circumference to its diameter – is so alien in shape that his sex is indeterminable, leaving them only to guess that he is a boy. As plot devices go, the interdimensional birthing gizmo calls for a significant suspension of disbelief from the reader. It is utterly absurd, even for those of us who are not theoretical physicists and/or don't know anything about birthing babies, for a machine used in delivering a child to send him to another dimension – let alone how a woman could birth a pyramid. But Bradbury's strength is his way of humanizing supernormal happenings. Pete and Polly undergo understandable pain and challenges in caring for their baby. The uncredited illustration on the title page shows the new family 'coptering home, Py rather hard to make out in Polly's arms. Pete's face, under flight goggles on his forehead, expresses perplexity; Polly's, hope.

The story opens with Pete's disbelief: "He did not want to be the father of a small blue pyramid. Peter Horn hadn't planned it that way at all. Neither he nor his wife imagined that such a thing could happen to them" (47). The shock of unforeseen complications takes the new parents on a difficult path of anger and shame. It is worth considering the Latin origin of "complications," that plural word we use for medicine's unanticipated, unwanted and threatening outcomes: *complicare* means "to fold together" (*OED*), and as we shall see the child's state will eventually fold the family together like polygonal origami. When told before his wife that the pyramid is their son, Pete thinks a friend must be playing an April Fool's prank: "That's not human! That's a crime against God!" (48). Yet when given the option for the doctors to raise him at the Institute (evoking institutionalization), he says, "He still belongs to me and Polly. I'll raise him. I'll give him a home. Raise him like I'd raise any kid. Give him a normal home life. Try to learn to love him" (49).

The Shape of Things

By RAY BRADBURY

Neither Peter Horn nor his wife ever expected that their child would be a small blue pyramid of another dimension!

HE DID not want to be the father of a small blue pyramid. Peter Horn hadn't planned it that way at all. Neither he nor his wife imagined that such a thing could happen to them. They had talked quietly for days about the birth of their coming child, they had eaten normal foods, slept a great deal, taken in a few shows, and, when it was time for her to fly in the helicopter to the hospital, her husband, Peter Horn, laughed and kissed her.

"Honey, you'll be home in six hours," he said. "These new birth-mechanisms do everything but father the child for you."

She remembered an old-time song. "No, no, they can't take *that* away from me!" and sang it, and they laughed as the helicopter lifted them over the green way from country to city.

The doctor, a quiet gentleman named Wol-

47

Figure 4.4 Vincent Napoli's illustration on the title page for "The Shape of Things." (© Standard Magazines, Inc., 1948)

Breaking the news to Polly, her concerns inspire the worry that she is somehow to blame for what has happened. She asks the doctor if she made the baby the way it is, if its genes have made it monstrous, and when the doctor assures her it is healthy despite being in another continuum, she asks to see him. We are told, with the emphasis of inverted commas, "They brought the 'child'" (50). The scientistic marriage of monstrosity with "faulty" genetics occurs to her as an explanation. Syndromes certainly have genetic components but monstrosity is defined by any number of factors that fall outside the borders of objectivity. Leveling "bad" genes or the idea of an "unfortunate" combination of chromosomes at a condition is a persistent twentieth-century superstition that persists. When it comes to scapegoating birth defects and disabilities, the sins of the father myth has been replaced by the myth of deficiencies in that father's DNA, which, tapping back into the old cycle, may have been impaired through the sins of father's hard living.

Parents hope their unborn babies will arrive in good health: "perfectly normal." The mysteries of embryology and gestation astound us despite medical advances and pre-natal screening – no babies to date, to my knowledge, have accidentally been zapped to another dimension during a sonogram. And conception itself, though witnessed and recorded using an array of technologies, can only be *seen*, as Hillman notes:

> What goes on in that massive, virginly intact, single, round ovum that allows only this particular miniscule sperm among millions to enter? Or is the question more correctly addressed to the sperm? Is one of you more wily, more pushy, and more sympathetically congenial? Or is it just the randomness of "luck" – and what is luck, really? We know about DNA and the results of joinings, but we are left with the mystery that Darwin spent a life with, the mystery of selection.
>
> (*SC* 64)

Polly's insecurities come marinated in a value-basted understanding of genetics, but there may be another explanation for her worry of culpability: Is she an alcoholic? As the demands of caring for Py persist, she develops a drinking problem. Were she already prone to drinking before the birth, Polly may legitimately fear having insulted the fetus. Context is limited without description of the pregnancy, so we can only speculate. However, if she *were* drinking while pregnant, the doctor has made no such diagnosis, assuring her the baby is otherwise "perfectly normal." That is, it is only freakish in its appearance.

"The Shape of Things" can be read as a meditation on the plight of parents raising from birth a child whose needs go beyond the conventional. It measures their struggles and successes with compassion, challenging readers to empathize. From the 'copter ride home, after the doctors promise to find a way to reverse the effects, Polly expresses suicidal despair. She says she will hold herself together for six months, "And then I'll kill myself. [. . . If] the doctor can't help us, then a mind can't take it, a mind can only tell the body to climb out on a roof and jump" (50). Sent home with Bluebeard instructions that Py must not be seen by anyone, one of the culprits against her confidence in the task ahead is society. The quotation marks around *child* when Py is brought to her signal the intrusion of a master narrative. These invasive quotes occur again later – "Polly was walking the 'child' in the yard" (52) – when the neighbors first lay eyes on the pyramidal baby and assume it's an exotic pet acquired abroad. "He looks dangerous, but he's not," an inebriated Polly explains, "He's friendly as a baby. My husband brought him from Afghanistan the other day. Has anybody got a drink?" (53).

When Pete shoos off the neighbors, sarcasm and intoxication cannot hide the depth of her care: "Don't you want to see my baby? *Don't* you? Yes, he's my *child*, my very *own*! Isn't he simply beautiful!" (53). Pete responds by slapping her until she stops speaking, giving up so that he must carry her indoors. Pete's physical abuse comes from the hand of patriarchy, as well as frustration over the fact that men, who botched the birth, cannot fix the interdimensional "distructure," a word of Bradbury's coinage sounding a lot like "destruction." Pete has been struggling with the nearly yearlong ordeal as well, just not as obviously. And despite the dictated gender roles typical to mid-century white American families, when Polly begins drinking herself unconscious Pete takes over caring for the infant at night.

Meanwhile, Py seems to get along okay. Three sections briefly present Baby's point of view in the other dimension, where the environment is described as "a crystalline plateau" (49). Men appear as gray-white cubes and Polly as a white cube with three eyes: "There was something about this White Cube that Baby liked. There was an attraction. Some relation. There was an odor to the White Cube that reminded Baby of itself" (49). The baby emerges as the story's optimist, its great adapter. For while the adults lament his state of being, he only knows – and accepts – himself in this form, a most mythological form. The pyramid calls to mind some of the oldest examples of human architecture, both the towering structures at Giza and those hidden in the jungles of Central America. Theories behind their construction are diverse, sometimes fantastically attributed to supernatural forces, Atlantian technologies, aliens from outer space. No one can be utterly sure what they once meant to the cultures that built them; their mystery is left for us, along with connections to symbols in our own contemporary societies.

The pyramid has held day-to-day economic significance for Americans since 1935, when both sides of the Great Seal of the United States were first printed on the backside of the dollar bill. The seal's reverse depicts a truncated pyramid with the all-seeing Eye of Providence as the capstone. Scots-Irish-born Charles Thomson, who became one of the U.S.A.'s founding fathers and designed the Great Seal with help from William Barton, explained the reverse design to Congress in 1782: "The pyramid signifies

Strength and Duration: The Eye over it & the Motto allude to the many signal interpositions of providence in favour of the American cause. The date underneath is that of the Declaration of Independence and the words under it signify the beginning of the new American Æra, which commences from that date" ("Explanation of the Great Seal's Symbolism").[5] The perspective on children held by Zimmer, who Campbell joked would unpeel the symbolism of French onion soup when out to dinner, might season our sense of Py's shape and how it reflects his character: "The child is the self reborn in pristine perfection, the perfect being that we ought to be, that we are striving to become, and that we hoped to become, so to say, when we entered our present body. It is the symbol of the entelechy, or secret model, of our destinations" (180). Pyramidal Baby is a mysterious embodiment of providence, a force the adult characters have shrugged off.

Speaking to Herman Harvey in 1962, Bradbury expressed belief in the healing function of art: "I would like to say to the creative people – especially to writers; this is my field after all: 'You are in the same profession as the doctors of the world.' [. . . The] writers come along, and help to cure the minds. They are working in the same field as with psychologists and psychiatrists" (Aggelis 9). He viewed the office as sacred, casting the writer as doctor, witchdoctor, medicine man, shaman. With this sanctifying appraisal, he stressed the responsibility of offering readers a way of expelling the anxieties a story evokes:

> It is up to the artist, then, to look into that tension and see if he can relieve it, not by playing the Pollyanna, not by giving happy endings, but by making sure that the sickness is a whole, and that the sickness finally results in a cleansing by being really sick.
>
> (Aggelis 11)

"The Shape of Things" is a story that relieves its tension, in which a family eventually finds an imperfect but psychologically balanced compromise with the fate unanticipated events have rendered. Eller notes that the story's first draft did not end gently: "In his initial version, Bradbury had chosen psychological trauma so severe that the child was driven insane" (Textual Apparatus, *Collected Stories: Vol. II* 349). That version was rejected by several editors.

The solution, both for Pete, Polly, and Py *and* for the story's publication, sees the parents transported into the same dimension as their baby. Though the doctors are unable to reverse the effects, they can reproduce them. Once the parents agree to sacrifice their typical forms in our dimension and lead life as moving shapes, the family is united in the other continuum. What was first seen as a terrible deformity has been re-visioned, bringing forth an enriching transformation for all. In order to save their own life together, Peter and Polly buck the narrative that has trapped them into only seeing the culturally dictated monstrosity of their baby and, undergoing the same complications – or "folding together" – become origami figures of their own individual shapes, described through the eyes of Dr. Wolcott as "the White Oblong and the White slim Rectangle holding the Blue Pyramid" (55). On the other side, they finally see Py as the baby that he has been all along: "It was Peter Horn's son. A living, pink-faced, blue-eyed boy, lying in her arms, gasping and blinking and crying" (55). At last, for the Horns, union. As the old axiom goes: If you can't beat the dimensional distructures caused by the simultaneous short-circuitings and malfunctionings of the new birth-mechs and the hypnosis machines, join 'em.

But what about the children?

In "Bradbury on Children," Lahna Diskin applies Mr. Howard's prejudice in "Let's Play 'Poison'" (1946) to Bradbury's canon: "'You are another race entirely, your motives, your beliefs, your disobediences [. . .] You are not human. You are – children'" (543):

> In his fiction, children live and move in a dimension where they are generally exempt from the dilemmas that afflict their elders. Each sphere of activity – home, town, wilderness – has heightened or enhanced elements which, to them, give it a psychological credence that it does not possess for the adults with whom they share it.
>
> (49)

But the divide, at least for Mr. Howard, is more an unfortunate example of fates coinciding with his worst fear than an illustration of a sound theory. Mr. Howard, a teacher, has come to his pedophobic conclusion after profound trauma: sixteen of his students defenestrate a boy to his death and go unpunished when deemed too young, at eight and nine, to have understood what they were doing. His inevitable breakdown sends him out of the classroom and to a new city, where, of course, one day, as a favor to a friend, he is put in the unenviable position of substitute teaching. Taking out his stagnant grief on a new group of kids, they pay it back by burying him alive and cementing him under a patch of sidewalk bearing his name. Diskin rightly points out, "His dread of children inspires dread in the children who know him" (49), which makes it extreme to adopt his discrimination, deeming them "another race entirely," in the service of understanding Bradbury's fictional children. In his short stories, they enjoy a broad range of significances, only sometimes behaving as ruthlessly as Golding's do in *Lord of the Flies*. Especially in relation to postwar American families, these characters don't fit neatly into Othering generalities and are best taken case by case.

And yet "The World the Children Made" is another take on the wicked capacities of children, especially in relation to new technologies in the home. Collected after its first publication in *The Saturday Evening Post* (23 Sep.

1950) as "The Veldt," Diskin files it under "the theme of the insidious struggle for total power and control that children wage behind the façade of innocence" (46). Peter and Wendy, their names pointing directly at characters in J. M. Barrie's *Peter Pan*, never even have to leave home to find Neverland; it and any other environment they wish to conjure is right there in the home, thanks to the state-of-the-art nursery. Set in a technologically convenient future, the Hadleys' Happylife Home is as automated as the home that continues to function after nuclear war in Bradbury's "There Will Come Soft Rains," published earlier the same year in both *Collier's* (6 May) and *The Martian Chronicles*.

But whereas that story picks up after human life is blasted away, this focuses on a family at terrible odds with and within their own home. Imaginings of a house humming "with a soft automaticity" (26), a "shoe tier" (66), an "automatic scrub bath" (62), an "air closet" pneumatic flue that spirits family members to their "slumber rooms" (65) and beds that rock them to sleep – and the centerpiece nursery: "all dimensional superreactionary, supersensitive color film and mental-tape film behind glass screens [with] odorphonics and sonics" (26) – are printed alongside advertisements for the Universal Stroke-Sav-r: "America's Fastest Iron" (62) and the General Mills Automatic Toaster: "the only *double* automatic toaster you can buy" (68). This disparity reveals that those of us living in the second decade of the twenty-first century are daydreaming about the future from a vastly different technological baseline than middle class Americans were in 1950.

Al Parker's title page spread is one of the most exciting pieces of magazine art to accompany Bradbury's work. The turmeric yellow of the savannah highlighted with green foliage on distant trees and watery blue sky present Technicolor vibrancy for the landscape projected from the nursery's walls and floor. The male lion that will eat George Hadley, split vertically by the hinge gap, lurks in the grass on the backside of the door as he leans in. The house beyond is plainly white, sterile, brightly lit, devoid, and casting harsh light, enough to define shadows behind Peter and Wendy, while the world they have made teems, an idealized natural environment. They seem interrupted, Peter standing imperiously with hands on hips while Wendy is sprawled on the ground, spoon in hand, ready to get on with the tea party. Their backs to us, we can only guess at the expressions on their faces. They are also similarly and sparingly clothed, in orange: both wear knee boots but she has a skirt while he wears what look like boxer-briefs. Their shirtlessness is odd, particularly Wendy's, given that their wardrobes are otherwise gendered. Perhaps Parker is trying to "futurize" their clothing; Bradbury does not describe their costumes. George, in red t-shirt, is merely looking in on the kids, the sort of thing a parent does when their children are occupying themselves without want of attention. His position in relation to the lion is most telling, both facing us, both being the patriarch of family and pride respectively, both opposing each other with increased tension as the story progresses.

Figure 4.5 Al Parker's illustration for "The World the Children Made." (Illustration © SEPS licensed by Curtis Licensing Indianapolis, IN. All rights reserved.)

That lion is not so much a creation of the nursery as it is an intuitively compiled representation of the children's psyche. The room only projects what Peter and Wendy project upon it: "Remarkable how the nursery caught the telepathic emanations of the children's minds and created life to fill their every desire" (62). Were it a room of mirrors we would speak of reflection of their projection, but those walls work more like television screens: instead of matching a projection, which a mirror does, the room amplifies a projection. In Jungian terms, the room facilitates inflation: "an IDENTIFICATION with the collective psyche caused by an invasion of unconscious archetypal contents or as a result of extended consciousness. [. . . As Jung put it,] An archetypal content 'seizes hold of the PSYCHE with a kind of primeval force and compels it to transgress the bounds of humanity'" (*CDJA* 81, 82). The children's sense of themselves as "world" creators has overstepped the bounds of their reality.

George and Lydia become concerned after she notices that Africa has become the children's favorite nursery environment. Of course, it isn't Africa at all, but their conception of it. The distinction is lost on the Hadleys: "[The] walls began to purr and recede into crystalline distance,[6] it seemed, and presently an African veld appeared in three dimensions, on all sides, in color, reproduced to the final pebble and bit of straw" (26). Heat and smells accompany the visual display, convincing in what is only a *simulation* of authenticity:

> And here were the lions now, fifteen feet away – so real, so feverishly and startlingly real that you could feel the prickling fur on your hand, and your mouth was stuffed with the dusty upholstery smell of their heated pelts, and the yellow of an exquisite French tapestry, the yellow of lions and summer grass, and the sound of the matted lion lungs exhaling on the silent noontide, and the smell of meat from the panting, dripping mouths. (26)

What of the lion, a creature unknown to these American characters living in the future? Without experience of or interactions with real life lions, this pampered family has invited the so-called King of the Beasts into their home.

Stressing "[t]here can be no single interpretation of the dream lion," Hillman challenges us to see *the lion* of the lion: "It is a lion inside an image, and it is this image as a whole that transmits the lion to our consciousness. The image is its carrier. To take the lion only as such, to see it only as a meaning, lifts it from its habitat in the dream in which its meanings are enfolded" (*Animal Presences* 92). Dealing as we are with a story, not a dream, we must be careful to not isolate it from its nursery habitat within the story. Consulting ARAS provides further insights from a depth psychological perspective:

> In dream images such as a great cat prowling in the house or the backyard, psyche warns us that physically or affectively we are identified

> with a big cat libido and need to get some distance. To respond to such urges by killing, caging or degrading the great cat is to brutally repress one of nature's most extraordinary incarnations of creative aggressiveness and sovereign instinct. The resolution seems to be in balance and boundaries.
>
> (*Book of Symbols* 268, 270)

The Hadleys' problem with these lions is not that lions have been conjured; it is rather how these lions have been confined. When George and Lydia retreat, they are distressed to see the nursery door "tremble as if something had jumped against it from the other side" (62). Peter and Wendy, resenting denied permission to travel to New York unattended, possess a strong desire for control. If anything, the illusion of creation in the nursery, of easily framing the fearful symmetry not of tigers but of lions, has dramatically skewed the family dynamic.

Gheerbrant and Chevalier, tracing the lion through Christianity, Islam, Hinduism, Buddhism, ancient Egypt, and psychoanalysis, find what could serve as a profile for George: "Although [the lion] may be the embodiment of power, wisdom and justice, overweening pride and self-confidence, on the other hand, may turn him into the symbol of the father, the master and the monarch dazzled by his own power and blinded by his own light to become the tyrant when he believes he is the guardian" (611). George and Lydia have forfeited their responsibilities as parents to the conveniences of comfortable living. Both are infantilized, sleeping in separate (this is 1950s middle class America, after all) beds that rock them to sleep like cradles. Lydia, for lack of anything to do, voices a desire to return to life *without* automated amenities even if it means taking up the predictable gender roles: "I feel like I don't belong here. The house is wife and mother now, and nursemaid" (62). She expresses her feelings of inadequacy in the presence of devices more efficient than her and draws attention to how George, too, has changed. It turns out George, patriarch of the home, has been smoking, drinking, and taking sedatives a little more every day. Considering the family as a pride, with its strict gender roles, he is the lion whose authority stands challenged. When he fearfully wanders into the nursery and attempts to reset it, he calls up the Emerald City: "I demand Oz!" (62). As if sensing a coward already in the room, the veldt resists with its decidedly uncowardly lions.

Prompted at last to ponder the inner lives of his children, of which he knows next to nothing, the best he comes up with are, "Death thoughts. They were awfully young, Wendy and Peter, for death thoughts. Or no, you were never too young, really. Long before you knew what death was you were wishing it on someone else. When you were two years old you were shooting people with cap pistols" (62). Fantasies of violence and death aimed at other people emerges normalized, understandable, and not that surprising to him – suggesting these cubs are definitely his. Later when he consults his friend David McLean, a psychologist, it is drastically recommended that he tear down the nursery and bring Peter and Wendy in for treatment every day for the next year. The immediacy with which George shuts off the nursery, however, is tyrannical. Impatiently attempting to reassert his control over the children's, he goes about murdering the house. "Lord, how we need a breath of honest air!" he complains, turning off all of the mechanical devices until "[t]he house was full of dead bodies, it seemed. It felt like a mechanical cemetery" (66). Peter cries out not to the Lord but to the ceiling, "as if he were talking to the house, the nursery" (66). Father and son worship very different gods. Rage finally finds expression through Peter's mouth, telling his father that he hates him and wishes him dead. George meets his death wish with a tardy invocation for life: "Now we're really going to start living. Instead of being handled and massaged, we're going to live" (68).

Not for long. Preparing for a vacation to Iowa – not a destination most kids beg to visit – George and Lydia are called downstairs to the nursery by the children. Or rather, lured. Shut inside the expanse of veldtland, they succumb to their children's lions. When McLean checks in on everybody, he only finds Peter and Wendy, calmly picnicking in Africa, their great cats nearby at the watering hole. "'A cup of tea?' Wendy asked in the silence" (68), and the story ends. There are shades here of the 1882 short story by Frank R. Stockton, "The Lady, or the Tiger?" Stockton leaves his character's fate up to the reader, describing an elaborate punishment in an Orientalized society, whereby the accused is made to choose between two doors in an arena while thousands watch. Behind one door is a beautiful lady; behind the other is a ferocious tiger. If the door reveals the lady, he is taken off to marry her; if it reveals the tiger, he is eaten as entertainment. Stockton complicates the character's door choice with the ambiguity of a princess's gesture to the right, but what he finds behind the door is never told.

If there is any ambiguity in the ending of "The World the Children Made," we might ask where responsibility lies and how far does it stretch? Surely George and Lydia share some culpability with the children, but the fact that such a potential deathtrap is available for purchase points a finger at the manufacturer or even a lack of regulation in the law. The temptation is to label the nursery as an allegory for television, then rising across the United States in 1950. However, instead of blaming the messenger, I think the story acts better as a parable about parenting. As in "The Small Assassin," readers are never privy to the thoughts of the children; instead, we follow the perspectives of the adults. The story anticipates a chasm in communication within American families as distraction provided by doohickeys becomes more prevalent. George and Lydia Hadley's symbolic failure is not in simply a sin of materialism, but in underestimating Peter and Wendy's capacities and, worse, not investing in knowing who they are.

This brings us to "Jack-in-the-Box," published in Bradbury's first collection, *Dark Carnival* (1947), a story about a boy whose mother oversteps her responsibilities from parenting to dictating. Drawing inspiration from a newspaper article about an abused child in Chicago raised in seclusion with no outside contact, Bradbury created thirteen-year-old Edwin, Mother, and their World: a mansion built by his father that he has never left. This is a story of abuse perpetrated on an only child by a severely neurotic mother whose pathological manipulations are losing their stranglehold on his life. Diskin draws attention to the story's psychological elements: "Perhaps more than any other child in Bradbury's fiction, Edwin is an innocent incarcerated by adult neuroses, subjugated by the delusions and defenses erected as compensation by adults in retreat from life. Like his toy, the jack-in-the-box, he is confined, even trapped" (45). But Edwin's capacities are outgrowing the life his mother has provided. In his cornerstone essay on myth, "The Psychology of the Child Archetype," Jung discusses how individuation begins with this image of the child: "[The child archetype] represents the strongest, the most ineluctable urge in every being, namely the urge to realize itself" (1940/1968, *CW 9.I*, ¶289). Edwin, nearly fourteen, is an adolescent, a teenager, and he wants to become himself.

The story begins with a preamble in second person plural and present tense: "Let us imagine a Jack-in-the-box, stuffed, compressed in upon its coiled body, its head against a locked lid" (159). The metaphor may be obvious but it carries nuances, going on to claim it has remained shut for thirteen years. A Jack-in-the-box often contains a spring-loaded jester or clown but can also feature a plush animal. There is usually a jangling melody, typically "Pop Goes the Weasel," that accompanies the turning of the crank. The toy is one of the first a child has, appropriate for one-year-olds, the simplicity of its hand crank making it a staple of practicing manual dexterity. The force with which the figure inside pops out is both startling and harmless, giving a fright babies are usually capable of handling, for they quickly stuff it shut to do it all over again. A thirteen-year-old has profoundly outgrown this kind of toy, an amusement of infancy. Once presented, Bradbury does not return to the metaphor of the animal in the Jack-in-the-box. After a page break, he switches to mostly third person and past tense in telling the story of Edwin and Mother.

"Edwin" is Old English for "rich friend" (*BTN*), a curious name for a friendless boy. "Mother" is entirely archetypal, and if we are to unbox Edwin's vitality we must examine her insanity. Described as "blazingly lovely, like an angry white flower" (160), she is also spooky in a sense Bradbury assumes readers would recognize from their own communities: "She was the pale woman you saw in old houses in third floor cupola windows, each morning at nine, each afternoon at one and four, each evening at eight, and, also, if you happened to be passing at three in the morning, there she would be, in her window, silent and white, high and alone and quiet" (160). Her causes for self-and-son-cloistering have become a debilitating mythos, going unchecked through lack of interaction with others. Moriarty warns that, "Myths and cosmologies aren't daydreams that never engage with reality. They are, very often, damaging actions, damaging ways of being in the world" (*TGLT2* 101).

Mother's way of being is just such a myth, where her dead husband is called God, the mansion he built is the World, and automobiles and planes and people lurking out beyond the ring of chestnuts and elms and walls of her property are "Them," "Beasts" (160), "Things" (162), "Beings" (164), "Wicked Killers" (169), "Monster[s]" and "Chaos" (171). We glean through this warped view that the boy's father was knocked down and killed by a car or truck, realities she has hidden. Her imprisonment of the boy has led to a geographical orientation within the mansion, whose frontier grows with a newly opened room upon the occasion of each birthday. At six he gained access to school on a floor called the Highlands, seven provided a playroom, eight a music room, nine was the kitchen, ten the phonograph room, eleven a conservatory with a grass floor "carpet that really grew" (171), twelve access to Mother's makeup room, thirteen a private space for him to keep as he liked, and now, at fourteen, he received "A dim brown closet" (171). This room turns out to be an elevator, which she explains as flying them to a higher floor. She gifts it by jogging his fourteenth birthday ahead two months when his uncontainable curiosity threatens her authority.

One of the more disturbing aspects of her need for control has her costuming herself to play the part of Teacher Granleigh, who educates the boy daily. She provides him with a "book from which pages had been razored and torn and censored, from which certain lines had been inked or erased, from which all pictures had been ripped, some books glued shut, or locked in bronze straps, because Edwin might see, read, understand" (168). The book she thrusts into his hands is the Diary, a cosmological scripture of her own making that even starts "In the Beginning . . ." (168). He has not copped on that Mother and Teacher are one and the same, though he dares to figure it out and poignantly refuses to accept it in the end. Edwin has been cut off from society and the outside world of his own yard thanks to Mother's powerful myth of isolation: "He was to grow into a Presence. He was to fit the odors of God and the voice of God, he was one day to stand tall and dark and very malignantly pale by that window and make the house boom with his shout. He was to be God, himself, and nothing was to stop this. Not the sky or the trees or the Things beyond the trees" (165).

This is clearly a perversion of the goal of parenting. While plenty of mothers think their sons are the best thing since sliced cheese, few set about actually deifying them. The pressure is too great for anyone to match such expectations, especially in a state of confinement. Mother's inability to let her son grow as he must, versus how she wants him to, proves too much for her already shot nerves. On his preemptive birthday she goes on a champagne bender, shattering bottles down flights of stairs and smashing glasses in the hearth after he has gone to sleep. He finds her in the morning dead, but, having never learned about death, he does not know that she is gone. Early on he asks her, "What's – dying? You talk about it all the time. Is it a – *feeling*?" (161). Denied an answer, Edwin assumes she is asleep and dreaming.

Jung might say Mother is suffering the ill effects of a mother-complex, specifically in an inflection he labeled Hypertrophy (Ancient Greek for "excess nourishment") of the Maternal Element: "Driven by ruthless will to power and a fanatical insistence on their own maternal rights, they often succeed in annihilating not only their own personality but also the personal lives of their children" (1954/1968, *CW 9.I*, ¶167). Hillman blames this phenomenon not on the collective obsession with children but on its less identified counterpart, the obsession with parents: "The elevation of the parents, of the mother in particular, to the neglect of all other realities – societal, environmental, economic – shows that adulation of an archetype can obliterate common sense. [. . . The] archetypal myth of the completely surrounding mother, insulating from all influences, prevails over the actual world of collective pain" (*SC* 79). Absolute blame for life's pain is too much to pin to the vast majority of parents; by the same token, assuming absolute responsibility for how one's children "turn out" is altogether inappropriate. If children are not at first autonomous, depth psychology maintains they *are* autochthonous, in the sense that their spirits arise where we find them, exhibiting personality and being beyond our control from their earliest days.

And while Mother succeeds in destroying herself, Edwin finally emerges. Hillman insists that children require contact with the natural world in order to flourish: "Imagination does not grow all by itself in the household, or even out of imaginative tales told by parents. Children are 'by nature' at home in the world; the world invites them to grow down and take part" (*SC* 87). Edwin exhibits early signs of this, thrilling at the sight over the trees from a tower window he accesses when its door is left unlocked. Mother's death is what finally releases him, bravely venturing in search of Teacher. Having found her costume and one of her grey gloves folded under Mother's dead body – and refusing to connect the dots in a defensive decision against breakdown – he crosses the threshold of his small World: "If I go beyond the trees I'll die, he thought. Mom said so. What's dying? What is it anyway, what's it like? Is it another room? A blue one? A green one? There's a big green one, ahead. Oh, Mother, Teacher" (175). He begins to run, and in running to yell, and in yelling, leaving his Universe behind, to laugh. After a page break, we are suddenly introduced to a policeman puzzling over something he just witnessed: a boy running down the street laughing, touching everything, and yelling. As he explains to a pedestrian, "He kept yelling, 'I'm dead, I'm dead, I'm glad I'm dead, I'm dead, I'm dead, it's *good* to be dead, I'm dead, I'm dead, I'm glad I'm dead!'" (176). In a way Edwin really has died, as the cosmology forced upon him has been obliterated by his new and overwhelming expansion of experience. And while he is unhabituated to society, a feral, somewhat-civilized child, there is a sense of hope that, instead of being ruined by the abuse he suffered under his mother, he will thrive.

Nuclear families

At last we come to stories of families trying to "get it right," to live out American myths of happiness and individualism. These families stick together despite overwhelming circumstances. 1957 saw the publication of *Dandelion Wine*, a lyrical representation of Bradbury's own childhood in Waukegan, Illinois, set in the summer of 1928. Early in the novel, spread across three chapters and interrupted by other episodes, is the story of Leo Auffmann's Happiness Machine and what it brings to his family. We are concerned, however, with that story as it stands on its own, published the same year in *The Saturday Evening Post* (Sept. 14). No mention of *Dandelion Wine* accompanies "The Happiness Machine," no indication that the story is published as an extract. Green Town of the novel is not named, wiping away the regional aspect that grounds the novel. The story was read on its own terms here, and so we shall approach it as such.

Greeting readers on page 43 is Fritz Willis's illustration of Leo Auffmann kneeling beside his eight-foot-tall, orange-painted Happiness Machine, with his wife Lena sitting inside. Lovely as Disney's Snow White and still, with eyes closed, as Sleeping Beauty, she sits amid gauges and switchery, her hands in her lap, a cardigan over her shoulders. A pink sign taped onto the door's window reads "*CAUTION!*" Leo, the concerned innovator and spouse, listens against the glass, attentive to her experience within the booth. He looks to be forty, his temples greying, his hair shellacked in its aging retreat. Three Dixon Ticonderoga pencils and paper are tucked into his breast pocket, the casual uniform of the at-home-inventor, including highwater trousers and canvas sneakers. A tank of helium, an oil can, a brown box for file cards, and a black box with dials and a needle (either an ammeter or a voltmeter), sit in the foreground. Note how Willis dresses Leo and Lena in clothing of 1957, not the 1928 of the novel.

The Auffmanns are Leo and Lena and their six children: Saul, Marshall, Joseph, Rebecca, Ruth, and Naomi. Leo is the town jeweler, which likely includes the repairing duties of horology as he is given to timepiece metaphors in his thoughts, let alone his mechanical knowhow. That fact of career and the history of Jews as jewelers, along with the names Saul, Joseph, Rebecca, Ruth, and Naomi being Hebrew (*BTN*), I posit that the Auffmanns are Jewish. Bradbury never provides their religious tradition – he seldom does in his canon, typically writing explicitly about priests when approaching issues of religion. But if we read this family as being Jewish, and of the story taking place contemporary with its publication in the late fifties versus the pre-Depression summer of *Dandelion Wine*, their relationship to life in America shifts dramatically. They are post-Holocaust American Jews, a minority for whom the pursuit of happiness carries a distinct and poignant significance. The opening paragraph, introducing Leo Auffmann with a description of men outside the cigar shop smoking, resonates in hindsight of the Shoah. Their smoke is described as looming "Clouds of annihilation" (43). Leo was

It was the most incredible apparatus ever built. But not even the inventor knew the amazing things it could do. . . .

The Happiness Machine

By RAY BRADBURY

In front of the corner cigar store this evening the men were gathered to burn dirigibles, sink battleships, blow up dynamite works and, all in all, savor the very bacteria in their mouths that would someday stop them cold. Clouds of annihilation loomed and blew away in their cigar smoke about a nervous figure who could be seen dimly listening to the sound of shovels and spades and the intonations of "ashes to ashes, dust to dust." This figure was that of Leo Auffmann, the town jeweler who, widening his large liquid-dark eyes, at last threw up his child's hands and cried out in dismay.

"Stop! In heaven's name, get out of that graveyard!"

"Leo, how right you are," said Grandfather Spaulding passing on his nightly stroll with his grandsons Douglas and Tom. "But, Leo, only you can shut these doom-talkers up. Invent something that will make the future brighter, well-rounded, infinitely joyous. You've invented bicycles, fixed the penny-arcade contraptions, been our town movie projectionist, haven't you?"

"Sure," said Douglas. "Invent us a Happiness Machine!"

The men laughed.

"Don't," said Leo Auffmann. "How have we used machines so far—to make people cry? Yes! Every time man and the machine look like they will get on all right—boom! Someone adds a cog, airplanes drop bombs on us, cars run us off cliffs. So is the boy wrong to ask? No! No."

His voice faded as Leo Auffmann moved to the curb to touch his bicycle as if it were an animal.

"What can I lose?" he murmured. "A little skin off my fingers, a few pounds of metal, some sleep? I'll do it, so help me!"

"Leo," said Grandfather, "we didn't mean ——"

But Leo Auffmann was gone, pedaling off through the warm summer evening, his voice drifting back, ". . . I'll do it."

"You know," said Tom in awe, "I bet he will."

Watching him cycle the brick streets of evening, you could see that Leo Auffmann was a man who coasted along, enjoying the way the thistles ticked in the hot grass when the wind blew (Continued on Page 154)

Inside the machine, Lena could be heard saying, "Oh!" and then again, "Ah!" in a startled voice.

Figure 4.6 Title page with Fritz Willis's illustration for "The Happiness Machine" (*The Saturday Evening Post*, 14 Sep. 1957). (Illustration © SEPS licensed by Curtis Licensing Indianapolis, IN. All rights reserved.)

the name of Bradbury's father, but while there may be aspects of him in the character of Leo Auffmann, they would enter as privileged information the common reader would not possess. It is more compelling to downplay this autobiographical detail in favor of considering the character a middle class American *Jewish* father.

When challenged by Douglas, Tom, and Grandfather Spaulding,[7] to "Invent us a Happiness Machine!," Leo is reluctant: "How have we used machines so far – to make people cry? Yes! Every time man and machine look like they will get on all right – boom! Someone adds a cog, airplanes drop bombs on us, cars run us off cliffs" (43). Later, "pleasured in sleepless nights of brooding on the great clock of the universe running down or winding itself up" (154), he accepts the challenge. While contemplating the stages of life, "Getting born, growing up, growing old, dying" (154), and what can be done about improving the last three, Leo imagines possibilities. Here again is the positivist bugaboo metaphor of life as a machine, first in Leo's imagination being described as a clockwork cosmology and then in the potential for a device that *does* happiness in service of life's thresholds. We recall Abram's criticism of the metaphor of mechanism in the previous chapter: "The mechanical model of the world entails a mentalistic epistemology, the assumption that the most precise knowledge of things is a detached, intellectual apprehension purged of all subjective, situated, or bodily involvement. It is an abstract, disembodied knowledge" (71).

Leo is trapped under the restricting dome of the mechanical model, the metaphor, hiding in plain sight, routing his imagination away from life-affirming potentialities. Equipped only with a mechanical way of imagining, he can only conceive of fixing life's sorrow by creating another machine – with a mechanism for happiness and, by proxy, happiness reduced to mechanism. It is interesting to note that, on the magazine page, standing alongside the text in which Leo dreams his machine is a sidebar advertisement for Victor Business Machines – two adding machines and a cash register – real world "business machines" standing sentry for the Economy alongside Leo's hopes for his Happiness Machine. He has no monetary profit in mind, just the ethic that "sometimes you got to build for others" (154). This project, however, is flawed from conception. Early construction sees him appraising the materials as inert, meaningless, "dead tools and the inanimate lumber" (156), a devaluing attitude that is symptomatic of a ruling metaphor that Abram says "denies our perceptual experience [. . . and] our sensory involvement in the world" (69) and what Moriarty called commonage consciousness: "the one consciousness that is manifested in rocks, animals, human beings, and stars" (*TGLT1* XVII).

The chief barometer of well-being in the Auffmann family is Lena. "Eat, sleep, breathe, Leo," she says, criticizing his analytical obsession with life's mechanistics, "and stop staring at me like I'm something new in the house!" (154). In asking her to help him arrive at a definition of happiness, they have their first fight in six months. When he finishes construction, her concern for him trumps its unveiling. Her issue is that while his machine may not be an offense against God, it is nevertheless sapping him of his life, separating him from his family, and she worries that it may even kill him with stress.

Their home functions under the stereotypical gender roles we might expect from the American fifties, with Lena cooking for the family and doing the housework. At this point in the story, a two-page advertisement for Lennox home heating spreads across two magazine pages, bisecting the layout horizontally, taking up the lower half, and reinforcing the white middle class patriarchal narrative. Page 156 shows cartoon drawings of a girl going from ill in bed to smiling at breakfast thanks to a Lennox Super-Quiet Blower; next to her a cartoon woman/mom, hair in kerchief and bent over dusting, changes to a smiling form with a sparkling white napkin thanks to the Lennox Hammock Air Filter and the claim that, "You've less housework, fewer cleaning bills with Lennox!" Beyond the gutter, on page 157, a cartoon man/dad goes from lamenting an empty pocket to smiling with money in hand thanks to the Penny-Pincher Heat Exchanger; "More families buy LENNOX," according to the ad. Happiness Machines, indeed, judging by the curves of those cartoon mouths.

This is the monolithic representation of the American Family we are actively trying to avoid in our exploration of archetypal valence. We are not told if the Auffmanns have a Lennox furnace, but Lena expresses the practical aspects of life – and death – as they know it: "Also, how does death look when you hide in there with all that Happiness?" she asks him (156). She challenges him on his sense of their family life, asks him to consider her day-to-day routine of seeing the children off to school, doing the wash and running errands, cooking, polishing silver. She is fine with this, she says, but she feels unseen. Lena is cast as neither victim nor abuser in the family; she comes off as confident, articulate, and practical. Despite the very life she thrusts back in his face, Leo, being stuck in his programmatic way of seeing the world, marvels at her as if she, too, is a machine. The way he perceives her hands, as if they think for her, and how she never seems to brood for long, is to him the stuff of miracles, "a natural and gentle circuiting he could not and cared not to blueprint" (154).

The other family member who indicates the family's equilibrium is Saul, presumably the eldest child. He is the first to test out the Happiness Machine, sneaking into it when his father is exhausted upon its completion. Before putting two and two together, Leo hears Saul sobbing in his room and his attempt to comfort his son fails. Staying until his boy falls to sleep, Leo goes down and checks the garage, finding the Machine still hot. Realizing Saul had used it – and left wondering why he would need to – he is startled by movement:

> Above, quite suddenly, something white was exhaled from Saul's bedroom window. Leo Auffmann's heart thundered. Then he realized that the window curtain had blown out into the open night. But it had seemed as intimate and shimmering a thing as a boy's soul escaping his room. And Leo Auffmann had flung up his hands as if to thwart it, push it back into the sleeping house.
>
> (156)

In this instant he experiences a flash of his own illusionment, the unconscious breaking through his mechanical mode with enough force to excite his heart. To explain this phenomenon, Moriarty borrows the Hindu concept of *mayashakti* – the power that projects the world illusion – which we catch ourselves experiencing when we mistake a coiled rope for a snake:

> Viksepashakti it is called, the power by which a snake is projected into a rope, by which a world is projected into Divine Ground.
>
> Avaranashakti it is called, the power that veils the rope by projecting a snake into it, that veils Divine Ground by projecting a world into it. (*TGLT2* 5)

Leo has unconsciously projected his son's soul into the billowing curtain, calling his attention to his failure in tending to his boy's spiritual needs while obsessing over the machine.

Leo, a reluctant lion-father made of slightly more attentive stuff than George Hadley in "The World the Children Made," finally takes his cue and goes back up to lock Saul's window and guard over him as he sleeps. Both stories bear relation to the rise of television, but reading the Happiness Machine as a stand-in for TV misses the nature of this so-called family man's solo project aiming to provide his family with happiness, that subjective feeling held up, for better or worse, as an unalienable right in the U.S.A. There is only so much a father can provide. He will never, for instance, harbor and nourish a growing fetus within his own flesh. But whether he is a single parent or parenting in tandem, shrewdly practical needs are of utmost importance in the raising of a child or children: they must be fed; they must be sheltered, clothed; their health needs attention, as do the individual demands of their spiritual development. To move an abstract concept that has no absolute definition to the top of that list – in Leo's case, happiness – throws everything off balance and risks collapsing the family altogether.

The incident with Saul upsets Lena enough to threaten separation. As she goes through "sorting out the community property" (156), which consists of a comedic doling out of Dickens novels according to how their titles reflect the current situation, she agrees to try out the Happiness Machine for herself. The family watches her enter, listens as she experiences its offerings. She narrates as it shows her Paris, London, Rome, the Pyramids, the Sphinx, plays *The Blue Danube*, spritzes perfume, makes her think she is dancing. Breaching Leo's expectations, she weeps: "Oh, it's the saddest thing in the world! [. . .] I never even thought of being in Paris in my life. But now you got me thinking: Paris! So suddenly I want to be in Paris and I know I'm not!" (157). Their children are distressed by her distress, leading to her final verdict, in which she declares the machine a liar and bringer of sadness. His failure, in her eyes, is that he overlooked the fact that those who use the machine will have to get out of it and go back to lives that cannot match its enticing projections. Disbelieving her, he gets into the machine to test her claims but it overheats and catches fire. His sons drag him out and once the machine is engulfed in flames, Lena finally lets Saul call the Fire Department.

Looping back into the story at the end, Grandpa Spaulding, Douglas, and Tom reappear to watch the Auffmanns' garage burn. They chat with Leo, the self-effacing schmuck, after his family heads indoors to prepare dinner, giving him the chance to express his own revelation: "You want to see the real Happiness Machine? The one they patented a couple thousand years ago. It still runs; not good all the time, no! but it runs. It's been here all along" (158). Leading them to the front window he exhibits the Auffmanns inside going about their business as a collective. He is said to experience "gentle sorrow," "quick delight," and "quiet acceptance as all the bits, the pieces of this house mixed, stirred, settled, poised and ran steadily again" (158). Infected by the mechanical metaphor, the Spauldings watch him tend to his family, described like a mechanic tuning up an engine as he deals with his wife and children. It is a patriarchal ending, his assuming the role of maintenance man for the family machine in which the wife and children are parts. And while lifting us out of the story on the hopeful note that Leo finally appreciates the dynamism of his own family, one wonders if American families living under a mechanistic cosmology can structure their lives in such a way that the mystery of existence, that soul blowing through the window at night, can manifest beyond projection and be appreciated.

Capstoning the trouble with happiness, the final story we shall discuss in light of Bradbury's American families is "The Vacation." One of his shorter pieces, it was published in the tenth holiday issue of a groundbreaking and controversial magazine at a watershed moment in American history: *Playboy* (Dec. 1963). Since magazines are dated a month ahead of publication to ensure their presence on stands until the next issue appears, "The Vacation" was likely being sold on November 22, 1963, that cataclysmic day for the U.S.A. Examining short stories published between WWII and the assassination of President John F. Kennedy, this particular story takes us as close as possible to the end of that period.

Beyond the story, the issue of *Playboy* preserves a few last glimpses of an America that was not dreaming its young President could be murdered. Jack Davis offers a lampooning Christmas card of the grinning Kennedy clan trailing in a multitude of family members into the distance (128). Humorist Robert Paul Smith contributes an ill-timed opinion piece titled "Everybody Shinny on His Own Side," its lowercase editorial blurb reading, "*a smart rap on the first family's knuckles for the way it sticks its fingers in america's cultural pie*" (123). Taking umbrage with what he perceives as President and Mrs. Kennedy's desire "to be the cultural leader of the United States" (219), Smith closes with direct address: "But as President – I'll make you a deal, Jack. If you won't make statements about art, I won't buck for Commander in Chief. | You see, neither of us knows what part, if any, of our culture, if any, will be part of history. That comes under the Department of Posterity" (219). This cheeky jab was rendered chilling while still selling on newsstands, the immediacy of tragedy guaranteeing American culture in 1963 would be preserved beyond snapshot in twenty-six seconds of 8mm Kodachrome.

Phill Renaud's long brush strokes of beige and mud sketch out a desolation across all but the upper fourth of the story's opening pages, a red line of railway cutting across a strip of blue sea and yellow and mud sky above the horizon. A man heaves a pick behind a handcar while woman and child, she in yellow sunhat and he in red shorts, wander away. We can see that expressionism is mainstream enough by 1963 to appear in *Playboy*, a style we have not encountered in the illustrations accompanying earlier stories in this thesis. There is also an aspect of American Regionalism present, which makes sense given Renaud's studies at the Chicago Academy of Fine Arts. The art is exact in its roughness, peering through the empty outline of the title in its block capitals.

All of this matches the tone and feel of the story, its three characters nearly indistinct as individuals beyond their sexes and roles within a family. Bradbury presents "a man, his wife and their small seven-year-old son" (102). The man, costumed impractically in "his business suit and vest and

Figure 4.7 Phill Renaud's title illustration for "The Vacation." (Illustration © Phillip Renaud, 1963. Reproduced with permission of the Estate of Phillip Renaud. All rights reserved.)

tie and hat," is at times "Papa," "the husband" (102), and "Dad" (110). His wife, who wears a "great shadowing straw hat which had been tied over her golden hair with a bright yellow ribbon," is also "the woman" (102), though her introduction as his wife puts her under his possession, existing foremost in relation to him and, by proxy, patriarchy. Their son is also "the boy," but surfaces as his parents do not with a name: Jim (102), diminutive of James, the name of two apostles in the New Testament. This badge of identity, a name, sets him apart from his parents, illustrating an understanding in depth psychology that in the first half of life, the psyche focuses on defining oneself as an individual, and the latter half, occurring after a crisis of middle age, seeks to reunite us with the collective mystery of being.

This trio of characters forms that potentially dogmatic archetypal image of the American Family. Here it is: the white middle class American father, mother, and child, together, committed, and existing without outside influence, the American Family as island unto itself. For this profoundly vulnerable social unit, as the story goes, is the last one to exist: "They had wakened one morning and the world was empty" (102). No bodies, no carnage, nothing but the works and architecture of humanity – and these three people – are all that is left of people in America. When we join the family, they are traveling by handcar on a rusting railroad track toward Monterey and Palo Alto, with tentative plans to travel in the coming years on this extended "vacation" to Sacramento, Seattle, Yellowstone, Tucson, Florida, New York, Chicago, Mexico City. The handcar is a curious choice of transport, dependent as it typically is on cooperative physical effort to make it go. The family vehicle relies on family involvement to get them anywhere, although, being restricted to rail lines, their path is set ahead of them. When we first meet the family, they have to stop because, as the man can see, "There's a break ahead. We may have to wait while I set a few back in place" (102). This is not the freedom of the American highway, although we recall in "The Scythe" how the Joerg family, following the seemingly free road, inevitably arrive in the Valley of Death. Roads in America, though forming a vast circulatory system for the nation, are still pathways, not granting absolute access to the land; railroads are twice as fickle.

The cause of the mass disappearance, similar to the evangelical Christian concept of the rapture, is an absolute mystery. The family has no answer for it; neither does the narrator. Just as there is no explanation for the catastrophe that ruins America in Cormac McCarthy's *The Road* (2006), there is none here, although both settings differ profoundly. Bradbury's situation is made ironic by the fact that the night before it happens, the man asks his wife, "'I wonder when He will get tired of us and just rub us all out? [. . .] Wouldn't it be nice' – he lit his pipe and puffed it – 'if we woke tomorrow and everyone in the world was gone and everything was starting over?'" (102). When she entertains the idea and asks, in that age of nuclear fear, if he would "press a button right now and make it happen," he does not hold back. Wishing nothing like calamity, just the mass disappearance of his own species, he is happy for every other living thing to stay: "Everything except man, who hunts when he isn't hungry, eats when full, and is mean when no one's bothered him" (102). She lets him talk but expresses a devastating con to his list of pros: "Wouldn't we be *lonely*?" (102).

They took to this "new world," as Bradbury calls it, "with remarkable calm at first, perhaps because they had not liked the city for so many years and had had so many friends who were not truly friends, and had lived a boxed and separate life of their own within a mechanical hive" (102). And yet the sudden and persistent absence of people, even the disingenuous ones, shows early signs of becoming unbearable. "'I feel guilty,' she said. 'They gone and we here. And . . . I feel happy. Why? I *should* be unhappy'" (110). The husband's response expresses the emptiness of his own selfishness: "Our only responsibility *is* being happy" (110). And again, as in "The Happiness Machine," Bradbury presents a father prioritizing happiness as the family's responsibility, overstepping the exceptionally American unalienable right to its mere pursuit. And this is no post-Flood narrative. When the wife worries that they must be fruitful and multiply, the husband refuses: "No. Let Jim be the last" (110). His vision is one in which another species may arise and match happiness with curiosity in order to build settlements and societies humans wouldn't understand. Their son, by this decree, will be far lonelier than either of them. Their refusal to expand the family is a damnation to their isolated community of three.

The man finally feels the pang of loss, a delayed response, crying into the sand. He offers up a wish running counter to the one before, in which everything lost returns overnight: "All the foolishness, all the noise, all the hate, all the terrible things, all the nightmares, all the wicked people and stupid children, all the mess, all the smallness, all the confusion, all the hope, all the need, all the love. Wouldn't it be nice?" (110). Jim retreats in tears to the seashore below and casts a message in a bottle into the water. There is no reason to expect it will be found and read, not in this empty world. The woman wonders what he has written, if it was their wish or something for himself, perhaps a wish that she and her husband would disappear and leave him free. When he returns to the handcar, "She searched his colorless eyes, could not read the answer; dared not ask" (110). The colorlessness of his eyes is another emptying, a voiding of vitality in the organs of seeing. And again, at the end, when they re-board the handcar with a pail full of shells, his seven-year-old sight is distant. He is able to look ahead and leave this place with ease, giving it a wave before they go. Thinking back, earlier in the story, to when the family has to stop on the tracks – "There's a break ahead. We may have to wait while I set a few back in place" (102) – this family is railroaded, much the way Americans were by the actions of Lee Harvey Oswald. The extracted quotation stretching across the bottom of Phill Renaud's two page painting could very well apply to the passing of the era that President Kennedy's assassination marked: "'we're let out, darling,' he'd said, 'and we'll never come back to the silly damn dull routines'" (100–101). Nothing shatters a people's identity as a civilized group and shocks routine quite like the murder of their political leader by one of their own.

Writing the following year of the mythic significance of President Kennedy's funeral, Campbell viewed it as an unprecedented collective "weekend of unanimous meditation": "To my knowledge, this was the first and only thing of its kind in peacetime that has ever given me the sense of being a member of this whole national community, engaged as a unit in the observance of a deeply significant rite" (*Myths to Live By* 53–54). Unforeseen, on the other side of December 1963, would be the Beatles, President Johnson's War on Poverty, "Great Society," and Jobs Bill, escalation of American military action in Vietnam, the Civil Rights Act of 1964 followed by the Voting Rights Act of 1965, popularization of lysergic acid diethylamide, increased broadcasting of color television, the Black Panthers, the first heart transplant, the first Super Bowl, the first handheld calculator, Warhol's Campbell's Soup cans, Thurgood Marshall becoming the first black Justice of the Supreme Court, the assassinations of Kennedy's brother Robert and Martin Luther King, Jr., the protest of the Democratic National Convention in Chicago, Shirley Chisholm becoming the first black woman elected to Congress, a presidential win for Richard Nixon, the Tet Offensive and the My Lai Massacre, hippies, Yippies, John and Yoko, Tiny Tim, R. Crumb, Woodstock, the Occupation of Alcatraz by Indians of All Tribes, Neil Armstrong becoming the first living thing to imprint the surface of the moon, the Weathermen and their declaration of war against "Amerikan Imperialism," the Kent State massacre, Watergate, and so on, and so forth. All of that and more awaited readers of the man, the woman, and the boy. They are, these characters in this story, turned out, cast away. It is an attempt at sending off the archetypal image of the American Family, an exploration of how isolating and trapping that construct is as an ideal. There is no safety for them in a country where the President is not safe, and so, as this short fiction and that major historical moment coincide, the patriarchal family of the middle class white majority at the time is unmasked as not enough. It will not do.

Family myths

"Each of us to our own. None of us the same. All wild. That's how the Family goes." So muses Mother in "The Traveler" (*Stories of Ray Bradbury* 36). Worthy of their own study, Bradbury's Elliott clan, known as the Family, appears in seven of his short stories. Four were published during the era at hand: "The Traveller" (*Weird Tales*, Mar. 1946), "The Homecoming" (*Mademoiselle*, Oct. 1946), "Uncle Einar" (*Dark Carnival*, 1947), and

"The April Witch" (*Saturday Evening Post*, 5 April 1952).[8] The Elliotts are a lineage of paranormal oddballs living in a rural Illinois mansion, a sort of Midwestern Addams Family – Charles Addams, whose own macabre Family debuted in *The New Yorker* in 1938, provided the art for publication of "The Homecoming" in *Mademoiselle*. The Elliotts diverge from the families we have considered in that they know they are weird, strange, set apart from mainstream Americans. They openly invert the imposing archetypal image of the American Family, opposing its bland, white bread narrative of stability by presenting individualities ranging from vampirism to great green wings to the ability of assimilating with and directing another person's soul.

And yet from the Joergs to the family on "vacation," stories featuring white American families trying to make do, we witness a valence of experiences that defy simplified taxonomical classification under the heading of American Family. Bradbury defies such an act, presenting in microcosmic fictions a diversity of hopes and fears – and responses to those hopes and fears – by American characters of the era. There is either a myth of the postwar American Family that gathers under its heading all of these inflections and more – meaning all families of the era, from all racial and socioeconomic circumstances, must be included – or, as I would prefer to frame it, myths of American families, expressing the gamut without the constriction of a unified theory. Thinking, as Moriarty puts it, philomythically, "Myths are instinct with wonder. Like nothing else perhaps in our culture, they uncompromisingly mediate the difficult strangeness of self and of world. Therefore the philomythos has as good a chance of reaching and living in the Truth as the philosophos has" (*TGLT3* ix). Bradbury's suite of short family myths rescues us from reducing the diversities within white American families to one dominating image of the nuclear family. As soon as we discover the subjectivities alive within seemingly similar, "perfectly normal" families, the static symbol of the patriarchal postwar, nineteen-fifties, pre-Johnson white American family cannot hold. This is showing true respect toward an archetype, honoring its medley of forms, actively refusing to confuse one of its common articulations for its whole.

Notes

1 As collated meticulously by Jonathan R. Eller and William Touponce in *The Collected Stories of Ray Bradbury: A Critical Edition, Vol. I: 1938–1943* (Kent, OH: Kent State University Press, 2011).

2 In Chapter 5, we examine "Golden Apples of the Sun," in which a space rocket captain, on the edge of the sun, also imagines a primordial human first wielding fire. Joerg and the captain both experience a need to fill in an ancestral back story that can only be speculated.

3 Marvel's Incredible Hulk did not appear until May 1962.

4 Hillman names D.W. Winnicott, Melanie Klein, René Spitz, John Bowlby, and Anna Freud.

5 In *Breakfast of Champions* (1973), Vonnegut clowned around the symbol:

> If they studied their paper money for clues as to what their country was all about, they found, among a lot of other baroque trash, a picture of a truncated pyramid with a radiant eye on top of it, like this:

> Not even the President of the United States knew what that was all about. It was as though the country were saying to its citizens, "*In nonsense is strength.*" (*NS* 507–8)

Figure 4.8 Vonnegut's illustration of the Eye of Providence in *Breakfast of Champions* (1973).

6 I am reminded of Py's other-dimensional environment, "a crystalline plateau" (49) in "The Shape of Things." Here we have something like interdimensionality built into the home as an entertaining feature, as opposed to imposed debilitating physiological features.

7 More autobiography: Douglas was Bradbury's middle name, Spaulding his father's middle name.

8 The other three appeared decades later: "On the Orient, North" and "West of October" (*The Toynbee Convector*, 1988), "From the Dust Returned" (*Magazine of Fantasy & Science Fiction*, September 1994). One of Bradbury's final novels, *From the Dust Returned* (2001), ties all seven Elliott Family stories together, a full fifty-five years after the first was written.

Chapter 5

Hope for wholeness

Bradbury's heliocentric individuation

When astrophysicist Neil deGrasse Tyson was asked by *TIME Magazine* for the most astounding fact about the universe, he unfurled the following lyrical narrative based upon current scientific understandings of the origins of the cosmos:

> The most astounding fact is the knowledge that the atoms that comprise life on Earth, the atoms that make up the human body, are traceable to the crucibles that cooked light elements into heavy elements in their core, under extreme temperatures and pressures. These stars, the high mass ones among them, went unstable in their later years. They collapsed and then exploded, scattering their enriched guts across the galaxy, guts made of carbon, nitrogen, oxygen, and all the fundamental ingredients of life itself. These ingredients become part of gas clouds that condense, collapse, form the next generation of solar systems, stars with orbiting planets. And those orbiting planets now have the ingredients for life itself. So that when I look up at the night sky and I know that, yes, we are part of this universe, we are in this universe, but perhaps more important than both of those facts, is that the universe is in us.
>
> ("*TIME*'s Ten Questions")

Astrophysics has long been a political venture, seeking to sagely explain human beings' place in the scheme of existence. During the Cold War, the tone from the scientific establishment on stellar matters was markedly grave.

Collier's readers in March 1952 found, in the second paragraph of the cover feature, a fear-mongering call to the stars: "What you read here is not science fiction. It is serious fact. Moreover, it is an urgent warning that the U.S. must immediately embark on a long-range development program to secure for the West 'space superiority.' If we do not, somebody else will. That somebody else very probably would be the Soviet Union" ("What Are We Waiting For?" 23). Eight more issues, the final published in April 1954, focused on the conceived actualities of space exploration, introducing it as a national project that was, above all speculation, possible. These articles, featuring rocket scientist Wernher von Braun and conceptual paintings by

Chesley Bonestell, also inspired three episodes of *Disneyland*, a weekly TV show, two airing in 1955 and one in 1957. These propagandistic articles and shows helped convince Americans, with the urgency of anticipated competition with a hostile Russia, to support what became known as the Space Race. In this same decade, one of the most popular writers of stories imagining life in space was Ray Bradbury. His space tales in the nineteen-fifties, kicking off with *The Martian Chronicles* (1950), are particularly telling when considering how Americans, by the time Kennedy became President, put their faith in the space program. An enormous psychological shift in the mainstream had to occur and Bradbury played a popularizing role in it. Americans had to accept a new myth about themselves, as being space-faring people, in order for it to actually happen. But where *Collier's* pointed to the moon, Bradbury points readers to the sun.

"[T]he sun is a symbol of the source of life and the ultimate wholeness of man," Jung ascertained. "Now, the sun is an antique symbol that is still very close to us" (1936/1968, *CW 12*, ¶112). His scholarly interest in mythology's relation to psychology began with a solar connection in 1909 when treating a man suffering from schizophrenia. The patient shared a vision of the sun where it had a long tube hanging from it; wind's source was the waving back and forth of this tube. Jung later came across a similar image in an esoteric book on myth recorded by a member of the cult of Mithras, an ancient religion practiced during the time of the Roman Empire. Presuming the "Solar Phallus Man" could not have seen the book on Mithras, Jung was spurred to explain the comparable visions arising independently across time and culture, whereby he began expanding his own model of the unconscious:

> The observation [of independent invention] was not an isolated case: it was manifestly not [to be sure] a question of inherited ideas, but of an inborn disposition to produce parallel thought-formations, or rather of identical psychic structures common to all men, which I later called the archetypes of the collective unconscious.
>
> (1956/1967, *CW 5*, ¶ 224)

Later still, Jung was inspired when meeting Pueblos in New Mexico (1923) and Elgonyi in Kenya (1925), in large part due to their cultural relationships with the sun:

> [The Pueblo's] life is cosmologically meaningful, for he helps the father and preserver of all life in his daily rise and descent. If we set against this our own self-justifications, the meaning of our own lives as it is formulated by our reason, we cannot help but see our poverty. Out of sheer envy we are obliged to smile at the Indians' naïveté and to plume ourselves on our cleverness; for otherwise we would discover how impoverished and down at the heels we are. Knowledge does not

> enrich us; it removes us more and more from the mythic world in which we were once at home by right of birth.
>
> (*MDR* 281)

Jung felt these different groups of people possessed in their solar appreciations something Westerners had lost, a vitality in their own understandings of existence detrimentally absent in our own. The stress on reason in the Western world has created a societal atmosphere in which many find claims that we are the sun's children utterly absurd. And yet twentieth and now twenty-first century scientists like Carl Sagan and Neil deGrasse Tyson have worked to reframe just that, insisting that we *are* "star stuff." This idea is not brand new; Sir Arthur Eddington, an English astrophysicist, noted in 1928 that, "We are bits of stellar matter that got cold by accident, bits of a star gone wrong" (Baker 143).

In Campbell's estimation, the sun, even when thought of as merely a giant thermonuclear furnace, holds a sacred significance within the unconscious in terms of individual growth and the expansion of consciousness:

> The sun is [a] symbol of rebirth, evoking that idea of not coming back at all, of not being reborn but of passing beyond the spheres of rebirth altogether to a transcendent light. The typical image for this is the sun. The moon carries darkness within it but wherever the sun goes there is no darkness. There are only the shadows of those forces that do not open themselves to its light.
>
> (*Thou Art That* 89)

The concept of illumination, be it physical, mental, or spiritual, is rooted by our existence in relation to the sun, which is the ultimate source of light from our vantage point on Earth. Here is where Campbell accepts a metaphysical aspect to reality, or even an ultimate reality experienced only through transcendence. Echoing Jung's solar realization upon meeting the Pueblos and Elgonyi, Campbell saw a lacking in the West's relationship to the sun, and with that dearth an opportunity to mythically reorient our understanding of ourselves and the sun in accordance with scientific discoveries: "The heliocentric universe has never been translated into a mythology. Science and religion have therewith gone apart" (*IROS* 17). The effects of the split between science and religion are impossible to fully quantify. Woody Allen's childhood flashback in *Annie Hall* (1977), in which his character explains to a psychiatrist that his depression began after reading that the universe is expanding, wouldn't strike the funny bone like it does if we were not so uncomfortable with the futility that accompanies such knowledge. "Well, the universe is everything and if it's expanding," Alvy explains, "someday it will break apart and that will be the end of everything." As astrophysicist Tyson states, we desire feelings of "connectivity" ("*TIME*'s Ten Questions"), which one typically will not find in the latest articles on the magnetic topology of sunspots.

With regard to the end of the war that made the U.S.A. a world power, J. Robert Oppenheimer's comments about witnessing the first atomic bomb test leave a hollow ring: "If the radiance of a thousand suns were to burst at once into the sky, that would be like the splendor of the mighty one" (Jungk 201). The physicist, who Doniger chides as "[liking] to think that he knew some Sanskrit" (*Other People's Myths* 157), was quoting the *Bhagavad Gita*, which makes up a portion of the *Mahabharata*, a sacred Hindu text. Oppenheimer's mythic observation is intriguing because of his privileged relation to the processes of fusion and, more so, fission. The war-changing process developed by scientists for the U.S.A. was nuclear fission, in which the nucleus of an atom is split through a chain reaction. This runs opposite to the ongoing process at work within the sun. "Nuclear fusion is the merging together of light atomic nuclei to form heavier ones" (Baker 140), a force understood but beyond the reach of scientists to this day. It was German-American physicist Hans Bethe who explained that fusion of hydrogen into helium is what causes stars to shine, demystifying the cause of our sun's property of illumination. Returning to the line from the *Bhagavad Gita*, where "the radiance of a thousand suns" might "burst at once into the sky," one senses the atomic bomb's failure to produce something constructive, for it is inauthentic, reaching only the level of simile, being "*like* the splendor of the mighty one." Harnessed fission was the profound discovery of the nineteen forties, while fusion continues to rise in the morning and set in the evening and shine well beyond human reach day after day. As essayist Max Beerbohm observed about fire's relationship with the sun, "It cannot compete with its archetype" (247).

At a time boasting fission, the suns in Bradbury's stories remind readers of the fusion above. This is not to be confused with concepts of perfection. "Health, like wholeness," Hillman writes, "is completion of individuality, and to this belongs the dark side of life as well: symptoms, suffering, tragedy, and death. *Wholeness and health therefore do not exclude these 'negative' phenomena*; they are requisite for health" (*Suicide and the Soul* 125). Wholeness is sometimes confused with wholesomeness, a condition caught up in subjective values. Wholesome is itself an oxymoron, for "some" suggests a portion while "whole" is entirety – this is not wholeness. The sun may be our best example of wholeness because its light, warmth, and gravity have been essential in life's existence on Earth, while being at the same time a massive, ongoing explosion that would eradicate all life if we came too close to it. It is, all at once, creation and destruction: wholeness.

Do Bradbury's symbolic suns remythologize our demythologized, scientifically defined sun so that we might behold it once again with mystery? When Campbell wrote in 1986 that "the heliocentric universe has never been translated into a mythology," had Bradbury been doing just that since the nineteen-forties? By examining how he inflects the sun in different ways in different stories, what form will appear when we consider these representations as a constellation? This chapter focuses on several of his short stories, published between 1948 and 1954, that reignite the sun with a spiritual light, recalling something he told an interviewer in 1964: "With amiable good will accept yourself as fool, dumbbell, clod, murderer, dreamer, dark shadow and lover of the sun. Man is Paradox" (Aggelis 23).

Death of a rocket man

The image below is the title page spread of Bradbury's short story "The Rocket Man," as it appeared in *Argosy* (Feb. 1952). Originally published a year earlier in *Maclean's* (1 March 1951), here it is presented with a lush illustration by James Bingham and an editorial hook: "He was one of the new breed. He was born on Earth, and he had touched the stars. His home, while he lived, would be Space." This publication is the one we carry forth in this study, most especially because it came out a month prior to *Collier's* inaugural cover-feature on space, titled "Man Will Conquer Space *Soon*: Top Scientists Tell How in 15 Startling Pages." Bingham's painting might be classified as twenty-first century Rockwelliana. The clean lines, panes of color, and stylized furniture all fit in with a 1950s vision of the future, but, as in Norman Rockwell's work from the same period, focus rests on the people.

Figure 5.1 Title page spread for "The Rocket Man" in *Argosy*, Feb. 1952. (Interior images from *Argosy* courtesy of Steeger Properties, LLC. Copyright © 2015 Steeger Properties, LLC. All rights reserved.)

The boy appears to be about ten, awestruck in the shadow of the black-clad man standing before him. The man, the Rocket Man of the story's title, commands an imperious stance, his head encased in a glass helmet casting his complexion blue and grey. Three dull electrons spin around his torso where we find, at his solar plexus, a red dot – Bingham's touch – a detail not found in the story but appropriate because "The Rocket Man" features another of Bradbury's nuclear families that cannot stay together. This scene does not play out in the story, unless this is showing one of the father's moments of return, making the boy a ten-year-old Telemachus. He is certainly not fourteen yet, the age the narrator was when his father died, but there is a child-Hamlet-meeting-ghost-Hamlet aspect to the image. The Rocket Man's uniform, described by Bradbury as "like a black nebula, stars glittering here and there, distantly, in the material" (46), comes out black as soot on the printed page. It looks as though he has been charred, as he will be by the story's sad end, suggesting to an *Argosy* reader picking it up that perhaps this is a spirit, one who died in fire. No account of afterlife visitation makes its way into the story, but it is no stretch to consider this image as depicting a man who has an impending rendezvous with violent death.

In contrast, the two-page spread from Canadian magazine *Maclean's* the previous year focuses on the saddest aspect of the story: a family in turmoil. The boy, on the edge of his self-rocking bed, wonders upward in dark, wrinkled pajamas at a cloud of green atomic dust wafting from a pair of cupped hands, presumably his father's. Behind him, his mother's tearful face,

Figure 5.2 Title page spread by Michael Mitchell for *Maclean's*, 1 Mar. 1951. (© *Maclean's* magazine, 1951)

fingers on her cheeks, precipitates in the nebula. Molecular swirls mark the cloud, representing a part in the story when the boy puts his father's suit into a centrifuge and releases the solar system's powders, which he examines under a microscope with imaginative effect: "brilliant motes of meteor dust, comet tail and loam from far Jupiter, glistening like worlds themselves" (46). Michael Mitchell's artwork conflates the story's tragedy by showing the Rocket Man's offering hands releasing both his son's wonder at his career in space exploration and his wife's unbearable grief about it. The boy's pajamas curdle in wrinkles upon him, caught as he is between both parents in a marriage that cannot work.

Narrated by Doug, "The Rocket Man" is a grown son's reflection on his family's strained dynamics when he was growing up, focusing primarily on his father's inability to provide his mother with emotional security. As noted in the previous chapter, Bradbury's middle name was Douglas,[1] but we are not so concerned with autobiographical aspects unavailable to readers at the time. Douglas comes from a Scottish surname meaning "dark river" (*BTN*), a connotation befitting a son entranced by his father's exploits in black space and carried along in his early life by currents beyond his control. We do not learn the amount of time that has passed since the events recounted but do know Doug was fourteen when he was most burdened as go-between for his mother and father, both of them unable to connect. The problem this family carries is a conflict with the father's career. As a Rocket Man, he is constantly absent, flying into space on missions that take him across the solar system. Like the clipper ship captain proverbially married to the sea, Dad's true love is outer space.

The Rocket Man is the only character whose given name is never revealed. Doug lets slip his own, and Lilly as his mother's – as in lilies, flowers of funerals and purity (*BTN*) – but the father is only ever named by two of his roles, Dad and the Rocket Man, and the story's title tells us which of those comes foremost. His name might as well be Willy Loman; it is never made clear why his rocket falls into the sun at the end, if by accident or to commit self-immolation. He is unable to reconcile his need to be himself with the demands of his marriage, no matter what tactics Mom employs to try to keep him grounded. His own attempt, by gardening, fails to ease the space-yearning anxiety. When tending his yard, he forces his attention downward, into the soil he is working, although it is obvious that he is doing his best to ignore the sky above. His relationship with Earth itself is no match for the pull of living beyond it, in the unknown frontiers above. This man needs a lot of space – *outer* space – and Lilly cannot handle his absences. Instead of incorporating this limitation into the way he lives his life, he hurls himself back and forth between two lives, the idle one with wife and son on Earth and the adventurous one that takes him to other moons and planets.

The tension here is that of a patriarchal family in which the father's work, while providing for the material needs of wife and son, separates him from the family for long stretches. Plenty of American families have dealt with this problem and, as opportunities in a growing infrastructure grew throughout the country in the mid-twentieth century, many husbands and fathers were called to lives on the road. The Rocket Man is a lot like a long haul trucker, a career that grew with the new interstate system of highways. Doug relates his clumsy attempts to hide his love for life out there: "'It's the best thing in a lifetime of best things.' Then he caught himself. 'Oh it's really nothing at all. Routine. You wouldn't like it'" (83). His effort to dissuade Doug mostly arises, it seems, from a desire to protect his wife; he knows that losing her son to space, too, would destroy her. His own ability to relate to his boy is undeveloped, occurring in intense bursts only after he's exhausted his appraisals of the earthly lacks of life on a rocket: "And I knew now we would talk, as we had always talked, for three hours straight" (83). In Dad-mode he listens to Doug, showing approval with chest slaps, but his advice always returns to his own condition as a Rocket Man, overriding his attention to his son. Asking, perhaps, too much, he implores his son for a promise: to never become a Rocket Man, even though the boy has given it a lot of thought. Not listening, he goes on to express the greatest struggle in his life: "I try to stay here. Last Saturday when I got home I started trying so damned hard to stay here" (84). This is hardly fair to Doug, a young teenager who just wants his father to hear him. The Rocket Man is already consumed before the sun consumes him.

When he promises the next rocket mission will be his last, it certainly is:

> His ship had fallen into the sun.
>
> And the sun was big and fiery and merciless, and it was always in the sky and you couldn't get away from it.
>
> (84)

Unable to accept this outcome, his mother shifts their lives to a nocturnal existence, entirely rejecting the sun. If the night sky before was a constant reminder of his time away in space, the sun has overtaken its pall with a dread far worse. But the sun is the divine circle, a mandala, the entirety of conscious, unconscious, and collective unconscious – the whole potentiality of every individual. The light-giving sun we see outside is reflected by a source of illumination within. The Rocket Man's fall into the sun indicates that he is ultimately consumed by himself, by his own potential. "The greatest limitation for man is the 'self'; it is manifested in the experience: 'I am only that!'" wrote Jung, "Only consciousness of our narrow confinement in the self forms the link to the limitlessness of the unconscious" (*MDR* 357). In his struggle to be true to himself, Dad returns to star-cinders in the sun.

His death sends Mom indoors, an ending not unlike that suffered by so many of myth's great exiles. Her grief is a bitter one, refusing to forgive the sun for claiming her husband, the father of her son. Previously she railed against the night sky, knowing it kept her husband away from her: "Mother wasn't afraid of the sky in the day so much, but it was the night stars that she wanted to turn off, and sometimes I could almost see her reaching for a switch in her mind, but never finding it" (46). Doug tells of buying her "some darker, greener shades" because "Once she said the light was too strong at night" (83). He is her protector, finding himself in the position of providing care for a parent before he is mature, an inverse of the parenting relationship that some children face. She, too, is consumed – by her husband's absences – reacting to him coldly when he does return home, unable to make eye contact with him.

The problem, as the Rocket Man understands it, is stated plainly to Doug: "'I'm not there for her,' said Dad" (83). Doug notes, however, that there actually were good times between them, days he witnessed where Mom and Dad were in sync, even happy. This joy was real but brief, for "at the end of such days when he was there to her, she would always cry. And Dad would stand helpless, gazing about the room as if to find the answer, but never finding it" (83). There is no balance in this family. The boy plays both caregiver for his mother and confidant for his father, roles that many fourteen-year-olds will not find themselves prepared to fulfill. The most remarkable character here may in fact be Doug, our narrator, who relays the tragic story of how his family came apart with maturity and a notable lack of acrimony. As a boy, he revered his father for his career in space, sympathized with his mother's emotional frailties, and never seems to blame any of them for what happened, not even himself, as children of suffering relationships sometimes do. He accepts that his father was enigmatic and that his mother was insecure, and certainly makes it clear that he loves both as individuals.

The Rocket Man is not the only character from this period in Bradbury's career to combust in the sun. In "A Little Journey" (*Galaxy Science Fiction*, Aug. 1951) we meet a con man preying on others' hopes for salvation, Mr. Thirkell, and an old woman, Mrs. Bellowes, who follows him to Mars to find God. A hundred other little old ladies have given everything they have to his divine promise. These women are eager in the elderly phase of life to experience a direct relationship with God. Mrs. Amelia Bellowes has previously invested her faith in Hinduism, spiritualists, astrologers, and evangelists, her openness to various traditions humanistic – yet, in none of them has she found what she seeks. Amelia, a variant of the name Amalia, means "work" (*BTN*), fitting for a character who prioritizes her spiritual quest, who is working at it.

Thirkell is a fraud and a materialist: "I don't know anything about space. He's not out there anyway. I lied. I don't know where He is, and I couldn't find Him if I wanted to" (156). When the ladies discover the lie, they overwhelm him, making him take them in his rust bucket rocket to meet God, as guaranteed. In a variation on Bradbury's story "Kaleidoscope" (*Thrilling Wonder Stories*, Oct. 1949), in which astronauts are scattered to deaths in space after a rocket collision, Thirkell's rickety rocket explodes and the travelers are scattered into blackness. Like the Rocket Man, the conman is destined for solar cremation:

> *There goes Mr. Thirkell,* thought Mrs. Bellowes.
> And she knew where he was going. He was going to be burned and roasted and broiled good, but very good.
> Mr. Thirkell was falling down into the Sun.
>
> (158)

And so Thirkell is blown by the actions of Mrs. Bellowes, herself a working bellows, to burn. The pilgrims are destined to die floating through space, spared fiery end for a suffocating whimper. Thirkell's trajectory sends him toward an overwhelming end, one he is not ready for, because he lived in denial of his self. As Martinez points out, "Literature, because of its multitude of renderings of numinous experiences, has the capacity to manifest complexity concerning successful and unsuccessful attempts at their integration" ("Reading for Psyche: Numinosity" 1–2). These are stories of failed integration.

In totality, Bradbury's sun engulfs the self-possessed and self-denying alike. The con man is fed to the sun's bright hellfire in a stroke of poetic justice, incinerated for his sins against a hundred old women – his death brought upon himself for unscrupulous deception and manipulation. The Rocket Man, who fights his own soul to live between a grounded family life on Earth and a dangerous adventure in the stars, is a tragic figure, losing his life under circumstances left mysterious. There is no knowing how it happened, why it happened, if it was a malfunction with his rocket or a deliberate act. He leaves his son with a discussion of the "million" ways to die in space, claiming "They never find you" (83), and though he may be right, hurtling into the sun is not a death he lists. His focus is on the immediacy of death out there in the void: "One thing," he said later, "it's quick in space. Death. It's over like that. You don't linger. Most of the time you don't even know it. You're dead and that's it" (84). This may have come as a comfort to the Rocket Man, knowing that he would not suffer, but there is no comfort in it for Lilly or Doug, whose pain over his death will not end, will linger, will be all they know for grief's long term. For them the life-giving and life-ending sun is a constant reminder of their personal loss and the painful absences that led up to it.

Venusian chronicles

In the anthology *Farewell Fantastic Venus!* (1968), Brian Aldiss collects fantastic and scientific writings about the second planet from the sun to show how Westerners have imagined it for centuries. The book came as a response to *Venera 4*, a Soviet probe that became the first piece of human technology to land on another planet. Venus, it turned out, was very hot and practically devoid of water, curious given the planet's extensive cloud cover. Those clouds, so reflective of the sun's light as to make it stand out with prominence in our morning and evening skies, lent our "sister planet" what Aldiss calls elusiveness: "An unsatisfactory sibling she has proved at last. And even to the imagination there has always been something cheating about her. She has been teasing, ambiguous, hiding herself near the sun, disappointing – a close relation who has yet stayed distant, blank-faced" (11). While space fantasies about Mars abounded over the last one hundred fifty years, Venus lagged in popular imagination, inspiring far fewer works.

Bearing distinction as author of *The Martian Chronicles* (1950), Bradbury also wrote several Venusian tales. Venus, not just a planet but the Roman Goddess of love, afforded one of his first big breaks when friend and writing tutor Leigh Brackett asked him to finish a Venusian novella under contract. "He said yes, and forthwith did so, without any outline or a stitch of anything to go on except the first 10,000 words," she recalled. "The result was 'Lorelei of the Red Mist', one-half pure Brackett, one-half pure Bradbury. I have heard all sorts of theories about how I did the action bits and he did the poetry, etc. Not so. It was not even a collaboration in the ordinary sense" (xii). Published in *Planet Stories* (Summer 1946), "Lorelei of the Red Mist" follows Hugh Starke, whose consciousness has been uploaded into the body of Conan, a tribute to Robert E. Howard's famous barbarian. His struggles with Rann, a siren from Venus's sea of scarlet vapors, and his efforts to overcome her unfeeling nature provide much of the novella's conflict. Following Brackett's lead, Venus is depicted as wet, a popular portrayal at the time; Robert A. Heinlein, in *Logic of Empire* (1943), and Henry Kuttner, in *Fury* (1947), also wrote swampland Venuses.

Bradbury independently produced two rain-soaked Venusian stories relevant to our task of tracking the sun's course through his short fiction, using the facts of its clouds and closeness to the sun to meditate mythically upon our relationship with our closest star. The first story we are concerned with is "Death-By-Rain," published in *Planet Stories* (Summer 1950), thereafter collected as "The Long Rain." In a feature recurring throughout many of his solar stories, the protagonist is only named archetypally by rank, here as the lieutenant. Following the crash of their rocket, the lieutenant, Simmons, Pickard, and a fourth crew member journey on foot through the wet, white, fungal jungle in hopes of finding a Sun Dome, one of one-hundred-twenty-six identical outposts Congressional funding from Earth has built in the wilderness. These Sun Domes are sanctuaries stocked with books and cocoa and illumination from an overhead light evocative of daylight as they know it: "There it would be, the yellow sun, just the size of the Earth sun and it was warm and continuous and the rain world of Venus would be forgotten as long as they stayed . . ." (37). The dome is at once a safe house, a destination, and a site for reunion with sunshine in the midst of a storming, inhospitable, otherworldly environment – an Earthly haven on Venus.

Venus experiences never-ending rains that bleach everything they spatter. The lieutenant, once brown, has turned pale in the rain, even his hair and eyebrows going white. This is not a purifying whiteness but the moldy, sickly whiteness of decay. The rivers, streams, and the Single Sea are described as mercury, silver, and milk; the blanched flora, which grow through life cycles fast enough to be watched, rot as soon as they are picked:

> The white, white jungle with the pale cheese-colored leaves, and the earth carved of wet Camembert, and the tree boles like immense toadstools, everything black and white. And how often could you see the soil itself? Wasn't it mostly a creek, a stream, a puddle, a pool, a lake, a river, and then, at last the sea?
>
> (37)

That description follows a paragraph about the Sun Dome, dousing the reader's chances of lingering over thoughts of the sun's comforts. The white rains and vegetation connote "infirmity and disembodiment, a lack of red-blooded vigor or a failure of courage. White is the pale horseman of death, the pallor of the corpse, bone stripped of flesh, shroud and wraith" (660). Venus's whiteness, however, is not elusive, something to be hunted down; it is overabundant to the point of suffocation.

The first discovery made by the four men is that they have unwittingly circled back to their rocket's crash site, which is already overgrown with flowering and suddenly rotting fungus. "Good Lord, we're not any closer to anywhere!" one of them complains (37). Their despair at the perpetuation of their aimlessness is soon interrupted by the appearance of a prodigious monster, one of Bradbury's finest and briefest creations:

> The monster was supported upon a thousand electric blue legs. It walked swiftly and terribly. It struck down a leg with a driving blow. Everywhere a leg struck a tree fell and burned. Great whiffs of ozone filled the rainy air, and smoke blew away and was broken up by the rain. The monster was a half-mile wide and a mile high and it felt of the ground like a great blind thing. Sometimes, for a moment, it had no legs at all. And then, in an instant, a thousand whips would fall out of its belly, white-blue whips, to sting the jungle.
>
> (37)

"Here she is!" one of the men cries, imbuing the monster with the feminine aspect commonly attributed to large storms (38). The electrical monster claims the unnamed crew member's life before moving on its way, charring him in its Greco-Roman temple-like undercarriage, described as "a great hall of pillars" (38). His end is likened to the death of a fly hitting an electric bug zapper and he is reduced to ashes. It is as if the storming weather has coalesced into a living creature, albeit one more atmospheric than corporeal, and its appearance is not unlike that of the Questing Beast in Arthurian legend. Encountered by Pellinore, Palomides, and Percival, the Questing Beast often has a serpent's head, a leopard's body, a lion's tail, the feet of a rabbit or a stag – and the call of thirty hounds barking. In Malory's *Le Morte d'Arthur* (1485), the Beast appears after Arthur's incestuous affair, and is never caught by Palomides despite his making it his quest to do so. The chaotic conflagration of form and appearance, not to mention its elusive and passing nature, are qualities shared with the electrical monster of Venus, named for Rome's Goddess of Eros.

To their elation, the lieutenant, Simmons, and Pickard eventually arrive at a Sun Dome; however, it stands decrepit and overrun with damp and moss. Simmons blames the Venusians, so elusive their only appearance in the story is by his word. He claims they likely came out of the sea, where they live; destroyed the dome; and took the survivors into the abyss, where they drown men slowly, taking eight hours to do it. The lack of an obvious enemy begins to gut Pickard, who shares a memory of being bullied in school. Then the adversary was obvious, but Venus offers no clarity. He complains at the inability to fight off something as ubiquitous as rain. Unable to define their tormentors, Simmons and Pickard are reduced to paranoia of malfeasant beings alive in the sea and the amorphousness of unperpetrated tortures upon their bodies and souls.

It is the lieutenant who holds himself together through this journey. A French word, lieutenant means "place holding," the *OED*'s first definition being: "One who takes the place of another; usually, an officer civil or military who acts for a superior; a representative, substitute, vicegerent." If he is holding the place of another, who would that be? Perhaps he is so attentive to his duties and how they uphold his society's aims and values that his individual desires are superseded. A hallmark of the hero is an appropriate degree of selflessness for the betterment of the collective, and where Simmons and Pickard worry so acutely about themselves he is able to hold himself at bay.

When they stop to rest, the lieutenant does not sleep, distressed by vegetation suddenly growing *upon* him. He and Simmons decide to push on, but Pickard has given in, "with the bubbles of rain breaking out in his whitened hair and manacles of rain jewels dripping from his wrists and his neck" (41). Pickard, chained into the Venusian equivalent of the thousand-yard stare, will drown upright. This moment provides inspiration for the story's title page illustration. Uncredited, the drawing, in EC Comics style, shows Simmons leveling his pistol at Pickard, the lieutenant reaching out to stop him. The trio, in jumpsuits and oxygen tank backpacks, is washed out on the page, vertical streaks of rain disrupting the art, lashing over them and the mangrove-rooted jungle growth. The action between Simmons and the lieutenant is offset by Pickard's still hopelessness: on his knees, his head is thrown back to a skyward, open-mouthed stare, his fist clenched just above the water. As it happens, Simmons shoots him dead, a mercy killing the

"I'll show you what to do with him," said Simmons.

DEATH-BY-RAIN

By RAY BRADBURY

Four men, crash-landed on Venus, world of eternal rain. Three men, slogging through drenching gloom. Two men, staggering senselessly on. One man, battering at the endless curtains of rain, RAIN, *RAIN!*

Figure 5.3 Illustration for "Death-By-Rain" in *Planet Stories*. (© Love Romances Publishing Co., Inc./Fiction House, 1950)

lieutenant reluctantly accepts. A page later, Simmons loses his hearing to the rain and commits suicide. "We weren't made for this," the lieutenant says for himself, to himself, "no Earthman was or ever will be able to take it. Your nerves, your nerves" (42). This final repetition may be where another river-colonizing casualty, Joseph Conrad's Kurtz, began his own descent, ending up at, "The horror! The horror!"

"If you have someone who can help you, that's fine," says Campbell, "But, ultimately, the last deed has to be done by oneself" (*POM* 149). Only once he is alone, after his crewmates have all died terrible deaths, does the lieutenant finds the Sun Dome. He wastes no time when "a faint yellow smudge" appears, "his feet crashing into mirrors and glass, his arms flailing at diamonds and precious stones" of rain (42). Unlike the derelict Sun Dome, this one is fully furnished and functional, and when he enters his worries lift:

> The sun hung very high in the blue sky of the room, warm, hot, yellow, and very fine.
>
> He walked forward, tearing off his clothes as he went.
>
> (42)

Thus the story ends. There is no denying the vitalizing quality of this sun, even if it is an artificial light. The sun in the Sun Dome is one of renewal; our last image of the lieutenant is him stripping as bare as pre-Fall Adam in its light and warmth. Mythologically speaking, in entering the Sun Dome and denuding his body, he undergoes what Campbell describes as the deed of one entering a temple for worship: "The one who enters the temple compound and proceeds to the sanctuary is imitating the deed of the original hero. His aim is to rehearse the universal pattern as a means of evoking within himself the recollection of the life-centering, life-renewing form" (*Hero with a Thousand Faces* 40). The lieutenant's harrowing of Venus gives way to a religious experience in this manmade sanctuary that links him back to the naked potential of living a human life on Earth. He has passed through what Campbell calls the "sun door": "The meaning is that the grace that pours into the universe through the sun door is the same as the energy of the bolt that annihilates and is itself indestructible: the delusion-shattering light of the Imperishable is the same as the light that creates" (*Hero with a Thousand Faces* 134). Bradbury's lieutenant, in his achievement, is the Campbellian hero.

If we are to read "Death-By-Rain" as a myth of individuation, the lieutenant's goal in reaching the Sun Dome is to escape the storming shapelessness of forces and conditions he will never be able to control. The place of calm consciously carved out of the mess of vegetation and elemental furies is not the ego, for that exists only in the individual characters and is terribly vulnerable when exposed to gales of the unconscious. The Sun Dome is rather an environment properly balanced toward the pressures outside, a sanctuary within the drowning maelstrom. And so the Sun Dome exists prior to the crew's crisis – not superheroically hewn out of the unforgiving wilderness by the lieutenant alone – just as the potential for wholeness already exists within each of us before we actualize it. There is a sense in life that balance is not merely achieved, it is also a state to which one arrives, however briefly, often at the expense of self-sacrifice. Perhaps this story's title as first published in *Planet Stories* is more appropriate than its subsequent one, "The Long Rain"; "Death-By-Rain" not only suggests the deaths of the crew members, of Pickard and then Simmons, but also that of the rain-bleached lieutenant who is reborn whole upon walking through the solar door.

The other Venusian tale relating to the sun is "All Summer in a Day," first published in *The Magazine of Fantasy and Science Fiction* (March 1954). It tells of first generation Venusians, set to experience *the* meteorological event of their nine-year-old lives: the brief parting of clouds that will usher in their first memorable view of the sun. It seems this is the same Venus presented in "Death-By-Rain," with its constant rain and fast-growing, fast-rotting vegetation: in seven years, "[a] thousand forests had been crushed under the rain and grown up a thousand times to be crushed again" (641). If we orient this story in relation to that one, though both stand alone, the human presence on Venus is at a further stage of development. There is no mention of Sun Domes, and survival is not an immediate problem; the planet's storming environment has been countered with an underground city colony. Families now live on Venus with the story set in "the schoolroom of the children of the rocket men and women who had come to a raining world to set up civilization and live out their lives" (641).

One of the nine-year-old students, who are described as "so many roses, so many weeds, intermixed" (641), is unique for being born on Earth and remembering the unclouded sun. Margot is vilified for this, "hated [. . .] for all these reasons of big and little consequence" (643), and locked away in a closet so that she misses the event. William, her chief imprisoner, becomes an indistinct member of the class once he voices the idea of shutting her away. From that point on, the boys and girls are portrayed collectively, through the sun's appearance and brief hour of illumination, until the first raindrop falls into a girl's open palm. When the sun disappears again for seven more years of rain, they experience guilt for what they have done to Margot. The story ends with them, suffering regret, letting her out of the closet.

The name Margot is a French diminutive of Margaret, which, we recall from Vonnegut's numerous Margarets, is Ancient Greek for "pearl" (*BTN*). Like the pearl, a semi-precious mineralization formed through the agitation of grit in an oyster's shell, Margot has had to protect her soul under an opaque barrier of clouds: "Margot stood alone. She was a very frail girl who looked as if she had been lost in the rain for years and the rain had washed out the blue from her eyes and the red from her mouth and the yellow from her hair. She was an old photograph dusted from an album, whitened away, and if she spoke at all her voice would be a ghost" (642). She is a poet, writing "*I think the sun is a flower, / That blooms for just one hour*" (642), amid an artless class of intermixed roses and weeds. This is a story in which the majority feels insecure in the presence of a true individual. She has known the sun – they have not – and the mystery of her knowledge against their own lacking raises spite and envy. Margot becomes a painted bird, suffering among children of rocket men and women who have gone to Venus for financial gain, opting for overcast existences where the brief appearance of sunlight is astronomical. In a social group like this, the presence of one who isn't at odds with the others but who *is* odd for her originality and grounding poses a threat to the structure and order of the entire colonial endeavor.

A vitalized individual, even an ailing one like Margot, does not always inspire vitalization in others; sometimes he or she inspires ire from those living without vitality. The problems of living in seemingly endless rain are compounded for this generation of children born out of sunlight. They did not choose to be born on Venus, and growing up there is difficult. They are all victims of their parents' decision to "come to a raining world to set up civilization and live out their lives" (641). It is only through experiencing the sun firsthand that the classmates gain appreciation for it and what Margot has been denied for so long. There is no redemption for the class, but there is the dawning of guilt and shame for their cruel action. They are shown to gain a new awareness after they discover together the vitalizing aspects of the sun by experiencing its light and warmth.

The sun on Bradbury's Venus is as elusive as the surface of Venus from our perspective on Earth. The clouds of Venus, which exist in fact, provide a setting where sunlight rarely and briefly touches life directly. The wet, fungal landscape is another imagining of the unforgiving frontier, a wilderness where civilization is unwelcome. And yet the sun does shine on Venus, reproduced in miniature in the Sun Domes, remembered by a sun-sick expatriate in a poem, and anticipated and then embraced by a class of ignorant children. In showing the detriments that living without the sun inflicts upon characters in these stories, Bradbury champions the effects of living in its light. And while Bradbury is remembered as a fantastic chronicler of Mars, Venus coincided with the end of his life: he died 5 June 2012 during the transit of Venus, an extremely rare astronomical event in which the planet passes directly between Earth and the sun. As Mark Twain famously came in and went out with Halley's Comet, Bradbury's death – and life – stand punctuated in conjunction with Venus and the sun.

Sun of a preacher man

In "The Man" (*Thrilling Wonder Stories*, Feb. 1949), a team of rocket men arriving on an alien planet discover they have just missed the arrival of a messianic figure. The Captain is skeptical but becomes convinced of the visitor's holy nature, resolving to hunt him down across the reaches of space. Here we see the outcome of a materialistic glory hound who has glimpsed others living vital lives and strikes off to find and take that vitality for himself. His awakening is to the hunger of his own spiritual impoverishment. It is all a mistake, however, because after he leaves we find out that the messiah has not left the planet and is still there. The Captain will be following nothing through space but the projected trail of his own folly.

"In This Sign . . .," published in pulp digest *Imagination* (April 1951), presents the opposite scenario: Father Peregrine is an Episcopal priest sent to Mars to tend to the spiritual needs of the colonists. Instead he encounters sun-like spheres of blue light in the Martian hills. These he takes for souls, and again we are presented with a solar symbol of the wholeness of the psyche. Notes Jung: "In Neoplatonic philosophy the soul has definite affinities with the sphere. The soul substance is laid round the concentric spheres of the four elements above the fiery heaven" (1936/1968, *CW 12*, ¶109). Indeed, these Martian spheres turn out to be souls, pure and transcendent of corporeal existence. Whereas in "The Man" the Captain takes off on a hunt to shake down a messianic traveler, Father Peregrine takes it upon himself, against protestations of his fellow priests, to prove the alien spheres of light are sentient and, furthermore, to save them spiritually. When they finally reveal their sentience to him, introducing themselves as the Old Ones, he and his colleagues are humbled into turning their ministry once again to their own people, the humans residing in First Town.

This story is better known under the title "The Fire Balloons" and today stands as part of *The Martian Chronicles*, though it was not included in the first publication (May 1950).[2] We proceed with the title "In This Sign . . .," for it raises an otherwise missing association. *In hoc signo vinces*, Latin for "in this sign you will conquer," is ascribed to a vision experienced by Constantine I. According to Eusebius, "his own eyes beheld the trophy of the cross declared in the sky above the sun, organized out of light, and telling with its own writing: By this conquer" ("Eusebius," translation mine). Revelations cannot get much more imperial than this one, urging the first Christian Emperor of Rome to conquer the empire's enemies with the cross of Christianity. Father Peregrine does not set out to conquer, unless we read his aim at spreading salvation as an imperial cause – which historically it has been in many instances. In a curious way, he flips Constantine I's vision, swapping out the symbol of the cross seen above the sun for a solar sign he crafts as a sphere of fire.

Much has been made critically about *Chronicles'* allegory for the American frontier myth but "Sign" remains largely unanalyzed in this respect. The priestly crew of the rocket *Crucifix* recalls historical clergymen who encountered American peoples. Bartolomé de las Casas (1484–1566), the first ordained priest in the Americas, Spain's *Protectoría de indios*, protested the abuses he witnessed perpetrated by the Spanish against the people of Hispaniola. There were also the French and Belgian Jesuits who traveled into the North American interior between 1632 and 1650 to spread Christianity, conforming to an extent with the peoples they lived with in hopes of conversion. And Jonathan Edwards the younger (1745–1801), an abolitionist and theologian, was fluent in Mahican after growing up in an integrated Massachusetts community. He eventually wrote a short book on the subject, *Observations on the Mahican Language* (1788). Like these real world forbears, Father Peregrine is drawn to the indigenous population of Mars. Seeing in them the potential for realizing his desired destiny as a savior of souls, Christianity is presented as a colonizer's toolkit. And Peregrine's brand of Christianity is, as it was for the Jesuits, malleable in the forms of its symbols.

The Very Reverend Father Joseph Daniel Peregrine's name is loaded with Judeo-Christian meanings. Joseph is Hebrew for "He will add" and Daniel for "God is my judge," invoking the Biblical God's capacities for providing and judging. Joseph and Daniel are also Old Testament figures revered for their skills in the interpretation of dreams, both promoted to significant roles in the kingdoms of Egypt and Babylon respectively. Bradbury's Joseph Daniel is himself a visionary, recognizing disembodied souls where other priests see "blue balloons." There is also the Joseph of the New Testament, who steps in as the adoptive father of Jesus after God urges him to do so in a dream, and Joseph of Arimathea, who prepares Jesus' body after death for entombment, a father's role. Bradbury's protagonist, a spiritual father by occupation, also adopts a fatherly attitude to the Old Ones, deciding to raise their souls with the Good Word.

Peregrine's surname calls to mind the species of falcon, a raptor, a bird of prey, but also holds a diversity of meanings, originating from Latin: pairing *pereger* ("beyond the borders") and *ager* ("land") to mean "one beyond his own land" (*OED*). That meaning persists in English: "Foreign; outlandish, strange; imported from abroad," "A pilgrim; a traveller in a foreign country," "Travelling; wandering." Peregrine also casts other intriguing inflections: a peregrine was "A free resident in ancient Rome having no rights of citizenship," and in Roman Law a peregrine praetor had the duty to "administer justice between peregrines [. . .] or between Roman citizens and peregrines"; the peregrine tone was "one of the tones used in Gregorian plainsong in the recitation of Psalm 114 (113 in the Vulgate), and later adapted as an Anglican chant"; and peregrine also has a use in astrology, being the property "[o]f a planet: situated in a part of the zodiac where it has none of its essential dignities." Hillman would wholeheartedly have us heed these bygone definitions:

> We need to recall that we do not just make words up or learn them in school or ever have them fully under control. Words, like angels, are powers which have invisible power over us. They are personal presences which have whole mythologies: genders, genealogies (etymologies concerning origins and creations), histories, and vogues; and their own guarding, blaspheming, creating, and annihilating effects.
>
> (*A Blue Fire* 28–29)

Father Peregrine exhibits some, if not all, of these aspects of his name. He is "one beyond his own land," a foreigner and pilgrim to Mars, a human Other to the Old Ones, who are to him Other humans. Though a peregrine himself, he acts to bring justice via salvation to the phosphorescent spheres, becoming an Episcopal praetor of sorts. Astrologically, Father Peregrine and the other priests' notions, born of Earth, are themselves peregrine on Mars. One of Peregrine's chief concerns is sin, having "written a little book: THE PROBLEM OF SIN ON OTHER WORLDS" (58), to which his skeptical colleague Father Stone argues, "No Adam and Eve on Mars. No original sin. Maybe the Martians live in a state of God's grace" (64). Stone winds up being partially correct about their grace, but the priests' consuming worry about Earthly sin is, in an astrological light, situated far from Earth on Mars "where it has none of its essential dignities." Understood as a kind of predator, Father Peregrine's preferred prey are salvation-starved souls.

Father Stone and Brother Mathias are the only other characters bearing names. Mathias echoes Matthias from the New Testament, who fills Judas's vacancy as the twelfth apostle to Christ (*Acts* 1:18–26), peculiar in that he becomes one of the twelve after Christ has died and risen. In "Sign," Brother Mathias, who initially regards the blue spheres to be "the body of a soulless animal" (67), is also a latecomer, in that the salvation the priests hope to deliver unto the Old Ones has already been attained. Father Stone, a dogmatic priest who dismisses the Old Ones as "[b]lue [. . .] circus balloons" (60, 66) and "[m]onsters" (61), consistently upholds church doctrine. He is a foil in the narrative, his skepticism rising against Peregrine's belief in the Martian souls. His ways, like those in stone, are set; and yet he undergoes a greater transformation than Peregrine in the end, after the Old Ones have communicated their state of grace. "The way I see it is there's a Truth on every planet. All parts of the Big Truth," he says, "For this Truth here is as true as Earth's Truth" (71). Stone, after all, can crumble.

During their initial encounter with the floating blue orbs, Fathers Peregrine and Stone are nearly buried in an avalanche. In a swoop of blue light they find themselves unharmed by falling rocks. Peregrine is convinced the speechless fire spheres acted to save them and goes about trying to prove they possess not only consciousness but good will, what he calls humanity. His experiment has him stand at the edge of a cliff and throw himself off in the hopes the spheres will deliver him safely to the ground. The taking of one's own life being a sin, he rationalizes his test: "It wouldn't be suicide, would it, if I did it out of Love . . .?" (65). In this act the priest tempts the blue fires, and this tempting bears relation to one of Satan's three temptations of Christ. In *Matthew*, it is the second temptation (*King James* 4:5–7); in *Luke*, the third (*King James* 4:9–12). Setting Jesus on the pinnacle of the temple in Jerusalem and daring him to jump off, Satan uses Old Testament scripture (*Psalms* 91:11,12) that says God will send angels to the rescue "lest at any time thou dash thy foot against a stone"; Christ counters with "Thou shalt not tempt the Lord thy God," also from Old Testament scripture (*Deuteronomy* 6:16). Bradbury underscores this connection with Peregrine, anticipating "himself *dashed* on [the rocks] and sent to glory" (italics mine 65). Yet he is tempted not by a devil but the desire to know if the blue orbs are intelligent. Also, Peregrine tempts not God but the spheres, unless we consider his hope that God will forgive him if he is wrong a challenge. This potentially suicidal behavior is altogether peculiar for a priest, but Peregrine is consistently portrayed as a maverick to his own religious tradition.

His leap is the focus of Malcolm Smith's illustration in *Imagination*. Another instance of EC Comics-style art, the Martian landscape is presented

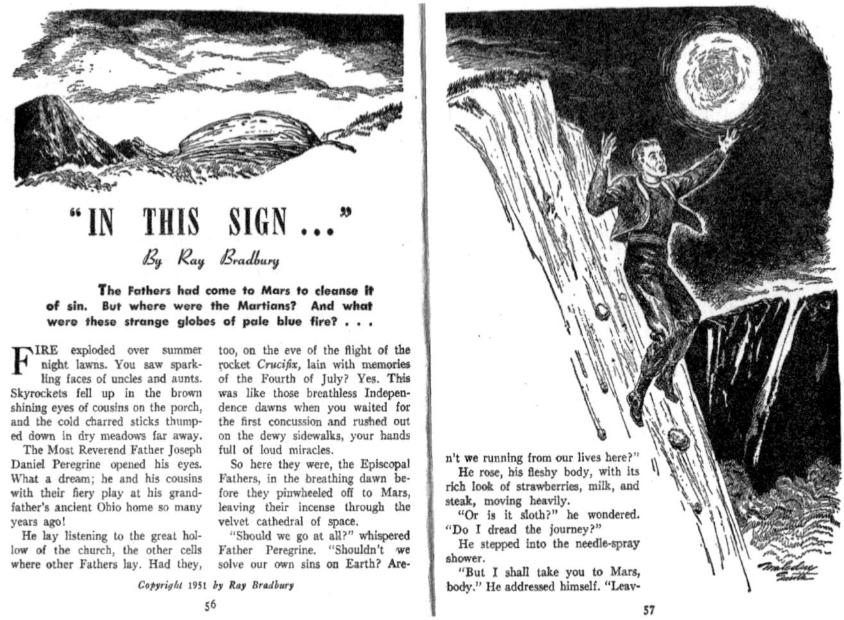

"IN THIS SIGN . . ."

By Ray Bradbury

The Fathers had come to Mars to cleanse it of sin. But where were the Martians? And what were these strange globes of pale blue fire? . . .

FIRE exploded over summer night lawns. You saw sparkling faces of uncles and aunts. Skyrockets fell up in the brown shining eyes of cousins on the porch, and the cold charred sticks thumped down in dry meadows far away.

The Most Reverend Father Joseph Daniel Peregrine opened his eyes. What a dream; he and his cousins with their fiery play at his grandfather's ancient Ohio home so many years ago!

He lay listening to the great hollow of the church, the other cells where other Fathers lay. Had they, too, on the eve of the flight of the rocket *Crucifix*, lain with memories of the Fourth of July? Yes. This was like those breathless Independence dawns when you waited for the first concussion and rushed out on the dewy sidewalks, your hands full of loud miracles.

So here they were, the Episcopal Fathers, in the breathing dawn before they pinwheeled off to Mars, leaving their incense through the velvet cathedral of space.

"Should we go at all?" whispered Father Peregrine. "Shouldn't we solve our own sins on Earth? Aren't we running from our lives here?"

He rose, his fleshy body, with its rich look of strawberries, milk, and steak, moving heavily.

"Or is it sloth?" he wondered. "Do I dread the journey?"

He stepped into the needle-spray shower.

"But I shall take you to Mars, body." He addressed himself. "Leav-

Copyright 1951 *by Ray Bradbury*

56

57

Figure 5.4 Title spread by Malcolm Smith for "In This Sign . . ." (© Greenleaf Publishing Company, 1951)

as rocky with a dark, crosshatch sky. Father Peregrine falls feet first, his arms out, doubt in his face. Hovering just beyond his fingertips, one of the Martian spheres is a white circle with short pen strokes at the center and white lines around the corona, implying motion. Before we have read the editorial hook about "strange globes of pale blue fire" (56), it looks like the sun. As a moment chosen for illustration, it emphasizes the Fall. When Peregrine leaps and is saved again by the blue spheres of light, he resolves, like the Jesuits in North America in the 1600s, to reformulate Christianity to meet the alien souls on their own terms – or, rather, what he *perceives* to be their own terms. "We are giving them God in an understandable image," he explains to his colleagues, outlining his plan for a church catering to Martian needs:

> What is a shape? Only a cup for the blazing soul that God provides us all. [. . .] I would not let a Martian sphere burn in hell either, for it is a sphere only in mine eyes. When I close my eyes it stands before me, an intelligence, a love, a soul, and I must not deny it. [. . .] We shall give them Christ in their own image.
>
> (67–8)

This is iconoclasm in its etymological sense: "breaking an image" (*OED*). By his estimation, the spheroids need a church and a cross for worship, but the church will be open-air and the cross a glass sphere filled with firelight, a form he imagines they will relate to. He understands the cross is an archetypal image specific to his own faith and his own form as a human being as well as a Christian. He takes the cross's role as expressing the archetype of salvation, which he recognizes as universal or, at least in this case, bridging planets. Peregrine's genius, which is the genius of effective missionaries, is recognizing that different archetypal images may be used to express one archetype, and their individual efficacy in evoking that archetype depends greatly on a viewer's subjective perspective, informed by his or her society, ethnicity, and experience.

Peregrine expounds upon the diversity of racial Christs pictured in different cultures on Earth: the Chinese worship a Christ who looks Chinese, the Virgin of Guadalupe has dark skin, and so on. Their role as priests, he instructs, will be to believe in the spheroid Christ as much as the Martians, transcending their own symbol for another. "Sign" ends with a humbled Father Stone telling Father Peregrine that the glass globe Brother Mathias crafted for the Martian souls is "Him. It *is* Him, after all" (71). This revelation anticipates a point made by Trappist monk Thomas Merton in 1968:

> The true symbol does not merely point to something else. It contains in itself a structure which awakens our consciousness to a new awareness of the inner meaning of life and of reality itself. A true symbol takes us to the center of the circle, not to another point on the circumference. It is by symbolism that man enters affectively and consciously into contact with his own deepest self, with other men, and with God.
>
> (1)

Merton, a Catholic, involved himself in interfaith dialogue, reaching out and ingratiating himself to monks of Eastern traditions.

If Peregrine possesses genius in the way of recognizing symbols, he also possesses acute ineptitude in reading his audience. Once the open air church is built and swept, the altar set with the newly-crafted glass globe, the Martian spheres descend from the sky and inform all priests present that they are the Old Ones. They introduce themselves as enlightened beings who were spiritually saved by one of their own long ago, so long ago that the history has been lost. They have not sinned for eons, existing in a state where their "clime is rich in thought" (70). They thank him for his efforts at salvation, but "have no need for it, for each of us is a temple unto himself, and needs no place wherein to cleanse ourselves" (70).

Curiously, Father Peregrine repeatedly returns to a childhood memory when encountering the Old Ones. They call to his mind the fire balloons that he and his grandfather would lift into the night on the Fourth of July, a tradition in their celebration of the U.S. holiday of Independence Day. In "Take Me Home," Bradbury's last publication in his lifetime, he recounts this memory of the fire balloons and his grandfather as coming from his own childhood in Illinois:

> Twenty-five years later, I wrote "The Fire Balloons," a story in which a number of priests fly off to Mars looking for creatures of good will. It is my tribute to those summers when my grandfather was alive. One of the priests was like my grandpa, whom I put on Mars to see the lovely balloons again, but this time they were Martians, all fired and bright, adrift above a dead sea.
>
> (66)

The Martians even become identified as those fire balloons, earning capitals in Peregrine's final moment with them: "And then the Fire Balloons blew away and were gone, and he was like a child, on his knees, tears streaming from his eyes, crying to himself, Come back! Come back! and at any moment Grandfather might lift him and carry him upstairs to his bedroom in a long-gone Ohio town . . ." (71). Childlike qualities are evoked in this climactic confrontation with the cool *senex* wisdom of the Old Ones, and with them the sensation of an outgrown phase of life. Yet the effect upon Peregrine is not one of negative regression. On the contrary, it recalls Jesus blessing children in *Matthew* (*King James* 19:14), "for of such is the kingdom of heaven."

Regarding their form, one of literal enlightenment, the Old Ones have attained a state of being strikingly similar to the spiritual goal of Gnosticism. There are a multitude of readings of ancient Gnostic traditions, as well as a multitude of traditions theologians have classified under the umbrella of Gnosticism. Campbell viewed this multitude as a distinct quality of those traditions: "[In] Gnosticism [. . .] there was a diversity because [. . .] individuals have differing spiritual capacities and requirements, so that [. . .] no one can safely pretend to have grasped Truth once and for all" (*MGOC* 378). Gnostics depended upon a subjective, individual experience of and with the godhead, which they believed exists within and without the confines of matter. Gnosticism is of particular interest here because of its relation to Christianity and Jungian psychology. Historically, Gnosticism arose during the height of the Roman Empire, and many of its groups embraced Christ while teaching that salvation from the body is achieved through knowledge.

The Council of Nicaea declared Gnostic texts heretical in 325 AD; their traditions suppressed, the Gnostics dwindled, their works lost until a trove of gospels surfaced in Nag Hammadi, Egypt, in 1945. The library contained fifty-two texts, most of them unknown to the modern world. When discovered, one codex sold on the collector market, eventually being bought in 1951 by the Carl Gustav Jung Institute in Zürich. For this reason, the first codex of the Nag Hammadi library is known as the Jung Codex. Jung was profoundly affected, professionally and personally, by what he saw in Gnostic imagery as empirical evidence of a relationship with the collective unconscious that predated his own. He hoped his findings through studying

Gnosticism and medieval alchemy, another tradition centered on divine essence in matter, would lend credibility to his theories. Segal's reading of Gnosticism and Jung is helpful: "Jung deems the Gnostic quest for salvation a form of therapy: a process of discovering and exploring who one really is" (*Allure of Gnosticism* 35).

In Jungian terms, the Old Ones have not individuated but given themselves over to the unconscious wholly. Their state as bodiless souls is as imbalanced as a totally rational, atheistic rejection of soul. Depth psychology seeks balance in life through maintaining dialogue between consciousness and the unconscious. The Old Ones and, indeed, Father Peregrine – who asks them, "May I come again, someday, that I may learn from you?" (71) – seek a spiritual escape from the body. Says Segal, "[Gnostics] urge the escape of the spark from both the body and the material world and the restoration of both it and the godhead to their pristine state. That state *is* one of unity, but the unity is of all divinity, not of divinity with matter" (*Allure of Gnosticism* 33, 34). Regarding that spark, we recall the Old Ones' description of taking "on the look of lightning and blue fire" (70). Even before he meets the Old Ones, Peregrine expresses disassociation between his spirit and his body, addressing his physique as a separate entity: "I shall take you to Mars, body" (57). In these ways, Father Peregrine is far more Gnostic than he is Episcopal, accepting divinity present in all things and beyond the body as opposed to one that must be gained through faith in the body and blood of Jesus Christ.

The path of the spiritual ascetic is one most Americans of the twentieth century did not undertake. Such a transformation is outside the experience of the typical secular Westerner and most American Christians. Father Peregrine does not even represent the average Episcopal priest, his "little book: THE PROBLEM OF SIN ON OTHER WORLDS, ignored as somehow not serious enough by his Episcopal brethren" (58). "In This Sign . . ." offers a challenge to Christianity, an ancient religious tradition facing the problem of relevancy in the modern era where secularism, supported by law, is an American benchmark. Peregrine is not a demythicized Westerner but a devout practitioner encountering Other traditions. An attempt to understand spiritual devotion plays out in this story, addressing not priests but a general reader. And while most readers will not come away with a serious desire to commune with enlightened floating spheres, the wonder of such an exchange is ignited. Something remains, even for one who is not Christian, a desire to touch the mysterious source of life's vitality and come away with it. For just such an encounter, secularly inflected, we finally turn to one of Bradbury's most lyrical short stories.

The golden apples of the sun

Irish mystic John Moriarty begins the Overture to his philomythic trilogy, *Turtle Was Gone a Long Time* (1996–1998), by invoking Neil Armstrong's first moonwalk: "It is my belief that, yes, it was a small step for Neil and, however glamorous in appearance, a quite insignificant step for humanity" (*TGLT1* IX). He read the moon landings as mere feats of transportation that failed to advance the human spirit at a comparable magnitude. Building from Sir Francis Bacon's idea of advancement, Moriarty uses that historic journey to introduce concepts of movement in the development of consciousness: "Movement local is movement from one to another place [. . .] Movement essential, as its name suggests, is movement from one to another state of being" (*TGLT1* IX). His work is an attempt in the demythologized West to "reinstitute commonage consciousness [. . .] On commonage lands there are no fences. Nor, I believe, are there fences in consciousness. Differently inflected, it is the one consciousness that is manifested in rocks, animals, human beings and stars" (*TGLT1* XVII).

And here we find an analog to "The Golden Apples of the Sun," a story pairing movement local and movement essential. Appearing in the November 1953 issue of *Planet Stories*, it also came out that same year as the titular story of Bradbury's third collection, *The Golden Apples of the Sun*. Joseph Mugnaini's illustration, printed on the first page of the story, overwhelms a triangular spaceship in coronal columns of fire. Stick figures can be seen peering out of windows in the side hull as a cupping clam extends from an open hatch. In the distance are two small spheres, one black and one white, perhaps Mercury and Venus. The uncredited art in *Planet Stories* depicts a more traditional rocket, this time descending toward the fires of the sun. The imagery of both, with flame boiling out of the photosphere, is unmistakably hellish, setting the reader up for a tale of eternal damnation. And yet this is a story presenting the constructive opposite of everlasting suffering: individuation.

Before approaching Bradbury's most significant sun story, there is a point to be made about specific anticipations and readings of the impact of space exploration in the twentieth century. It was 1996 when Moriarty expressed his conclusion about the significance of the American program named Apollo (and I would be negligent to not note the solar connection there). Recent history reminds us that to date the Americans are still the only people to visit the moon, a journey last taken in 1972, which now makes it more than forty years since anybody stood sole-deep in lunar soil. There has been, in the wake of Apollo, a general apathy in the U.S.A. surrounding space exploration, as well as conspiracy theories insisting that the moon landing was a hoax. And yet several people predicted that the new frontier of space would awaken human beings to a new level of consciousness.

In 1948, English astronomer Sir Fred Hoyle said, "Once a photograph of the earth, taken from the outside, is available [. . .] a new idea as powerful as any in history will be let loose" (*Cry for Myth* 300). That anticipated photo arrived in 1968 when Apollo 8 astronaut William Anders took a picture from lunar orbit that came to be known as *Earthrise*, enjoying prominence as a six-cent postage stamp the following year. As for the transformative effects Hoyle predicted, Martin Heidegger was affected: "I was shocked

The Golden Apples of the Sun

By RAY BRADBURY

Toward the sun . . . south toward the vastest of all burning hearths soared the refrigerated, ice-sheathed rocket . . . run by proud and vain men hoping to sting the lion and escape the maw.

"SOUTH," said the captain.

"But," said his crew, "there simply *aren't* any directions out here in space."

"When you travel on down toward the sun," replied the captain, "and everything gets yellow and warm and lazy, then you're going in one direction only." He shut his eyes and thought about the smoldering, warm, faraway land, his breath moving gently in his mouth. "South." He nodded slowly to himself. "South."

Their rocket was the *Copa de Oro,* also named the *Prometheus* and the *Icarus,* and

21

Figure 5.5 Uncredited illustration for "The Golden Apples of the Sun" in *Planet Stories.* (© Love Romances Publishing Co., Inc./Fiction House, 1953)

[. . .] We do not need atomic bombs at all [to uproot us] – the uprooting of man is already here. All our relationships have become merely technical ones. It is no longer upon an earth that man lives today" (56). Astronaut Rusty Schweickart also experienced a shift in perspective following his service as the twenty-third American to travel into space:

> Outside on the front porch of the lunar module you watch the sun rise over the Pacific and it's an incredible sight, beautiful, beautiful! [. . .] You begin to realize that your identity is with that whole thing [. . .] And from where you see [Earth], the thing is a *whole*, and it's so beautiful. [. . .] I've used the word 'you,' because it's not me or the others on the lunar module. *It's life that's had that experience.*
>
> (*Cry for Myth* 299–300)

Campbell, who, like millions, witnessed the first lunar landing from the comfort of his home, shared a spiritual appreciation for the event:

> . . . the actual fact of the making and the visual broadcasting of that trip has transformed, deepened, and extended human consciousness to a degree and in a manner that amount to the opening of a new spiritual era.
>
> (*Myths to Live By* 234–5, 239)

Campbell's comments were made in 1970, the year after Apollo 11.

Twenty years later, *Voyager 1* captured a photo of Earth from a distance of 3.7 billion miles. Astronomer Carl Sagan embraced the photo, titling a book after it, *Pale Blue Dot* (1994). In his introduction, Sagan mythologizes the smallness of Earth in the picture, reminding readers that everything that has ever happened to them and their ancestors took place "on a mote of dust suspended in a sunbeam" (xv–xvi). Lamenting that a collective shift in consciousness had not yet taken hold in 1991, Rollo May made a similar appeal: "[T]he exploring of the heavens is a myth out of which we can achieve a new international ethics and understanding, a new raison d'être for humanity. Though it has not yet changed us, we can believe that it will become a new myth out of which we may achieve a new international morality" (*Cry for Myth* 298).

These individuals shared what was for them a profound transformation of spirit in their relation to the planet, but that experience was not and has not been shared by all of humanity. Moriarty's sense that the moon landing was "a quite insignificant step for humanity" accepts that space exploration has failed to inspire masses. Hoyle, Fuller, Heidegger, Campbell, Sagan, and May, none of them having taken space journeys, shared their individually mythologized understandings of the endeavor with others. They hoped that everybody on the planet could be transformed the way astronauts like Schweickart had been, and that hope was driven by a desire for globalism. Their globalism, itself a myth, would be moral, humanist, and Western – and whether one supports their hope or not, to date it has not taken hold.

That idealism, the hope for an individuating West, was coming alive in the American psyche during the run up to the Space Race, and can be seen in "Golden Apples," Bradbury's story of direct encounter with the sun. Here we encounter the captain of a spaceship who, in a marriage of Moriarty's movement local and movement essential, achieves commonage consciousness as a result of the journey. The plot is simple: the crew of a rocket ship, the *Copa de Oro*, travel to the surface of the sun, collect a sample from its edge, and turn around. Along the way there is the phenomenal experience of the feat, including the death of a crewmate, but there is also the inward journey of the captain's memories of a Midwestern childhood, as well as his daydreaming speculations about the first people to wield fire. Bradbury's Prometheus undergoes a spiritual shift in accomplishing the fire theft, undertaken not alone but with a crew, and does not suffer divine punishment.

Harold Bloom, who "respects Bradbury as a benign moral fabulist while sadly noting how slender are his characterizations" (VII), takes this tale to be his finest: "To call 'The Golden Apples of the Sun' a short story is to endanger it. You cannot read it side by side with Chekov, Flannery O'Connor, Hemingway, or Borges. It is a parable, and probably Bradbury is best thought of as a fabulist, a teller of moral tales" (2). Touponce and Eller acknowledge views like Bloom's as missing the nature of Bradbury's project, which "[seeks] to undermine" that very "view of culture depending on hierarchies of meaning ('high' culture verses 'low')" (*Ray Bradbury: The Life of Fiction* 39). Bradbury once confronted an interviewer on this point: "I can read Yeats one minute and then watch *The Empire Strikes Back* and enjoy both equally. What's wrong with that? Do you want me not to do that?" (Aggelis 120). Here he iterates the same dictum put forth by filmmaker Werner Herzog: "The poet must not avert his eyes": artists should consume and metabolize the products of their culture beyond hierarchies.

Touponce offers a cogent analysis of the story as psychological reverie, portraying "modern consciousness which often forgets, in its urge towards progress and technology, its Promethean debt to the unconsciousness" ("Existential Fabulous" 217). By setting much of the story in the captain's imagination and memory, Bradbury reflects the concept of the outward space journey back onto and into the personal psyche of a single character. Touponce is right that "the emotive-cognitive" lens cannot be our sole viewfinder ("Existential Fabulous" 217), although we do need it to build a complete case for Bradbury's achievements. The collective must also be considered, for this is not as much a story of a Prometheus as it is of Prometheans, an unnumbered crew working together to risk the opportunity of collecting a sample from the sun.

The captain and crew's national identities are never defined. The spaceship itself carries a Spanish – not English – name, *Copa de Oro*, which is both Spanish for "Cup of Gold" and the common name of *Eschscholtzia californica*, the state flower of California. Also, works from American and European literature are referred to throughout, including Irish and English authors. Bradbury is taking the reader beyond Americanness to a cast of characters whose signifiers are not based along national or ethnic lines, aiming at the idea of what is universally human. This was not an unpopular view in the United States at the time; the U.N. mission to create and ratify the Universal Declaration of Human Rights in 1948 and 1949 was led by former First Lady Eleanor Roosevelt, who played a major role in the new international coalition formed in hopes of preventing a new worldwide catastrophe – hopes that were being tested in Korea. That spirit, of a responsibility to the citizens of the world, their betterment, and the myth of progress, is alive in the captain and crew. Theirs is a humanist quest, a collective endeavor born out of shared need.

There is also the global matter of the atomic bomb and that solar-fusion/human-fission-inspired inferiority discussed at the beginning of this chapter. When the captain remembers the inevitable question – why did they undertake this task? – his answer is expressed collectively with "we" and "our":

> Because the atoms we work with our hands, on Earth, are pitiful; the atomic bomb is pitiful and small and our knowledge is pitiful and small, and only the sun really knows what we want to know, and only the sun has the secret. And besides, it's fun, it's a chance, it's a great thing coming here, playing tag, hitting and running. There is no reason, really, except the pride and vanity of little insect men hoping to sting the lion and escape the maw. My God, we'll say, we *did* it! And here is our cup of energy, fire, vibration, call it what you will, that may well power our cities and sail our ships and light our libraries and tan our children and bake our daily breads and simmer the knowledge of our universe for us for a thousand years until it is well done. Here, from this cup, all good men of science and religion: drink! Warm yourselves against the night of ignorance, the long snows of superstition, the cold winds of disbelief, and from the great fear of darkness in each man. So: we stretch out our hand with the beggar's cup . . .
>
> (248)

We recall Schweickart's insistence on using "you," in its sense as the second person plural pronoun, when discussing work he accomplished as an astronaut. The crew's boon is not theirs alone but provides for the greater good as they understand it, which, in hyperbole of the era, stretches outward to the whole of humanity. "Golden Apples" becomes a vision recorded in 1953 of the scientific and spiritual potential of the U.S.A., on the behalf of all the world and even with it, to explore beyond orbit, moon, or Mars to a seemingly impossible frontier. At the center of the solar system, by this story's reckoning, we will find our collective center. Concurrent with the American public's serious consideration in the nineteen-fifties of entering low Earth orbit and colonizing the moon, Bradbury's story pitches those hopes farther and further, that is in distance and possibility, in movement local and movement essential, to the heart of the solar system – and the entire human race. Bradbury offers this story, first and foremost, as a citizen of the world and one of the countless children of the sun.

Two aspects that set "Golden Apples" apart from other fire theft stories are its future setting and the seizing of a yet-untapped source of energy. Every fire thief, from Grecian Prometheus to Vedic Mātariśvan to Ojibwe Nanabozho the Hare to Cherokee Grandmother Spider, lives in the past of his or her culture. Their stories, in part, explain how fire was first harnessed. Bradbury's fire thieves aboard the *Copa de Oro*, on the other hand, exist in an imagined future and seize a dreamed-of energy. I do not classify "Golden Apples" with religious apocalyptic (as in revelatory or eschatological) literature, as Bradbury was not a scribe of scripture, but we can certainly read the story in the context of the scientific narrative of the origin of the human use of fire.

While moving the robotic hand toward the sun, the captain imagines that moment a "million years ago" when "a naked man on a lonely northern trail" seized fire from a lightning-struck tree "and gave his people summer" in their cave (247). This daydream, inspired by paleoanthropology, is the best science can provide in the way of the origin of fire tending. As opposed to a history, it is a speculation, an empirical gray place outlying factual certainty. There is no way that science can answer this question: Who was the first person to wield fire? The gap between what is known and what is unknowable provides space in which a story can arise to satisfy, at least partly, our desire to understand how that invaluable practice began. The Prometheus of the modern scientific West, separated from us by time and species, is nameless, often and presumably a male cave dweller. Says Campbell:

> One of the earliest signs of a separation of human from animal consciousness may be seen in man's domestication of fire [. . .] The fascination of fire [. . .] may be taken as the earliest sign in the records of our species of that openness to fascination and willingness to adventure for it at great risk which has been ever the essential mark of the uniquely human – as opposed to common animal – faculties of our species.
> (*Myths to Live By* 240–241)

That line, the one that we imagine separates us from the animal kingdom, is, like all scientific concepts, open to revision.

Campbell, almost in harmony with Bradbury's captain, muses upon the force of fascination that we believe inspired our predecessor all those eons ago: "when that protohuman troglodyte Sinathropus, in his dismal cave, responded to the fascination of fire, it was to the apparition of a power that was already present and operative in his own body: heat, temperature, oxidation; as also in the volcanic earth, in Jupiter, and in the sun" (*Myths to Live By* 246). Sinanthropus, we pause to note, is no longer recognized as a genus by the scientific establishment; the Peking Man cranial remains are now classified as belonging to Homo erectus. Science, we remember, is a fluid field where new data alter understanding. "Golden Apples" provides speculation in time's opposite direction, into the unknown future, of how people will one day wield fusion. The science is not present – no astrophysicist will approve of the method presented, using a robotic hand and cup, for capturing a piece of the sun – but a narrative is provided that satisfies through imagination what human achievement is unable to accomplish to date. Both events, the very first use of fire, which happened, and the potential development of solar fusion, which many scientists hope will someday happen, are unknowable to us as specific events. Our only opportunity of experiencing them exists in our imaginations, which can satisfy, expand, even spur the desire to achieve the seemingly impossible.

Bradbury often makes references to texts in his work, but intertextuality begins stacking in "Golden Apples" from the title. "The Song of Wandering Aengus" by W. B. Yeats provides that title, the final line of the third and final stanza of the poem: "The golden apples of the sun" (47). Yeats portrays Aengus, a figure from Irish mythology, as having glimpsed a "glimmering girl / With apple blossom in her hair" who knows his name, disappears, and inspires an obsessive determination to find her again. From a Jungian perspective, the poem illustrates the concept of the *anima*, a feminine psychic image that manifests in dream and myth as go-between between a man and the unconscious. They are conceived to be "guides of the soul and they can become necessary links with creative possibilities and instruments of individuation" (*CDJA* 23). For Dante, this quality was projected upon Beatrice; for Poe, upon Virginia Clemm. Fiction abounds with anima figures, from Hermine in Hesse's *Steppenwolf* to Clarisse McClellan in Bradbury's *Fahrenheit 451*.

In "The Song of Wandering Aengus," it is a girl transformed from a silver trout, caught with a berry for bait. "Golden Apples" presents no recognizable anima figure, but does relate to the poem beyond the appropriation of its final line. Yeats's narrator, Aengus, mentions fire twice, first "a fire in my head" that drew him into a hazel wood to cut and fashion a fishing wand. Intending to cook the fish, he "went to blow the fire aflame" (47). There are two fires, the second being physical fire, the kind our ancestors domesticated, and the first being a mental conflagration, what Campbell called a power "present and operative" in our bodies (*Myths to Live By* 246). The two are linked: the fire he plans to cook the trout starts in his mind before he even has the tools to catch his meal. In a similar way, the sun's energy informed and shaped the life within the *Copa de Oro* long before it docks alongside the photosphere. The desire to touch the sun is inborn, it exists somewhere within us today, as it did eons ago, and here we still stand unable to tend the energy it provides. For Aengus the golden apples of the sun are the fruit he anticipates harvesting from his hoped-for relationship with the "glimmering girl / With apple blossom in her hair" (47); for the captain and crew of the rocket, the golden apples of the sun are "the knowledge of our universe for us for a thousand years until it is well done."

Prometheus and *Icarus* are given as alternative names for the rocket, invoking figures from Greek myth, the former already discussed and the latter the sky-flying youth who defies the wax limits of his father's technology, the sun's heat melting his wings' binding and plummeting him deathward into the sea. In a call and response conversation between captain and crew, which Touponce likens to "the form of questions and answers reminiscent of a small town classroom" (209), quotes and titles are paired with their respective authors. "Fear no more the heat of the sun," a line from *Cymbeline* (IV.i.327), is rightly attributed to Shakespeare. *Cup of Gold*, a historical novel about the pirate Henry Morgan by John Steinbeck (1929), and *The Crock of Gold*, James Stephens's Irish fantasy novel (1912), are also named by an unidentified crewmember. There is also a link between Yeats's poem and Stephens's novel, in that the Irish god Aengus appears in *The Crock of Gold* as Angus Óg. The crew has a firm grounding in literature; this is not a group of engineers educated solely in STEM.

What Bradbury achieves by listing many different golden cups is not unlike Gertrude Stein's "Rose is a rose is a rose is a rose." He piles cups upon cups so that cups become numinous. By not using the word *grail*, loaded as it is with Christianity, Bradbury recreates the grail for a demythicized reader. The motorized cup is a vessel; so is the rocket ship; so is the crew's collective psyche; so is the captain's individual psyche. The grail has already been crafted, seized, attained. What remains is the filling of that grail with solar fusion. The risk is being engulfed and immolated by the sun, which is the tragic fate of Bradbury's "Rocket Man" and the depersonalizing transformation of the Old Ones in "Sign"; the goal is to survive incorporation of the sun's essence. This is a delicate act, with the insides of the rocket frozen cold to counter the sun's heat.

There is also, lurking in the text, oblique reference to William Blake's poem "The Mental Traveller" (1803). Consider the final line of the third stanza:

> And if the babe is born a boy
> He's given to a woman old,
> Who nails him down upon a rock,
> Catches his shrieks in cups of gold.

Here are more cups of gold. Furthermore, Bradbury uses "shrieking" twice and "shrieked" once in this story of little more than two thousand words. Given the captain's daydreaming and remembering and nightmaring, he is presented as a futuristic mental traveler. His movement is not just local; it is also essential. Martin K. Nurmi remarks that "many critics, when they come to Blake's poem, either avoid it, admit defeat, or seize upon some aspect of it as a 'key' to its meaning. I do not think the poem can be unlocked by any single key" (109). Its obtuseness inspires or perhaps even demands initial readings producing wonder. Nurmi also acknowledges a debt to the fire-thieving Titan: "The nailing of the babe down to the rock, of course, reminds one of Prometheus" (111). We recall that his agonizing punishment for gifting human beings with fire sees him bound to a rock where nightly, forevermore, an eagle descends and gorges on his liver in beakfuls.

Why, with naming other literary works and authors, would Bradbury mask reference to Blake? "The Mental Traveller" describes an entire mythic cycle, whereas "Golden Apples" is close to vignette. The captain and crew are presented just prior to, during, and just after their encounter with the sun. The effect their feat will have on society does not play out. Where Blake builds an ouroboric vision of humanity's grand struggles with itself and its environment, Bradbury presents a single ordeal steeped in optimism that appeals to a positive hope for things to come. There is no telling how the crew of the *Copa de Oro* will be received upon their return to Earth, but they look forward to sharing their boon. And yet a sense of technological déjà vu arises between the captain's imagined ancestral fire thief and his own accomplishment. Where the use of fire defined humanity's separation from other animals, the harnessing of solar fusion is set up as being just as profound for life on – or from – Earth.

Cardinal points demarcate both inner and outer space in "Golden Apples." The story opens with a polar direction, directing them South:

> "But," said his crew, "there simply *aren't* any directions out here in space."
> "When you travel on down toward the sun," replied the captain, "and everything gets yellow and warm and lazy, then you're going in one direction only."
>
> (243)

The crew thinks of empty space in terms of movement local, unappreciative of metaphor. They regard the environment, or *lack* of environment, through which they travel literally, while the captain adopts a mythopoetic perspective on their trajectory. He is set apart as an individual, not only by rank but mental faculty. He knows their southwardness is a psychological south. Being the first to undertake a trip to the sun itself, a journey into unknown parameters, he is rescued by metaphor, which transforms the task into relatable terms. Once the deed is done, the cup filled with solar energy and safely stored in the hull, the story ends with another pole:

> "There's only one direction in space from here on out," he said at last.
> They waited. They waited as the ship moved swiftly into cold darkness away from the light.
> "North," murmured the captain. "North."
>
> (250)

Having integrated the southern sun, north is revealed – and once north is verified, east and west appear. For now, having come to a center of life, the captain calibrates the compass of his soul. We may not individually be the center of the universe, but when it comes to the phenomenology of life, lived within the boundaries of time and body, we are each our own center. The ability to orient the cardinal directions of our inner selves places each of us with confidence within the field of existence. The finer the sensitivity of that compass, the more complete, fulfilling, and whole life becomes. In Jung's opinion, this balance is the ongoing goal of individuation.

Campbell viewed the centering revelation to be the prime mythic understanding:

> God is an intelligible sphere – a sphere known to the mind, not to the senses – whose center is everywhere and whose circumference is nowhere. [. . .] And each of us is a manifestation of that mystery. [. . .] What you have here is what might be translated into raw individualism, you see, if you didn't realize that the center was also right there facing you in the other person. This is the mythological way of being an individual. You are the central mountain, and the central mountain is everywhere.
>
> (*POM* 89)

If the *Copa de Oro* is an ark where human psyche undergoes individuation, the crew represents different interior processes, conscious and unconscious, with the captain standing in for ego. Bretton, the first mate, is the only character named. He is also the only character to die, freezing when the ammoniated conditions break through his protective suit. Individuation is not a safe or easy process, and as consciousness expands certain aspects of the self will die to allow for new growth. He is not killed by the sun; rather, he is killed by their own over-compensation in preparing for their encounter with the sun. Bretton has several definitions, the *OED* pointing in its obsolete uses, tantalizingly, to the Breton *apple*.

Though Bretton's death is accidental, and his loss as second in command is distressing, it is significant in the end that the *Copa de Oro* will return home not with their Breton apple but with golden apples. Not everybody makes it to the point of fulfilling their potential. Those who do will find themselves changed, transformed, growing into new states of consciousness. All around us are the victims of life, the people who have suffered traumas they will never bounce back from, people impaired by the effects of drug use or abuses and torments from other people. "Golden Apples" reminds readers that life is permanently connected to the sun above. We have Promethean potential within; most will not actualize it, and others will suffer defeat in the process. Those who do discover their own center, and then the center of each person, place, or thing they encounter, encounter eternity – and once the eternal has been experienced, there is no going home. Where does Bradbury's individuated crew aboard the *Copa de Oro* head? Not home. They go north.

Wholeness myths

In Bradbury's "Pillar of Fire" (1948), William Lantry, who died in 1933, wakes undead from his grave in 2349 to a society where the dead have been outlawed. As the last corpse in the world, he undertakes a mad mission to reintroduce death to society by attending to a killing spree and the destruction of the Incinerators that stubble the landscape. Essentially crematoriums, the altars inside these Incinerators are adorned with the phrase: "WE THAT WERE BORN OF THE SUN RETURN TO THE SUN" (42). Zombie Lantry's campaign to reinstate darkness in a naïve culture is met without resistance or understanding, which serves to play on the ideas of paradise that many readers might expect to accompany utopia. Bradbury imagines a relationship to the sun that overcompensates the dearth in his own time and culture. The answer to appreciating the sun, in other words, is not sun worship; it is, rather, the act of encounter and integration. In his most famous novel, *Fahrenheit 451* (1953), the protagonist Montag struggles to conceptualize this, settling for the wholeness of solar *dis*integration:

> The sun burned every day. It burned Time. The world rushed in a circle and turned on its axis and time was busy burning the years and the people anyway, without any help from him. So if he burnt things with the firemen, and the sun burnt Time, that meant that everything burned! One of them had to stop burning. The sun wouldn't, certainly.
>
> (151)

Neither a clergyman nor a scientist, Bradbury engages both of the modern tribes of religion and science in his solar tales. The Rocket Man and conman Thirkell, leading lives terribly off balance, are cast into the sun itself, burned for their inability to lead sincere lives. The early conquistadors of Venus, which orbits both closer and somehow further from the sun thanks to its clouds, suffer death and near-death, yearning for sunlight, before their first descendants suffer melancholy and ennui, yearning even more for sunlight. A maverick priest encounters Martians afloat like small blue suns and sees in their Otherness the same animating force inside him. But it is the mission of the *Copa de Oro* that provides Bradbury's most significant encounter with the sun, for technology and the human spirit are there tempered in the sun's photosphere. The solar theft points far beyond low Earth orbit and the moon, both being destinations Americans had only recently begun to consider as places to physically venture, to the center of our solar system and, thereby, ourselves.

Campbell's assertion that "the heliocentric universe has never been translated into a mythology" stands questioned by the diversity of solar emblems shining through the stories we have examined (*IROS* 17). Bradbury was a writer of fiction concerned with the source of life, free from issues of fact and faith that are essential parts of science and religion. While rite and ritual may not accompany his stories, unless one counts purchase and reading as holy acts, they nevertheless offer opportunities for awakening individual wonder, which is a significant part of any established mythology. In his suns, we see "the source of life and wholeness of man" that Jung and Campbell traced through world mythological systems and the modern psyche.

It is curious that Ray Bradbury's name at birth was Ray Douglas Bradbury. Ray stood on its own, never being the full Raymond. Raymond has a Germanic origin, "composed of the elements *ragin* 'advice' and *mund* 'protector'" (*BTN*). "Advice" seems appropriate enough for a writer like Bradbury, who concerned himself with humanity and bemoaned the directions in which he saw civilization heading. The name also calls to mind Raymundus, the medieval alchemist whose recipe for preparing the *lapis*, the "treasure hard to attain," Jung quotes in "The Symbolism of the Mandala": "Take of the body that is most simple and round, and do not take of the triangle or quadrangle but of the round, for the round is nearer to simplicity than the triangle. Hence it is to be noted that a simple body has no corners, for it is the first and last among the planets, like the sun among the stars" (1936/1968, *CW 12*, ¶220).

But there is that other meaning of Ray, that is, as a sunbeam, a radiating line of light, radiance. The *OED* lists *ray* deriving from the Latin *radius:* "ray of light, spoke, radius of a circle, pointed rod, spur of a bird, spine of a stingray, radius bone of the forearm, in post-classical Latin also arm of a cross." As manifestations of radiations from a center, be it a physical, psychological, mystical center, or all of the above, it is a romantic but nevertheless linguistic point to end this study of solar myths with the observation that Ray Bradbury was aptly named for the tales he told.

Notes

1 See note 7 to Chapter 4.
2 *Chronicles* was only conceived as a whole after its individual stories were written, and when it was published in the U.K. as *The Silver Locusts* (1951), "The Fire Balloons" was included. The story found a wider American audience when published in *The Illustrated Man* (Feb. 1951) and was eventually instated in subsequent editions of *Chronicles* published from 1963 to the present, though in Bantam paperback reprints it remains absent (Eller and Touponce 129, 130). It is also the topic of Bradbury's last essay to be published in his lifetime, "Take Me Home," in *The New Yorker*'s 2012 Science Fiction Issue.

Figure 6.1 "Golden Apples of the Monkey House," reproduced with permission from the artist. (© 2014 Kevin Storrar)

Epilogue

Golden apples of the monkey house

When work on this study was well underway, *Golden Apples of the Monkey House* presented itself as a subtitle. I resisted it at first because it seemed too easy, the pairing of the titles of two of Vonnegut's and Bradbury's most fertile stories. But, taking the lead from Hillman – "Seize the image before the content" (*Healing Fiction* 92) – I settled upon it as a subtitle with faith that it would reveal its own resonances. What has become clear to me now is that *Golden Apples of the Monkey House* is a solid metaphor for the nature of the stories themselves in exploring their significance as mythic narratives.

The golden apples in Bradbury's tale of heliocentric integration, "The Golden Apples of the Sun," are fruits of growing consciousness, a forecast of human potential fulfilled at the level of our solar system. They are also harvested from a literary tradition of our living past, "The Song of Wandering Aengus" by Nobel Laureate W. B. Yeats, which itself draws upon ancient Irish mythology. The stories we have considered, including those of Vonnegut, are significant in the way they portray our dark and bright potentials, collective and individual. They were telling white middle class Americans that they came from somewhere and were going somewhere, that they were connected to life long ago and life far ahead of them. Removed as we are by not much more than half a century today, these stories continue to sell in collections, still speak to readers of these mysteries. Our study would not be possible if they failed in this respect.

The monkey house, from Vonnegut's "Welcome to the Monkey House," is not just the patriarchal structure we found in our discussion of the story. It is also, in a sense, our ancestral home, identifying our lineage as one of the natural order of life on our planet. It is a humbling image, humanity living within the greater animal kingdom in a monkey house. Theories of evolution, though disagreeing on details of mechanism and what drives the process, show us that our species has come about in relation to all other species in a complex branching manner whereby all living things bear relation and relatedness to each other. And so again we hear Moriarty say, "The ancient regime we innately are" (*TGLT2* 91), and Jung before him: "This whole psychic organism . . . preserves elements that connect it with the invertebrates and ultimately with the protozoa" (*CW8*: ¶322). Careful examination of the fossil record, genetic science, and neurobiology confirm as much, which ought to warn us about subscribing too much to human exceptionalism.

Bradbury's and Vonnegut's short stories are golden apples of the monkey house in that they show how we stand in this unique position as human beings with both an animal heritage *and* the ability to express our imaginations in mythic narratives. "They are fruits of the spirit which fall to him who pays his tribute to life," Jung might say (*CW7*: ¶369) – that is, fruits of *psyche*, which Haule calls "the rich biographical process by which we have gotten to and come to understand the present moment – both by its facts and in its implications – and simultaneously as springboard for an imagined future. Psyche is both identity and possibility" (81). Campbell understood that myths engage people metaphysically, cosmologically, sociologically, and pedagogically. These four broad tensions are entirely relevant to the here and now of getting along with one's life in relation to others' and the environment. Our amplification of the stories we have explored reveals that Bradbury and Vonnegut were invested in this kind of storytelling. Their tales express a host of hopes and anxieties relevant to a predominantly white middle class American audience of the mid-twentieth century, which all simultaneously exist in relation to the ancient and unborn hopes and anxieties of a collective humanity.

A post-Jungian approach, with its theoretical basis rooted in the appraisal of dreams and fantasies, yokes well with the criticism of short fiction, particularly for – though not limited to – those stories presenting fantastical elements. Amplification of the details, characters, and situations in a story, when guided by Campbell's four functions of myth, draws out the compensation offered by the story, its way of making up for what Jung called "the inadequacy and one-sidedness of the present" (1922/1966, *CW 15*, ¶130). The distinction between archetypal images and archetypes must always be respected in the spirit of Haule's observation that "no experiences are finding their way into the human genome . . . but cultural styles and experiences do stamp their imprint" (27). Archetypal images point to archetypes and archetypes are diversified by the archetypal images; this is a complementary relationship that, instead of reducing analysis to plugging inputs into a model, serves to expand our understandings of the tremendous valence of experience. Reading short stories with a post-Jungian approach parses them in a way that cultivates our knowledge of what people have, can, and might go through in life while respecting identities individual and collective.

The approach challenges us to enact a Thou-I perspective in what Rowland calls the (w)rite of reading: "[It] can include those dimensions of mental processing often left out of modern reductionist disciplines, such as intuition, feeling, tacit knowledge, and aesthetic considerations. [. . .] A Jungian approach to literature means that the text can be understood as expressing a particular historical moment while, at the same time, retaining the possibility of 'other' kinds of reading" ("Literature and the Shaman" 2). This variety of criticism, sincerely concerned with the complexities of psyche, is unique in that it honors the ethos expressed in a dictum American writer Richard Ford carries on from English literary critic F. R. Leavis: "literature is the supreme means by which you renew your sensuous and emotional life and learn a new awareness" ("Bringing the News"). When we allow ourselves to be sensitive to stories, they teach us and can illuminate pathways of interconnectedness that are entirely practical in the scheme of life. This should not surprise us, given the therapeutic foundation of analytical and archetypal psychology.

Eliot Rosewater, in Vonnegut's novel *God Bless You, Mr. Rosewater* (1965), crashes a convention of science-fiction writers held at a motel in Milford, Pennsylvania. He heaps them with praise because, in his estimation, though they "couldn't write for sour apples, [. . .] they were poets just the same, since they were more sensitive to important changes than anybody who was writing well" (*NS* 202). Whether or not Vonnegut and Bradbury wrote in pleasing ways comes down largely to personal preference, but our readings of those stories written across the first couple decades of their careers prove they both possessed profound sensitivity to the shifting conditions of their time and culture. By considering the stories in the periodicals where they were first published, the artwork, advertisements, editorials, and varied articles help timestamp each one in a collective context. We find in them an array of dreams and fears present in the white middle class American psyche that needed to be expressed. "It's only recently that I've come to understand that writers are *not* marginal to our society," Vonnegut said in 1974, "that they, in fact, do *all* our thinking for us, that we are writing myths and our myths are believed, and that old myths are believed until someone writes a new one" ("Kurt Vonnegut on Breakfast of Champions").

A story from Campbell's life that Bill Moyers shares in opening *The Power of Myth* bears relation to the way these writers wrote:

> In Japan for an international conference on religion, Campbell overheard another American delegate, a social philosopher from New York, say to a Shinto priest, "We've been now to a good many ceremonies and have seen quite a few of your shrines. But I don't get your ideology. I don't get your theology." The Japanese paused as though in deep thought and then slowly shook his head. "I think we don't have ideology," he said. "We don't have theology. We dance."
>
> (*POM* xix)

Vonnegut and Bradbury danced. In writing the short stories we have examined, they were trying to earn a living wage while providing narratives relevant to the ups and downs of middle class American life. Their art sold in the mainstream to Americans who could afford subscriptions to weekly publications or a monthly digest picked up from the drugstore on allowance money. Their projects in the forties and fifties were not high art meditations financed by benefactors and printed in limited edition monographs. On this point, Rosewater iterates a low vs. high defense: "The hell with the talented sparrowfarts who write delicately of one small piece of one mere lifetime, when the issues are galaxies, eons, and trillions of souls yet to be born" (*NS* 202). Bradbury's family grew with four daughters; Vonnegut's to six children, after adopting three of his sister's boys when she died. The drive to write and publish short stories arose from the imperative of providing for a family. The nature of producing short stories, each being a fifty-yard dash compared to the marathon nature of writing a novel, paired with a diverse market, ranging from genre pulps to women's magazines to adult publications, allowed Vonnegut and Bradbury to switch gears as they pleased. Perhaps more than any other American writers of their generation, they sold short stories expressing most of the mainstream motifs of the day, never settling with any one genre.

Our role in the present study has been to consider the mythic nature of Bradbury and Vonnegut's early commercial work. By rounding up and unpacking stories by each author in turn, we have witnessed individual idiosyncrasies borne out of the experience of expressing stories arising from and with collective tensions of the day. Dawson rightly points out that literary works "engage with material that might be attributed to the collective unconscious. But all of them *also* give expression to dilemmas of an emphatically *personal* significance to their author" (*The Effective Protagonist* 16). And so Vonnegut provided war stories that challenged American attitudes of victory and victoriousness after WWII and wrote several others that expressed how fragmentary and incohesive white American identity could be for its citizens, be they upper, lower, or middle class. Bradbury took aim at the American family, penning tales of nuclear units struggling for molecular cohesion, but also appealed to the human hope for more, for attainment, for expansion of consciousness in his stories of wholeness. And here we see that their projects were not so vastly different, for fragmentation suggests wholeness, and wholeness is susceptible to fragmentation. Individuation is present in stories by both writers and neither is consistently pessimistic or optimistic about its realization. Both acknowledge life as the struggle of being alive while suggesting a way of becoming that transcends mere mechanics. Think of Professor Barnhouse's humane use of dynamopsychism and Harrison Bergeron's pronouncement – "Now watch me become what I can become" (9) – before Diana Moon Glampers guns him down. And what about Bradbury's Edwin, outgrowing and escaping his mansion "world," and the Rocket Man who, unable to ground himself in home life on earth, is eaten by our marvelous sun? Sometimes life "works out." Sometimes it doesn't.

Campbell rejects the ever-elusive meaning of life, arguing instead for the living of life:

> There's no meaning. What's the meaning of the universe? What's the meaning of a flea? It's just there. That's it. And your own meaning is that you're there. We're so engaged in doing things to achieve purposes of outer value that we forget that the inner value, the rapture that is associated with being alive, is what it's all about.
>
> (*POM* 5–6)

"Myths," he maintains, "are clues to the spiritual potentialities of the human life" (*POM* 6). Tracking these clues through the stories we have read closely has not been an endeavor at reduction but expansion. As Walker urges, Jungian literary criticism "must enrich the understanding of a text and increase the fund of perceptions associated with our reading" (148). Potentialities "we might not have seen from any other perspective" ask to be brought forth, in awareness, in our efforts to appreciate their revelations (Walker 148). Successful short stories are not typically "about" something, being, as Susan Lohafer notes, "strangely indescribable" (*NSST* 301). They are paradoxically explicit-and-suggestive experiences followed from the page, as irreducible as songs. One person's summarizing 'about' will never sit fully aligned with another person's – and neither will ever present the totality of what the story provides.

So too is it with the post-Jungian approach to archetypes. We do not seek reduction, easy explanation, a set path of psychological phylogeny. We seek to expand awareness of those aspects of life we are living without seeing, drawing attention to unconscious elements that influence us more than we know. Each archetype carries a diversity of meanings, associations, understandings, effects. In exploring these diversities, we gain an appreciation for the dynamism inherent in an archetype. We understand it is irreducible to any one idea. War is inflected in all wars and representations of war, Independence is only ever understood independently, and the Hero has faces beyond number. Archetypes are the themes of being alive and the narratives built around them, differing culture to culture, shift in significance for the individual over the course of his or her life – or even a day in the life. An archetypal perspective on myth both honors and struggles with the commonality of life's ineffable complexity. "Our psyche is set up in accord with the structure of the universe," wrote Jung, "and what happens in the macrocosm likewise happens in the infinitesimal and most subjective reaches of the psyche" (*MDR* 368).

Human beings have not always been writers but we can be certain that storytelling arose in the prehistoric past. Hillman, speaking from his experience as a psychoanalyst, advocates the foundational aspect of oral literature: "I have found that the person with a sense of story built in from childhood is in better shape than one who has not had stories, who has not heard them, read them, acted them, or made them up" (*Healing Fiction* 46). As he puts it, we found ourselves in story, supporting Jung's insistence that in helping a patient, "The crucial thing is the story" (*MDR* 145). Campbell answered Jung's call – "What is your myth – the myth in which you live?" (*MDR* 195) – by offering up *Myths to Live By* (1972) and a career defending the relevancy of mythologies old and new. This relates to the written short story in that the art form activates what Lohafer calls "storyness." As short story criticism branched into short story theories in the final decades of the twentieth century, critics made arguments for foundational and numinous qualities unique to the form.

Lohafer, in league with cognitive psychologists, claims that "Storying is a way of processing experience in the interests of human well-being. The sense of storyness [. . .] is a cognitive integer – and that accounts for the primacy of the short story as a narrative form" (*NSST* 310). May insists the form arose historically as it did – and has persisted – because it fulfills a basic need for enfranchising life, which the Enlightenment disenfranchised with positivism and models of an inert existence deprived of soul: "Because short fiction is so bound up with the experience of the sacred and mythic perception, it is no accident that the short story as we know it today got its most important impetus as an art form from the Romantic effort in the early years of the nineteenth century to regain through art what had been lost in religion" (*NSST* 139). Moriarty, who "yearned for a philomythic *Mabinogion*, a suite of myths, traditional or modern, that would mediate the highest truths to us," might have fashioned one from short stories as much as he did from scriptures, Upanishads, and American Indian tales. "Like nothing else perhaps in our culture," he says, "[myths] uncompromisingly mediate the difficult strangeness of self and of world" (*TGLT3* IX). The same is being said of short stories.

Few scholars have regarded Vonnegut and Bradbury's short stories with critical attention. With the work presented here, a contribution is submitted in the hope that others recognize these stories' value beyond entertainment. Vonnegut may have derided his as work "sold in order to finance the writing of the novels" (*Welcome to the Monkey House* XIV), but presented with historical contextualization and a theoretical approach, they stand up to scrutiny and reveal many other stories lurking in their characters and complexes. Here I argue that there is pleasure, too, for the scholar, who need not place him or herself at odds with readers. Zimmer, in "The Dilettante Among Symbols," urges us to "take delight in symbols" of storytelling, "evoke fresh speech from them," and "be always ready to begin anew" (*King & the Corpse* 2, 4, 6). That attitude dovetails with the playfulness encountered repeatedly in the short stories Vonnegut and Bradbury wrote, as well as their essays on writing. Says Bradbury:

> You can never tell when you might want to know the finer points of being a pedestrian, keeping bees, carving headstones, or rolling hoops.

> Here is where you play the dilettante, and where it pays to do so. You are, in effect, dropping stones down a well. Every time you hear an echo from your Subconscious, you know yourself a little better. A small echo may start an idea. A big echo may result in a story.
>
> (*Zen* 40)

Vonnegut also attributed some appeal of the short story to play: "the story has boundaries like a playing field. The story can't go simply anywhere. This, I feel, invites readers to come off the sidelines, to get into the game with the author. [. . .] Where, outside the Groves of Academe, does anybody like a story where so much information is withheld or arcane that there is no way for readers to play along?" (*BSB* 11). And so this is how they danced, with one hand extended to readers with invitation, to take and eat of the golden apples of the monkey house.

Primary sources

Ray Bradbury

Bradbury, Ray. "All Summer in a Day." *The Magazine of Fantasy and Science Fiction* Mar. 1954: 122–127. Print.

———. *Bradbury Speaks: Too Soon from the Cave, Too Far from the Stars*. New York: Harper Perennial, 2006. Print.

———. *Bradbury Stories*. New York: HarperCollins, 2003. Print.

———. *The Collected Stories of Ray Bradbury, A Critical Edition: Volume I: 1938–1943*. Eds. William F. Touponce and Jonathan R. Eller. Kent, MI: Kent State University Press, 2010. Print.

———. *The Collected Stories of Ray Bradbury, A Critical Edition: Volume II*. Eds. Jonathan R. Eller and Robin Condin. Kent, MI: Kent State University Press, 2014. Print.

———. *Dandelion Wine*. New York: Doubleday, 1957. Print.

———. "Death-By-Rain." *Planet Stories* Summer 1950: 35–42. Print.

———. *Fahrenheit 451*. New York: Simon & Schuster, 2012. Print.

———. "The Fire Balloons." *The Stories of Ray Bradbury*. New York: Everyman's Library, 2010. 218–235. Print.

———. "The Golden Apples of the Sun." *Planet Stories* Nov. 1953: 21–24. Print. Also in *The Golden Apples of the Sun*. New York: Doubleday, 1953. 243–250. Print.

———. "The Happiness Machine." *The Saturday Evening Post* 14 Sep. 1957: 43, 154, 156–158. Print.

———. *The Illustrated Man*. New York: HarperCollins, 1952. Print.

———. "In This Sign . . ." *Imagination: Stories of Science and Fantasy* April 1951: 56–71. Print.

———. "Jack-in-the-Box." *Dark Carnival*. Sauk City, WI: Arkham House, 1947. Print.

———. "The Jar." *Weird Tales* Nov. 1944: 49–56. Print.

———. "Let's Play 'Poison.'" *Bradbury Stories*. New York: HarperCollins, 2003. 542–547. Print.

———. "A Little Journey." *Galaxy: Science Fiction* August 1951: 152–158. Print.

———. "The Long Rain." *The Stories of Ray Bradbury*. New York: Everyman's Library, 2010. 253–266. Print.

———. "The Man." *Thrilling Wonder Stories* Feb. 1949: 69–75. Print.

———. *The Martian Chronicles*. New York: Doubleday, 1950. Print.

———. "Pillar of Fire." *S Is for Space*. London: Pan, 1972. 36–78. Print.

———. "The Rocket Man." *Argosy* Feb. 1952: 44–46, 83–84. Print. Also in *Maclean's* 1 Mar. 1951: 14–15, 41–42. Print.

———. "Science Fiction: Before Christ and After 2001." *Science Fact/Fiction*. Eds. Edmund J. Farrell, Thomas E. Gage, John Pfordresher, and Raymond J. Rodrigues. Glenview, IL: Scott, Foresman and Company, 1974. i–ix. Print.
———. "The Scythe." *Weird Tales* Jul. 1943: 46–55. Print.
———. "The Shape of Things." *Thrilling Wonder Stories* Feb. 1948: 47–55. Print.
———. "The Small Assassin." *Dime Mystery* Nov. 1946: 66–75. Print.
———. *The Stories of Ray Bradbury*. New York: Alfred A. Knopf, 1980. Print.
———. "Take Me Home." *The New Yorker* 4 & 11 June 2012: 66. Print.
———. "The Vacation." *Playboy* Dec. 1963: 100–101, 102, 110. Print.
———. "The World the Children Made." *The Saturday Evening Post* 23 Sep. 1950: 26–27, 62–63, 65–66, 68. Print.
———. *Yestermorrow: Obvious Answers to Impossible Futures*. Santa Barbara, CA: Capra, 1991. Print.
———. *Zen in the Art of Writing*. Santa Barbara, CA: Capra, 1990. Print.

Kurt Vonnegut

Vonnegut, Kurt. "2BR02B." *Worlds of If* Jan. 1962: 59–65. Print.
———. "All the King's Horses." *Collier's* 10 Feb. 1951: 14–15, 46–48, 50. Print.
———. *Armageddon in Retrospect*. New York: G.P. Putnam's Sons, 2008. Print.
———. *Bagombo Snuff Box*. New York: Berkley, 1999. Print.
———. "The Big Space Fuck." *Again, Dangerous Visions*. Ed. Harlan Ellison. Garden City, NY: Doubleday, 1972. 246–250. Print.
———. "The Big Trip Up Yonder." *Galaxy Science Fiction* Jan. 1954: 100–110. Print.
———. "The Euphio Question." *Collier's* 12 May 1951: 22–23, 52–54, 56. Print.
———. *Fates Worse Than Death: An Autobiographical Collage*. New York: Berkley Books, 1992. Print.
———. *God Bless You, Dr. Kevorkian*. New York: Washington Square, 2001. Print.
———. "Harrison Bergeron." *The Magazine of Fantasy and Science Fiction* Oct. 1961: 5–10. Print. Reprinted in *National Review* 16 Nov. 1965: 1020–1021, 1041. Print.
———. *Letters*. New York: Delacorte, 2012. Print.
———. *Look at the Birdie*. New York: Delacorte, 2009. Print.
———. "The Manned Missiles." *Cosmopolitan* July 1958: 83–88. Print.
———. *Novels & Stories 1950–1962*. Ed. Sidney Offit. New York: Library of America, 2012. Print.
———. *Novels & Stories 1963–1973*. Ed. Sidney Offit. New York: Library of America, 2012. Print.
———. *Palm Sunday*. New York: Delta, 1999. Print.
———. "Report on the Barnhouse Effect." *Collier's* 11 Feb. 1950: 18–19, 63–65. Print.
———. "*Some Comments on Mark Twain's* A Connecticut Yankee in King Arthur's Court *by Kurt Vonnegut at the Age of Seventy-two*." *A Connecticut Yankee in King Arthur's Court*. By Mark Twain. New York: Oxford University Press, 1996. xxxi–xxxiii. Print.
———. "Thanasphere." *Collier's* 2 Sept. 1950: 18–19, 60, 62. Print.
———. *Wampeters, Foma & Granfalloons*. New York: Dell, 1974. Print.
———. "Welcome to the Monkey House." *Playboy* Jan. 1968: 95, 156, 196, 198, 200–201. Print.
———. *Welcome to the Monkey House*. New York: Delacorte, 1968. Print.
———. *While Mortals Sleep*. New York: Delacorte, 2011. Print.

Secondary sources

Abram, David. "The Mechanical and the Organic: On the Impact of Metaphor in Science." *Scientists on Gaia*. Eds. Stephen H. Schneider and Penelope J. Boston. Cambridge, MA: MIT Press, 1991. 66–74. Print.

Adams, Hazard. *Philosophy of the Literary Symbolic*. Tallahassee, FL: University Presses of Florida, 1983. Print.

Aggelis, Steven L. *Conversations with Ray Bradbury*. Jackson, MI: University Press of Mississippi, 2004. Print.

Aldiss, Brian W. and Harry Harrison. *Farewell Fantastic Venus!* Frogmore, St. Albans, UK: Panther, 1977. Print.

"All the King's Horses." *Kurt Vonnegut's Monkey House*. Writ. Stan Daniels. Dir. Allan King. Acorn Media, 1991. VHS.

Allen, William Rodney. *Conversations with Kurt Vonnegut*. Jackson, MI: University Press of Mississippi, 2003. Print.

———. *Understanding Kurt Vonnegut*. Columbia, SC: University of South Carolina Press, 1991. Print.

"American Studies: An Interview with Donald Pease." *The Minnesota Review*, Spring 2006. Web.

Andrade, Oswald de. "Cannibalist Manifesto." Trans. Leslie Bary. *Latin American Literary Review* 19.38 (1991): 35–47. Web. 7 Nov. 2013.

Annie Hall. Dir. Woody Allen. Perf. Woody Allen, Diane Keaton. United Artists, 1977. DVD.

Auden, W. H. *Another Time*. New York: Random House, 1940. Print.

Baker, Joanne. *50 Physics Ideas You Really Need to Know*. London: Quercus, 2007. Print.

Barth, John. "Mystery and Tragedy: The Twin Motions of Ritual Heroism." *The Friday Book, Or, Book-Titles Should Be Straightforward and Subtitles Avoided: Essays and Other Nonfiction*. Baltimore, MD: Johns Hopkins University Press, 1997. 41–54. Print.

Baumlin, James S., Tita French Baumlin, and George H. Jensen, eds. *Post-Jungian Criticism: Theory and Practice*. Albany, NY: State University Press of New York, 2004. Print.

Beerbohm, Max. *The Prince of Minor Writers*. New York: New York Review Books, 2015. Print.

Behind the Name: The Etymology and History of First Names. Mike Campbell, 1996–2013. Web.

Berryman, John. *The Dream Songs*. New York: Farrar, Straus and Giroux, 2007. Print.

Blake, William. *The Works of William Blake: Poetic, Symbolic, and Critical*. Eds. W. B. Yeats and Edwin John Ellis. London: Bernard Quaritch, 1893. Print. Web. 3 July 2012.

Bloom, Harold. *Bloom's Modern Critical Views: Ray Bradbury – New Edition*. New York: Infobase, 2010. Print.

Boddy, Kasia. *The American Short Story since 1950*. Edinburgh, Scotland: Edinburgh University Press, 2010. Print.

"*Bookworm*. KCRW, Santa Monica." *YouTube*, 11 Nov. 1999. Web. 20 Oct. 2012.

Boon, Kevin A. and David Pringle, eds. *At Millennium's End: New Essays on the Work of Kurt Vonnegut*. Albany, NY: State University of New York Press, 2001. Print.

Boyd, Brian. *On the Origin of Stories: Evolution, Cognition, and Fiction*. Cambridge, MA: Harvard University Press, 2009. Print.

Brackett, Leigh. *Sea-Kings of Mars and Otherworldly Stories*. London: Orion, 2005. Print.

"Bringing the News: An Interview with Richard Ford." *Fiction Writers Review* 11 April 2011. Web. 14 May 2015.

Brinkley, Douglas. "Vonnegut's Apocalypse." *Rolling Stone* 1007. 24 Aug. 2006.

Brogan, Hugh. *The Penguin History of the USA: Second Edition*. New York: Penguin, 2001. Print.

Brogan, Jacqueline Vaught. "Introducing Stevens: Or, the Sheerly Playful and the Display of Theory." *Teaching Wallace Stevens*. Eds. John N. Serio and Bobby J. Leggett. Knoxville, TN: University of Tennessee Press, 1994. 51–62. Print.

Campbell, Joseph. *Goddesses: Mysteries of the Divine Feminine*. Novato, CA: New World Library, 2013. Print.

———. *The Hero's Journey: Joseph Campbell on His Life and Work*. Novato, CA: New World Library, 2003. Print.

———. *The Hero with a Thousand Faces*. Princeton, NJ: Princeton University Press, 2004. Print.

———. *The Inner Reaches of Outer Space: Metaphor as Myth and as Religion*. Novato, CA: New World Library, 2002. Print.

———. *Man and Myth*. Highbridge, 1998. CD.

———. *The Masks of God Vol. II: Oriental Mythology*. London: Secker & Warburg, 1962. Print.

———. *The Masks of God Vol. III: Occidental Mythology*. London: Secker & Warburg, 1965. Print.

———. *The Masks of God Vol. IV: Creative Mythology*. London: Secker & Warburg, 1968. Print.

———. *Myths to Live By*. New York: Penguin Compass, 1993. Print.

———. *Pathways to Bliss: Mythology and Personal Transformation*. Novato, CA: New World Library, 2004. Print.

———. *Thou Art That: Transforming Religious Metaphor*. Novato, CA: New World Library, 2001. Print.

Campbell, Joseph and Bill Moyers. *The Power of Myth*. Ed. Betty Sue Flowers. New York: Doubleday, 1988. Print.

Carroll, Lewis. *The Annotated Alice: The Definitive Edition: Alice's Adventures in Wonderland & Through the Looking-Glass*. Ed. Martin Gardner. London: W. W. Norton & Company, 2009. Print.

Chevalier, Jean and Alain Gheerbrant. *The Penguin Dictionary of Symbols*. Trans. John Buchanan-Brown. London: Penguin, 1996. Print.
Coleman, Philip. "Hauntedness: Edgar Allan Poe and Chuck Palahniuk." *The Ghost Story from the Middle Ages to the Twentieth Century*. Dublin, Ireland: Four Courts, 2010. 166–79. Print.
——— and Stephen Matterson, eds. *'Forever Young'?: The Changing Images of America*. Heidelberg, Germany: Universitätsverlag Winter, 2012. Print.
Crumb, Robert. *The Weirdo Years 1981–'93*. San Francisco, CA: Last Gasp, 2013. Print.
Dawkins, Richard. *The Selfish Gene: 30th Anniversary Edition*. Oxford, UK: Oxford University Press, 2006. Print.
Dawson, Terence. *The Effective Protagonist in the Nineteenth-Century British Novel: Scott, Brontë, Eliot, Wilde*. Chippenham, UK: Ashgate, 2004. Print.
Dawson, Terence and Polly Young-Eisendrath, eds. *The Cambridge Companion to Jung: Second Edition*. Cambridge, UK: Cambridge University Press, 2008. Print.
"Day at Night: Ray Bradbury." *YouTube*, 11 Mar. 2011. Web. 12 Mar. 2014.
"Defense.gov News Transcript: DoD News Briefing – Secretary Rumsfeld and Gen. Myers. United States Department of Defense." *Defense.gov*. U.S. Department of Defense, 12 Feb. 2002. Web. 1 Mar. 2014.
"Definitions for Medieval Christian Liturgy: *Kyrie eleison*." *Liturgy Main Page*. Yale University, n.d. Web. 5 Nov. 2013.
Diskin, Lahna. "Bradbury on Children." *Bloom's Modern Critical Views: Ray Bradbury – New Edition*. Ed. Harold Bloom. New York: Infocase, 2010. 23–50. Print.
Doniger, Wendy. *The Implied Spider: Politics & Theology in Myth*. New York: Columbia University Press, 1998. Print.
Eggers, Dave, Jonathan Safran Foer and Nicole Krauss, eds. *The Future Dictionary of America*. San Francisco, CA: Common Assets Action Fund, 2005. Print.
Eller, Jonathan R. *Becoming Ray Bradbury*. Urbana, IL: University of Illinois Press, 2011. Print.
——— and William F. Touponce. *Ray Bradbury: The Life of Fiction*. Kent, MI: Kent State University Press, 2004. Print.
Ellison, Harlan, ed. *Again, Dangerous Visions*. Garden City, NY: Doubleday, 1972. Print.
"Eusebius – Constantine and the Sign of the Cross." *Vita Constantini, 1.26–31*. Early Church Texts, 2007. Web. 27 March 2014.
"Explanation of the Great Seal's Symbolism." *Great Seal*. John D. MacArthur, 2013. Web. 18 Nov. 2013.
Eyer, Diane E. *Mother-Infant Bonding: A Scientific Fiction*. New Haven, CT: Yale University Press, 1992. Print.
Fiedler, Leslie. "The Divine Stupidity of Kurt Vonnegut." *Kurt Vonnegut: Images and Representations*. Eds. Marc Leeds and Peter Reed. Westport, CN: Greenwood, 2000. 5–18. Print.
Ford, Richard, ed. *The Granta Book of the American Short Story*. London: Granta, 1992. Print.
———. *The New Granta Book of the American Short Story*. London: Granta, 2007. Print.
Franz, Marie-Louise von. *The Problem of the Puer Aeternus*. Toronto, Canada: Inner City, 2000. Print.

Frye, Northrop. *Anatomy of Criticism*. Princeton, NJ: Princeton University Press, 1990. Print.
———. *The Bush Garden: Essays on the Canadian Imagination*. Concord, ON: Anansi, 1995. Print.
Fussell, Paul. *The Boys' Crusade: The American Infantry in Northwest Europe, 1944–1945*. New York: Modern Library, 2003. Print.
Galeyev, Bulat. "Open Letter to Ray Bradbury." *Leonardo* 34.1 (2001): 25–26. JSTOR.
Gardner, John. *The Art of Fiction*. New York: Vintage, 1991. Print.
Ghostbusters. Dir. Ivan Reitman. Perf. Bill Murray, Sigourney Weaver, Dan Aykroyd, Harold Ramis, Ernie Hudson, Rick Moranis. Columbia, 1984. DVD.
Gill, Glen Robert. *Northrop Frye and the Phenomenology of Myth*. Toronto, Canada: University of Toronto Press, 2006. Print.
Goethe, Johann Wolfgang von. *Faust*. Trans. Walter Arndt. New York: Norton, 1976. Print.
———. *Great Writings of Goethe*. Ed. Stephen Spender. Trans. Michael Hamburger. New York: New American Library, 1958. Print.
Goldsmith, David H. *Kurt Vonnegut: Fantasist of Fire and Ice*. Bowling Green, OH: Bowling Green University Press, 1972. Print.
Golemba, Henry. "Rockets Rise on the Wabash." *The Great Lakes Review* 5.1 (1978): 1–6. Print.
Gould, Eric. *Mythical Intentions in Modern Literature*. Princeton, NJ: Princeton University Press, 1981. Print.
Haule, John Ryan. *Jung in the 21st Century, Volume One: Evolution and Archetype*. London: Routledge, 2011. Print.
———. *Young Goodman Brown and Other Tales*. London: Oxford World's Classics, 1987. Print.
Heidegger, Martin. "'Only God Can Save Us': The Spiegel Interview (1966)." *Heidegger: The Man and the Thinker*. Trans. W. Richardson. Piscataway, NJ: Transaction, 2010. 45–67. Print.
Hillman, James. *A Blue Fire*. New York: Harper Perennial, 1991. Print.
———. *Animal Presences*. Putnam, OK: Spring, 2008. Print.
———. *City & Soul*. Putnam, OK: Spring, 2006. Print.
———. *The Dream and the Underworld*. New York: HarperPerennial, 1979. Print.
———. *Healing Fiction*. Putnam, OK: Spring, 2009. Print.
———, ed. *Puer Papers*. Dallas, TX: Spring, 1987. Print.
———. *Re-Visioning Psychology*. New York: HarperPerennial, 1992. Print.
———. *The Soul's Code: In Search of Character and Calling*. New York: Bantam, 1996. Print.
———. *Suicide and the Soul*. Putnam, OK: Spring, 2011. Print.
———. *A Terrible Love of War*. New York: Penguin, 2004. Print.
Hillman, James and Sonu Shamdasani. *Lament of the Dead: Psychology After Jung's* Red Book. New York: W. W. Norton, 2013. Print.
Hockley, Luke. *Frames of Mind: A Post-Jungian Look at Cinema, Television and Technology*. Bristol, UK: Intellect, 2007. Print.
Hollingdale, R. J. *Nietzsche: The Man and His Philosophy*. Cambridge, UK: Cambridge University Press, 1999. Print.
Holmes, John Clellon. "The New Girl: An Appreciative Appraisal of the Emergent Modern Female . . ." *Playboy* Jan. 1968: 179–182, 186, 214–216. Print.
House of Names. Swyrich Corporation, 2000–2013. Web. 9 Oct. 2013.

Huskinson, Lucy. "Introduction: Ordinarily Mythical." *Dreaming the Myth Onwards: New Directions in Jungian Therapy and Thought*. Ed. Lucy Huskinson. London: Routledge, 2008. 1–18. Print.

"Inequality in the US: Interview with Economist Joseph Stiglitz." *SPIEGEL ONLINE INTERNATIONAL*. SPIEGEL, 1 Oct. 2012. Web. 6 Oct. 2012.

"It Is the Woman Who Pays." *Letters of Note*. Shaun Usher, 14 Nov. 2011. Web. 15 Oct. 2013.

Izod, John. *Myth, Mind and the Screen: Understanding the Heroes of Our Time*. Cambridge, UK: Cambridge University Press, 2003. Print.

Jones, Darryl, Elizabeth McCarthy, and Bernice M. Murphy, eds. *It Came From the 1950s!: Popular Culture, Popular Anxieties*. New York: Palgrave, 2011. Print.

Joseph Campbell and the Power of Myth. Dir. Bill Moyers. Prod. Apostrophe S with Public Affairs TV and Alvin. H. Perlmutter. Mystic Fire Video, 2005. DVD.

Jung, Carl Gustav. *Collected Works of C. G. Jung, Volume 5: Symbols of Transformation*, Trans. R. F. C. Hull. Princeton: Princeton University Press, 1967. Print.

———. *Collected Works of C. G. Jung, Volume 7: Two Essays on Analytical Psychology*. Trans. R. F. C. Hull. Princeton, NJ: Princeton University Press, 1966. Print.

———. *Collected Works of C. G. Jung, Volume 9 (Part 1): Archetypes of the Collective Unconscious*. Trans. R. F. C. Hull. Princeton, NJ: Princeton University Press, 1968. Print.

———. *Collected Works of C. G. Jung, Volume 10: Civilization in Transition*. Trans. R. F. C. Hull. Princeton, NJ: Princeton University Press, 1970. Print.

———. *Collected Works of C. G. Jung, Volume 12: Psychology and Alchemy*. Trans. R. F. C. Hull. Princeton, NJ: Princeton University Press, 1968. Print.

———. *Collected Works of C. G. Jung, Volume 15: Spirit in Man, Art, and Literature*. Trans. R. F. C. Hull. Princeton, NJ: Princeton University Press, 1966. Print.

———. *Jung on Mythology*. Ed. Robert Segal. Princeton, NJ: Princeton University Press, 1998. Print.

———. *Memories, Dreams, Reflections*. Trans. Richard and Clara Winston. London: Fontana, 1995. Print.

———. *The Portable Jung*. Ed. Joseph Campbell. Trans. R. F. C. Hull. New York: Penguin, 1976. Print.

———. *The Red Book: Liber Novus, A Reader's Edition*. Trans. Sonu Shamdasani. New York: W. W. Norton, 2009. Print.

"Jung Today: An Interview with Dr. John Ryan Haule." *Humanistic Paganism*. Humanistic Paganism, 30 Dec. 2012. Web. 14 May 2015.

Jungk, Robert. *Brighter than a Thousand Suns: A Personal History of the Atomic Scientists*. New York: Harcourt Brace, 1958. Print.

Karon, Jeff. "Science and Sensibility in the Short Fiction of Kurt Vonnegut." *At Millennium's End*. Albany, NY: State University of New York Press, 2001. 105–117. Print.

Keegan, John. *The Face of Battle*. New York: Penguin, 1978. Print.

Klinkowitz, Jerome and Donald L. Lawler. *Vonnegut in America*. New York: Delta, 1977. Print.

——— and John Somer. *The Vonnegut Statement: Original Essays on the Life and Work of Kurt Vonnegut, Jr.* New York: Delta, 1973. Print.

Knox, Jean. *Archetype, Attachment, Analysis: Jungian Psychology and the Emergent Mind*. Hove, UK: Bruner-Routledge, 2003. Print.

Kroetsch, Robert. *The Lovely Treachery of Words: Essays Selected and New*. Toronto, Canada: Oxford University Press, 1989. Print.

"Kurt Vonnegut on Breakfast of Champions." *NYPR Archives & Preservation*. WNYC, 5 Dec. 2013. Web. 8 Feb. 2014.

Leeds, Marc. *The Vonnegut Encyclopedia: An Authorized Compendium*. Westport, CT: Greenwood Publishing Group, 1995. Print.

——— and Peter J. Reed. *Kurt Vonnegut: Images and Representations*. Westport, CT: Greenwood Publishing Group, 2000. Print.

LePan, Douglas. *Weathering It*. Toronto, Canada: McClelland & Stewart, 1987. Print.

Martinez, Inez. "Ego Readings vs. Reading for Psyche." *Journal of Jungian Scholarly Studies* 5.2 (2009): 1–17. Web. 28 February 2015.

———. "Reading for Psyche: Numinosity." *Journal of Jungian Scholarly Studies* 7.4 (2011): 1–15. Web. 28 February 2015.

———. "Re-reading Sophocles's Oedipus Plays: Reconceiving Vengeance as Cultural Complex." *Journal of Jungian Scholarly Studies* 8.1 (2012): 1–23. Web. 28 February 2015.

———. "Unconsciousness and Survival: Kafka's *Metamorphosis* and Borowski's 'This Way for the Gas, Ladies and Gentlemen.'" *Journal of Jungian Scholarly Studies* 6.2 (2010): 1–25. Web. 28 February 2015.

Marvin, Thomas F. *Kurt Vonnegut: A Critical Companion*. Westport, CT: Greenwood Publishing Group, 2002. Print.

May, Charles E., ed. *The New Short Story Theories*. Athens, OH: Ohio University Press, 1994. Print.

———. *The Short Story: The Reality of Artifice*. New York: Routledge, 2002. Print.

May, Rollo. *The Courage to Create*. New York: W. W. Norton, 1994. Print.

———. *The Cry for Myth*. New York: Delta, 1991. Print.

———. *Love and Will*. New York: W. W. Norton, 2007. Print.

McInnis, Gilbert. *Evolutionary Mythology in the Writings of Kurt Vonnegut*. Palo Alto, CA: Academica, 2011. Print.

Meagher, Robert Emmet. *Herakles Gone Mad: Rethinking Heroism in an Age of Endless War*. Northampton, UK: Olive Branch, 2006. Print.

Merton, Thomas. "Symbolism: Communication or Communion?" *New Directions* 20 (1968): 1–12. Print.

Moriarty, John. *Seeking to Walk Beautifully on the Earth, Volume One*. Lilliput, 2007. CD.

———. *Turtle Was Gone a Long Time, Vol. I: Crossing the Kedron*. Dublin, Ireland: Lilliput, 1996. Print.

———. *Turtle Was Gone a Long Time, Vol. II: Horsehead Nebula Neighing*. Dublin, Ireland: Lilliput, 1997. Print.

———. *Turtle Was Gone a Long Time, Vol. III: Anaconda Canoe*. Dublin, Ireland: Lilliput, 1998. Print.

Morse, Donald. "Bringing Chaos to Order: On Kurt Vonnegut's Literary Remains." *Los Angeles Review of Books* 24 Feb. 2013. Web. 3 March 2013.

———. *Kurt Vonnegut*. San Bernadino, CA: Borgo, 1993. Print.

"The Mortification of James Watson." *TIME* 19 Oct. 2007. Web. 14 July 2013.

Müller, Friedrich Max. "Friedrich Max Müller." *The Rise of Modern Mythology 1680–1860*. Eds. Burton Feldman and Robert D. Richardson. Bloomington, IN: Indiana University Press, 1972. 480–487. Print.

———. "On the Philosophy of Mythology." *Chips from a German Workshop, Vol. V*. New York: Charles Scribner's Sons, 1881. 54–98. *Project Gutenberg*. Web. 17 Aug. 2012.

Neumann, Erich. *The Great Mother: An Analysis of the Archetype*. Trans. Ralph Manheim. Princeton, NJ: Princeton University Press, 1972. Print.

Nurmi, Martin K. "Joy, Love, and Innocence in Blake's 'The Mental Traveller.'" *Studies in Romanticism* 3.2 (1964): 109–117. JSTOR.

O'Connor, Frank. *The Lonely Voice: A Study of the Short Story*. Brooklyn, NY: Melville House Publishing, 2004. Print.

O'Flaherty, Wendy Doniger. "Origins of Myth-making Man." *New York Times Book Review* 18 December 1983: 3, 24–25. Microfilm.

———. *Other People's Myths: The Cave of Echoes*. New York: Macmillan, 1988. Print.

———. "The Survival of Myth in Science Fiction." *Mindscapes: The Geographies of Imagined Worlds*. Eds. George E. Slusser and Eric S. Rabkin. Carbondale, IL: Southern Illinois University Press, 1989. 16–33. Print.

Ovid. *The Metamorphoses of Ovid*. Trans. Allen Mandelbaum. New York: Harvest, 1993. Print.

Pease, Donald E. *The New American Exceptionalism*. Minneapolis, MN: University of Minnesota Press, 2009. Print.

Phillips, Kathy J. *Manipulating Masculinity: War and Gender in Modern British and American Literature*. New York: Palgrave Macmillan, 2010. Print.

"Q&A on William F. Buckley." *The New York Times Websites* 27 Feb. 2008. Web. 2 Oct. 2013.

Rackstraw, Loree, ed. *Draftings in Vonnegut: The Paradox of Hope*. Cedar Falls, IA: University of Northern Iowa Press, 1988. Print.

———. "The Paradox of 'Awareness' and Language in Vonnegut's Fiction." *Kurt Vonnegut: Images and Representations*. Eds. Marc Leeds and Peter Reed. Westport, CN: Greenwood, 2000. 51–66. Print.

———. "Quantum Leaps in the Vonnegut Mindfield." *At Millennium's End: New Essays on the Work of Kurt Vonnegut*. Ed. Kevin Alexander Boon. Albany, NY: State University of New York Press, 2001. 49–63. Print.

The Ray Bradbury Theater. Echo Bridge Home Entertainment, 2005. DVD.

Reed, Peter J. *The Short Fiction of Kurt Vonnegut. Contributions to the Study of American Literature, I*. Westport, CN and London: Greenwood, 1997. Print.

——— and Marc Leeds, eds. *The Vonnegut Chronicles: Interviews and Essays*. Westport, CN: Greenwood Press, 1996. Print.

Rensma, Ritske. *The Innateness of Myth: A New Interpretation of Joseph Campbell's Reception of C.G. Jung*. New York: Continuum, 2009. Print.

Rhodin, Tony. "Vonnegut's Final Chapter in Friendship." *Penn Live* 12 April 2007. Web. 21 July 2013.

Robertson, James Oliver. *American Myth, American Reality*. New York: Hill & Wang, 1980. Print.

Ronnberg, Ami and Kathleen Martin, eds. *The Book of Symbols: Reflections on Archetypal Images*. Cologne, Germany: Taschen, 2010. Print.

Rowland, Susan. *C. G. Jung and Literary Theory: The Challenge from Fiction*. Chippenham, UK: Palgrave, 1999. Print.

———. "Literature and the Shaman." *Journal of Jungian Scholarly Studies* 5.1 (2009): 1–13. Web. 28 February 2015.
———. "Writing about War: Jung, Much Ado About Nothing, and the Troy Novels of Lindsay Clarke." *Journal of Jungian Scholarly Studies* 3.1 (2007): 1–11. Web. 28 February 2015.
Sagan, Carl. *Pale Blue Dot: A Vision of the Human Future in Space*. New York: Random House. 1997. Print.
Samuels, Andrew, Bani Shorter and Fred Plaut. *A Critical Dictionary of Jungian Analysis*. London: Routledge, 1986. Print.
Schilbrack, Kevin. "Myth and metaphysics." *Thinking Through Myths: Philosophical Perspectives*. Ed. Kevin Schilbrack. London: Routledge, 2002. 85–100. Print.
Schopenhauer, Arthur. *The World as Will and Representation*. London: Ballantyne, Hanson, and Company, 1818. Print.
Schopenhauer, Arthur. "On the Sufferings of the World." *Studies in Pessimism: A Series of Essays*. Trans. T. Bailey Saunders. London: Swan, Sonnenschein & Co., 1892. 5–18. Web. 3 Oct. 2013.
Schrödinger, Erwin. *My View of the World*. Trans. Cecily Hastings. Cambridge, UK: Cambridge University Press, 1964. Print.
Segal, Robert A. "Bringing Myth Back to the World: The Future of Myth in Jungian Psychology." *Dreaming the Myth Onwards: New Directions in Jungian Theory and Thought*. Ed. Lucy Huskinson. London: Routledge, 2008. 91–105. Print.
———, ed. *The Allure of Gnosticism*. Peru, IL: Open Court, 1995. 26–38. Print.
———. *Theorizing About Myth*. Amherst, MA: University of Massachusetts Press, 1999. Print.
Shields, Charles J. *And So It Goes: Kurt Vonnegut: A Life*. New York: Henry Holt, 2011. Print.
Slusser, George Edgar, ed. *Bridges to Fantasy: Essays from the Eaton Conference on Science Fiction and Fantasy Literature*. Carbondale, IL: Southern Illinois University Press, 1982. Print.
———. *The Bradbury Chronicles*. San Bernardino, CA: Borgo, 2008. Print.
Smith, David Livingstone. *The Most Dangerous Animal: Human Nature and the Origins of War*. New York: St. Martin's Griffin, 2007. Print.
Smith, Robert Paul. "Everybody Shinny on His Own Side." *Playboy* Dec. 1963: 123, 219. Print.
Spock, Benjamin. *The Common Sense Book of Baby and Child Care*. New York: Duell, Sloan and Pearce, 1946. Print.
Stephens, James. *The Crock of Gold*. London: John Murray, 2012. Print.
Stevens, Wallace. "Anecdote of the Jar." *Selected Poems*. London: Faber and Faber, 1953. 27. Print.
Sugg, Richard P., ed. *Jungian Literary Criticism*. Evanston, IL: Northwestern University Press, 1992. Print.
Sumner, Gregory D. "Building the Monkey House: At Kurt Vonnegut's Writing Table." *Welcome to the Monkey House: The Special Edition*. Ed. Kurt Vonnegut. New York: Random House, 2014. 335–393. Print.
Tally, Jr., Robert T. *Kurt Vonnegut and the American Novel: A Postmodern Iconography*. London: Continuum, 2011. Print.
Thornbury, Charles. "Introduction." *John Berryman: Collected Poems 1937–1971*. New York: Farrar, Straus and Giroux, 1991. xvii–lx. Print.

"TIME's Ten Questions." *Neil deGrasse Tyson* 26 June 2008. Web. 14 May 2012.
Tolkien, J. R. R. *Tree and Leaf*. London: Harper, 2001. Print.
Toms, Michael. *An Open Life: Joseph Campbell in Conversation with Michael Toms*. New York: Harper Perennial, 1990. Print.
Touponce, William F. "The Existential Fabulous: A Reading of Ray Bradbury's 'The Golden Apples of the Sun'." *Mosaic* XIII.3–4 (1980): 203–218. Print.
Twain, Mark. *The Annotated Huckleberry Finn*. Ed. Michael Patrick Hearn. New York: W. W. Norton, 2001. Print.
———. *The Mysterious Stranger and Other Stories*. New York: Dover, 1992. Print.
———. *The Mysterious Stranger Manuscripts*. Ed. William M. Gibson. Berkeley, CA: University of California Press, 2005. Print.
Tyson, Neil deGrasse. *Space Chronicles: Facing the Ultimate Frontier*. New York: W. W. Norton & Company, 2012. MOBI file.
"Understanding Mythology with Joseph Campbell." *Thinking Allowed*. Prod. Jeffrey Mishlove. Spectrum Foundation, 1988. VHS.
Vico. *New Science*. New York: Penguin, 2000. Print.
Walker, Stephen F. *Jung and the Jungians on Myth*. New York: Routledge, 2002. Print.
Wallace, David Foster. *Brief Interviews with Hideous Men*. London: Abacus, 2001. Print.
Warner, Marina. *From the Beast to the Blonde: On Fairy Tales and Their Tellers*. New York: Farrar, Straus and Giroux, 1996. Print.
Weist, Jerry. *Bradbury: An Illustrated Life*. New York: William Morrow, 2002. Print.
Weller, Sam. *Listen to the Echoes: The Ray Bradbury Interviews*. New York: Melville House, 2010. Print.
"What Are We Waiting For?" Editorial. *Collier's* 22 March 1952: 23. Print.
"Why the South Must Prevail." Editorial. *National Review* 24 Aug. 1957: 148–149. Print.
Williams, Melanie L. *Secrets and Laws: Collected Essays in Law, Lives and Literature*. London: University College London Press, 2005. Print.
Woodard, Colin. *American Nations*. New York. Penguin, 2011. Print.
Woodman, Marion. *The Ravaged Bridegroom: Masculinity in Women*. Toronto, Canada: Inner City, 1990. Print.
Yeats, William Butler. *The Collected Poems of W. B. Yeats*. Ware, UK: Wordsworth Editions, 2008. Print.
Zimmer, Heinrich. *The King and the Corpse: Tales of the Soul's Conquest of Evil*. Ed. Joseph Campbell. Princeton, NJ: Princeton University Press, 1948/1973. Print.
Žižek, Slavoj. "What Rumsfeld Doesn't Know That He Knows About Abu Ghraib." *In These Times* 21 May 2004. Web. 1 Mar. 2014.

Index

For Product Safety Concerns and Information please contact our EU representative GPSR@taylorandfrancis.com Taylor & Francis Verlag GmbH, Kaufingerstraße 24, 80331 München, Germany

Batch number: 10725973

Printed by Printforce, the Netherlands